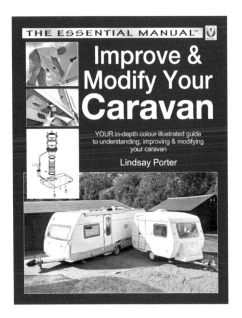

THE ESSENTIAL MANUAL™

Improve & Modify Your Caravan

YOUR in-depth colour illustrated guide
to understanding, improving & modifying
your caravan

Lindsay Porter

Other great books from Veloce –

www.veloce.co.uk

First published in April 2012 by Veloce Publishing Limited, Veloce House, Parkway Farm Business Park, Middle Farm Way, Poundbury, Dorchester, Dorset, DT1 3AR, England.
Fax 01305 250479/e-mail info@veloce.co.uk/web www.veloce.co.uk or www.velocebooks.com.

ISBN: 978-1-845843-28-1 UPC: 6-36847-04328-5

Contents

Introduction & acknowledgements

One of the great things that caravanners have in common, is that we're a little bit individual, a little bit different. Because of this, we all like to make our caravans reflect our needs, preferences, and personality.

That's why this book has been created: to give a flavour of what's possible and, in most cases, how you can do it yourself. Of course, there are some instances, particularly in relation to gas, electricity, and structural strength, where you need to bring in a qualified expert – and note the use of the word 'qualified.' When it comes to areas of safety, employing the services of someone with specific qualifications is vital.

Many of the jobs featured in this manual lie within the scope of the competent DIYer but, naturally enough, different jobs require different levels of competence, and you need to satisfy yourself that you have the required skills before tackling the work. A well carried out piece of work will enhance your caravan considerably, but a botched one will have the opposite effect.

So, if you're unsure, start with something simple and straightforward. Even if you don't feel up to tackling all of the jobs shown here, you can at least benefit from seeing the correct way of having them carried out, as well as seeing for yourself just what's available for your caravan.

The majority of the jobs shown here first appeared in *Caravan* magazine. I've always had a very enjoyable relationship with its staff, and its friendliness and helpful approach shine throughout its pages. It's a good read, and I'm grateful to them for having put up with me as a contributor for so long.

Many others have also contributed to this publication, and almost all of them are featured in its pages. In particular, Rob Sheasby and Dave Bradley-Scrivener have displayed their expertise on the mechanical side, while Zoe Palmer has done her usual job, making sense out of chaos when compiling the material, and bringing it all together. Without these three – and many others featured here – this book would not have happened. Many, many thanks to them all.

Lindsay Porter
Herefordshire

Foreword

Legend has it that Lindsay Porter forgot more last Wednesday than most of us will ever know about caravans. As a highly-regarded caravan guru, Lindsay has contributed his insightful ideas and features to caravan magazines for over a decade.

Lindsay has a unique knack of delivering complex concepts in a way that makes them easy for the layman to understand and follow – which is crucial when you're drilling holes in your beloved caravan. This, and a thoroughness bordering on obsession, makes him the perfect person to deliver a book here that will help the rookie or experienced caravanner to improve all aspects of their treasured van.

Do it properly, do it once – that's Lindsay's motto. Here at *Caravan*, we couldn't agree more.

John Sootheran
Managing Editor
Caravan

Safety first

Although the modern caravan is mechanically, relatively simple compared with a modern motor car, it's still extremely important to bear in mind some essential safety considerations before undertaking any work.

• By carrying out your own servicing and maintenance work on your caravan, you are taking on the responsibility for both your own safety, and that of those working with you. Work must be carefully planned in advance, with particular care being taken for safety, and sufficient time allowed (many accidents are caused by rushing).

• Before using specialist tools or materials, consult the necessary safety and operational instructions from the manufacturers and suppliers.

• Always disconnect the caravan's 12V DC and 240V AC electrical supplies before starting work.

• Always disconnect the gas supply at the source, and check that all the pilot lights are extinguished before starting work in a caravan.

• When working on the running gear or chassis, firmly chock the wheels.

• When using a jack, ensure that you locate and use the correct jacking points.

• Make sure you use axle stands before working underneath the caravan, and wind down the caravan's corner steadies, placing secure blocks beneath them if they no longer reach the ground.

• Wipe spilt oil, grease, or water off the floor immediately.

• Make sure that the correct tools are used for the job.

• Never take risky shortcuts, or rush to finish a job; plan ahead, and allow plenty of time.

• Be meticulous, and keep the work area tidy – you will avoid frustration, work better, and lose fewer items.

• Keep children and animals away from the work area, and from unattended caravans.

• Always wear eye protection when working underneath a caravan, and when using power tools.

• Before undertaking dirty jobs, use a barrier cream on your hands as a protection against infection. Preferably, wear thin gloves, available from DIY outlets.

• Remove your wristwatch, rings, and other jewellery before doing any work on the caravan – and especially when working on electrical systems.

• Always tell someone what you're going to be doing, and have them regularly check that all is well, particularly if you are working alone, or under the vehicle.

• Always seek specialist advice if you're in doubt about job. The safety of your caravan affects you, your family, and other road users.

• Always use genuine original equipment spares, built to the correct safety standards.

MAINS ELECTRICITY

• Always disconnect the caravan's mains electricity before commencing work.

• Never bypass the caravan's RCD (Residual Current Device) circuit breakers.

• Whenever you have undertaken work on a caravan's mains electricity system, have it checked by an approved electrician before using it.

• When working with power tools, use rechargeable tools, and a DC inspection lamp powered from a remote 12V battery. However, if you must use mains powered devices, ensure plugs are correctly wired; that, whenever necessary, they're properly earthed (grounded); and that the fuse is of the correct rating for the device. Don't use mains powered equipment in damp conditions, or in the vicinity of fuel, fuel vapour, or the caravan battery.

• Before using mains powered equipment, take one more simple precaution: use an RCD circuit breaker. This reduces the risk of electrocution by instantly cutting the power supply if there is a problem.

THE BATTERY

• Always disconnect the battery before commencing work on the 12V electrical system.

• Don't smoke, allow a naked flame, or cause a spark near the caravan's battery, even in a well ventilated area: a small amount of highly explosive hydrogen gas will be given off as part of the normal recharging process.

• When charging the battery from an external source, disconnect both battery leads before commencing charging. If the battery isn't of the 'sealed for life' type, loosen the filler plugs, or remove the cover, before charging. For best results, the battery should be given a low rate 'trickle' charge overnight. Don't charge at an excessive rate, or the battery could burst.

• Always wear gloves and goggles when carrying or topping up the battery. Even in diluted form the acid electrolyte is extremely corrosive and must not be allowed to contact the eyes, skin, or clothes.

GAS SYSTEM

In the UK it is an offence for anyone other than a trained engineer to carry out any work on a gas appliance. Furthermore, since April 2009, any person carrying out work on a gas appliance in the UK must be registered

with the Gas Safe Register – the CORGI system is no longer valid. Check the engineer's credentials before allowing him to work on your caravan – your life could depend on it!

BRAKES AND ASBESTOS

Whenever you work on the braking system's mechanical components, or remove front or rear pads or shoes:
• Wear an efficient particle mask.
• Wipe off all brake dust from the work area (never blow it off with compressed air).
• Dispose of brake dust and discarded shoes or pads in a sealed plastic bag.
• Wash hands thoroughly after you have finished working on the brakes, and certainly before you eat or smoke.
• Replace shoes and pads only with asbestos-free shoes or pads. Note that asbestos brake dust can cause cancer if inhaled.

A caravan's brakes are one of its most important safety items. Don't dismantle them unless you are fully competent to do so. If you have not been trained in this work, but wish to carry out the jobs described in this book, have a garage or qualified mechanic check your work before you use the caravan.

JACK AND AXLE STANDS

• Whenever you're planning to jack a caravan, it's essential that you use only the correct type of jack. It's also very important to locate the correct jacking points. If your caravan isn't equipped with a specific jacking point, only jack the caravan under the axle, and as close to the chassis as possible.

• Special care must be taken when any type of lifting equipment is used. Jacks are made for lifting the caravan only, not for supporting it. Never work under a caravan using a jack to support the weight. Jacks must be supplemented by adequate additional means of support, such as axle stands, positioned under secure, load-bearing parts of the chassis.

• When replacing a wheel, always

use the correct torque settings, and the correct 'North-South-East-West' sequence of tightening.

• Never overtighten the wheel nuts, as this can distort the wheel rim, and check wheel nut tightness with a torque wrench at regular intervals.

CHASSIS

Never drill a galvanised chassis; it could weaken the structure. Never weld any galvanised material, as it could create toxic fumes.

GENERAL WORKSHOP SAFETY

Always have a fire extinguisher of the correct type within easy reach when working on your caravan.

• If a fire does occur, **DON'T PANIC!** Use the extinguisher effectively by directing it at the base of the fire.

• **NEVER** use a naked flame near petrol, or anywhere in the workplace.

• **KEEP** your inspection lamp well away from any source of petrol (gasoline) and bottled gas.

• **NEVER** use petrol (gasoline) to clean parts. Use paraffin (kerosene), or white spirits.

• **NO SMOKING!** There's a risk of fire, or transferring dangerous substances to your mouth, and ash falling into mechanical components is to be avoided.

• **BE METHODICAL** in everything you do, use common sense, and think of safety at all times.

Part 1

Background information

Caravans are very personal items and everyone wants to make theirs as individual as possible. This chapter looks at some of the most popular methods of adding to a basic caravan. This could either be through the installation and fitting of items such as a cassette toilet, water filter, or TV aerial, or by simply buying more general accessories, like an awning or a generator. In most cases, there are a wide variety of models and makes to choose from, and it's really a matter of picking the one that most suits your individual needs.

CHECKING ELECTRICAL CAPACITY

One of the most important factors to consider before fitting any accessory, is the electrical power supply that it may require. A caravan site's mains electricity supply will vary from as little as 4 amps, to as high as 16 amps. If the demand from a caravan's electrical appliances exceeds the supply, the caravan's electrical circuit breakers will automatically cut in. Therefore, it's essential that the power demand of any accessory is known before it's fitted to a caravan. To calculate whether a site's supply is sufficient, it's necessary to know that:

Watts (W) = Volts (V) x Amps (A).

The mains voltage can be taken as a constant 230V. If, therefore, a particular site offers a supply of 10A, the maximum combined wattage of appliances in a caravan that can be powered by the supply is 2400W (10 amps x 240 volts = 2400 watts).

In order to help with your calculations, the chart opposite, reproduced courtesy of The Caravan Club, gives some typical appliance power consumption ratings. Be sure to check the specific rating of the appliances you use.

Battery capacity is quoted in amp-hours (Ah). This is approximately the result of multiplying the current taken from the battery, by the time the battery will supply the current before requiring recharging. The size of battery needed can be estimated from a combination of: the length of time that the equipment will be in use between charges; the amount of equipment in use; and the length of time that the equipment is switched on. This isn't an exact calculation, and it also depends on the age and condition of the battery, and the rate of discharge, – but it's a good guide. The current taken by a piece of equipment can be calculated by dividing its wattage by the nominal voltage (12V). For example: a 13W fluorescent light will take 13W ÷ 12A, ie just over 1A. A spotlight with a 5W bulb will take only 5W ÷ 12A, ie just over 0.4A. A water pump may take several amps, but is usually only working for a few seconds at a time. A colour television also takes several amps, so if you watch a lot of television on a site without a mains hook-up, you would need a larger battery.

The following table gives specimen figures for the power consumption of typical appliances found in a caravan. While this is only one example, and your usage may vary significantly, it does suggest that a battery of 60Ah is the minimum acceptable capacity in a well equipped caravan.

For other electrical equipment, check the rating plate, usually affixed to the rear or underside.

Mains and 12V appliance power consumption in amps

Typical appliance	Mains 240V AC	12V DC
Refrigerator	0.5	9.6
Colour television	0.2	4.2
Microwave cooker	5.0	
2kW kettle	8.3	
750W kettle	3.1	
1kW fan heater	4.2	
Low wattage panel heater	from 0.4	
Carver water heater	2.75	
Battery charger	0.03	1.5
Carver fanmaster	4.2 (slow) to 8.3	1.5 (max)
Water pump		2 to 3
Fluorescent lighting		0.5 to 1.5
Spot lighting		0.8 to 1.75
TV antenna		negligible
Powered jockey wheel		25 (running)
500kg electric winch (500lb load)		50 (typically)
Cassette toilet flush		2.3 max
Car type vacuum cleaner		6 (typically)
Air pump inflator		10 (typically)

Another important factor to consider when adding anything new to your caravan is its weight. An awning or a generator, for example, can weigh over 50kg, and this must be taken into account when loading it into the caravan.

Even the weight of a portable television stored in the wrong place can upset the behaviour of a caravan on the road.

The following chart, published by The Caravan Club, gives some idea of how much some popular caravanning accessories weigh. However, you will need to check the weight of each individual piece of equipment to be sure.

Sample accessory weights

Equipment	kg	lb
Awning, complete	20	44
Battery (12V) and carrier box	20	440
Spare wheel and tyre (155 SR 13)	13	29
Spare wheel carrier (chassis mounted)	4	9
Portable TV	15	33
Porta Potti (empty)	6	13
Toilet fluid (2.5 litres)	2	4
Water carrier (rolling type), empty	4	9
Fire extinguisher	2	4
Step	2	4
Lifting jack	2	4
Chocks/packing pieces (wood)	4	9
Additional LPG, above 15kg allowance, is a total of two full 7kg cylinders	15	33
TOTAL	**109**	**239**
Additional weight of toilet, full	12	36
Additional weight of water carrier, full	26	57
TOTAL	**147**	**322**

NOTE: Travelling with a full water container or toilet is not recommended.

Before fitting equipment to your caravan, make sure that you have thoroughly read and understand the fitting instructions, and that you have all the necessary tools. There's nothing worse than starting a job, only to discover that you're not able to finish it as a result of having the wrong tools, or are unable to understand the instructions. If you're in any doubt about how anything works or fits, contact the manufacturer or your local dealer for advice.

HOW A CARAVAN IS BUILT

I spent several days at Bailey of Bristol's state-of-the-art caravan factory, to present this unique, inside view of how a caravan is built, using a Loire model as an example, from design, to build, to the completion of a new model.

You might think of your caravan as a home-from-home, with its full range of household equipment in miniature, but the average house builder would think that the caravan builder's world is back-to-front.

A caravan's foundations are built similarly to a house – but upside down, being turned over when finished. Then, the carpets are fitted, followed by the rest of the interior, before moving on to finish the exterior. Finally, the ceiling is erected, then the roof.

It may sound odd, but there's are good reasons to building a caravan this way. So, let's start by taking a quick look at the way in which a caravan is constructed, and then we'll start on the first stages in the Bailey construction process.

Do bear in mind that each stage of every job is being carried out at the same time, although on different caravans, of course. Bailey builds components, and complete caravans, in batches, so while one part of the factory is making a set of Senator side walls for the next day's production, another will be making the roofs, and a third the interior furniture. At any given time on the caravan assembly line, a batch of Loires, for instance, will be being assembled with components built the previous day. So, although the photo-sequences have been presented in a chronological order of sorts, it doesn't reflect the true chronology of the process.

The first steps

Picture 1. The Loire chassis at the start of the production line process. At this point, the chassis is upside-down ...

Picture 2. ... and, once it's turned over, the carpets, followed by the interior fixtures and fittings, start to be added to the caravan's floor and bulkhead assembly.

Picture 3. You've probably seen cut-away drawings in car manuals, and this is the caravan equivalent! This gives an idea of how much of the interior is assembled before the walls and roof go on.

Picture 4. It's now starting to look like a caravan from the outside. But while there's still access, workers continue to fit wall lights, cables, and other items that would be difficult to get at with the roof in place.

Chassis and floor construction

Picture 5. Before the chassis components are brought together, a chassis sidemember is scribed with its unique VIN, using Bailey's Auto Scribe equipment. Bailey Director Simon Howard explains that scribing is preferable to stamping, because scribing is much more difficult to modify. The Bailey logo is included, making it even more difficult.

Picture 6. The galvanised chassis members are assembled onto a rigid jig, ensuring precise dimensional conformity. You can see, here, the way in which components are brought together on the edge of the assembly process, so that as little time as possible is lost fitting the parts together. In the foreground, there's a pile of spare wheel carriers, fitted with their respective wheels, while to the right of the picture, the axle for this chassis has been fitted with its wheels, so that it can be brought into place when the time comes. Beneath it, another batch of axles await their turn.

Picture 7. Outside, in the store, you can get an idea of the numbers that are involved in making Bailey the largest caravan manufacturer in the UK. These are all new axles, arranged by type, waiting to be fitted to future builds.

Picture 8. An electric hoist is used to bring over the axle. This reduces the amount of manual handling and physical labour involved. Bailey's axles are purchased, stored, and used in batches. This ensures accurate stock rotation, so that parts are never left lying around for too long.

Picture 9. Bailey pays a lot of attention to production ergonomics – it calls it "taking the task to the operative." Here, you can see that the chassis frame and axle are all at approximately waist height – the ideal height to avoid injury or strain.

Picture 10. The pre-drilled holes in the chassis ensure that the AL-KO axle can be fitted precisely, and only in the correct position.

Picture 11. With the axle fitted to the chassis, each wheel bolt is tightened to the correct torque, and is then marked with a yellow marker pen to show that the bolt has been tightened to its safe torque level.

Picture 12. The axle-to-chassis bolts are tightened using a compressed air gun, with a ring spanner to prevent the bolt from turning as the nut is tightened.

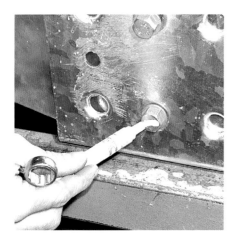

Picture 13. Again using a yellow marker, operative Paul Belford marks each bolt in turn, as it is correctly tightened. The wrench that Paul is using is a Desoutter calibrated air-driven torque wrench, combining accuracy with that all-important speed. This helps to keep the costs down.

Picture 14. A set of AL-KO Kober hitch assemblies will already have been brought in from the storage area, ready to be fitted to our Loire chassis. Bailey use all original manufacturer components in the assembly of its chassis.

Picture 15. With the hitch bolted to the chassis, Paul assembles the brake components ...

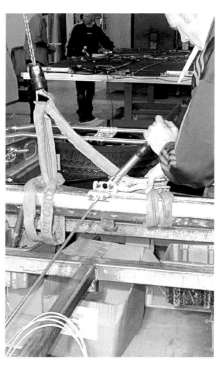

Picture 16. ... then turns his attention to the brake operating rod assembly on the underside of the chassis, once again using a torque wrench to ensure that bolts are correctly and safely fitted.

Picture 17. In the upside-down world of caravan manufacture, the spare wheel carrier is fitted to what will be the underside of the chassis. And, if you've ever tried to fit one as an accessory component, you'll appreciate just how much quicker it is to do it this way.

Picture 18. Meanwhile, an upside-down floor is being finished, ready for the chassis to be fitted to it.

Picture 19. The completed chassis, still inverted, is lifted by the electric hoist, and carried over to where it is to be fitted to the floor.

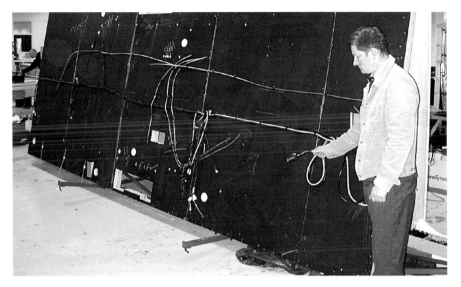

Picture 20. Bailey's Simon Howard demonstrates the very first stages building the floor assembly. You can see copper gas pipes and electrical cables already fitted at this early stage, even though none of it yet appears to make any sense. In fact, the only recognisable components are the 12V caravan-to-car connection plugs that Simon is holding here.

Picture 25. Manuel Rodrigez fits the heating ducting to the underside of the floor ...

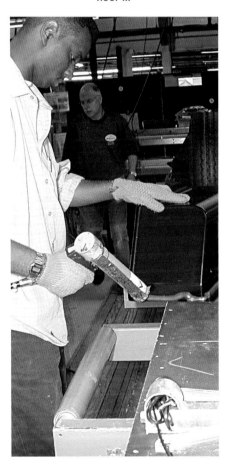

Picture 21. As many components as possible are fitted to the floor before the chassis is introduced to it ...

Picture 23. Team Leader Mark Baker starts to fit the underfloor waste pipes.

Picture 22. ... but many more, such as these corner steadies, can only be bolted into place once the chassis has been placed accurately upon the floor assembly.

Picture 24. All the waste water outlets are routed to the centre-offside of the caravan, so that waste water containers will be on the opposite side to the entrance door.

Picture 26. ... while Ali Mohammed places a generous bead of silicone sealant onto the caravan wheel box, before fitting the box to the floor assembly.

Picture 27. As the next floor is brought into position on the assembly bench, the floor turnover rig tips the completed floor and chassis assembly from the previous operation onto its side.

Picture 29. For the first time there's now a rolling chassis, and this is steered, much as you would with your caravan at home, until it's over the large jack used for raising it to the correct working height.

Picture 28. The turnover rig keeps going until the floor and chassis is on its wheels.

Picture 30. A group of operatives now work on the chassis. At the far end, you can see the bulkhead – one of the most important parts of the caravan for rigidity – has been bolted into place. The floor is now completely covered with carpet and Vinyl floor covering, the carpet being protected with a sheet of protective plastic. In the foreground, you can see the rolls of floor coverings on their stands, while to the right of the picture, the next chassis and floor assembly is waiting to be rolled over into position.

Part 2
General improvements

Picture 1. Würth has produced workshop consumables for car repairs for many years, but this was the first time I had used them extensively on a caravan. Included in the range shown here are upholstery cleaner, copper grease for keeping threads free of corrosion, and non-staining lubricants for locks and catches, and a whole lot more besides. I used the product shown in the following picture sequence, while my wife Shan took most of the photographs, and helped with the work between photohoots.

VALETING

It doesn't take long for your caravan to start looking tired and worn. By the time our Bürstner had seen its first birthday, it was looking remarkably neglected.

There are several reasons for this. One is that our atmosphere contains a lot of dirt, and this accumulates on the roof of caravans. From there, rain washes it down the walls, leaving those black streaks that we all recognise. But that's not all, as the rest of this section will demonstrate.

Picture 2. Areas where water can lodge are particularly prone to staining, and to providing homes for spiders. Whilst Shan and I think they're sweet little things, it was impossible to remove more than a minority of them before cleaning, though a hose of water seemed to help. Spiders' webs trap more dirt, leading to more staining.

Picture 3. One of the worst areas for mould to form is along the butyl or other mastic sealant, used along caravan joints. All sealed strips need checking for integrity, and it's ideal to check them all while cleaning.

Picture 4. On our caravan, the area at the base of the locker door is another gathering place for water and dirt as it drops out of suspension.

Picture 5. It's a good idea to open each hinge and flap. This complex door-and-window hinge on the Bürstner is a happy home for spiders, flies and, consequently, lots more dirt.

Picture 6. If you think that outdoor creatures have got it in for your caravan, you're not paranoid, you're right! Bird lime is not just unsightly, it can permanently mark paintwork, and should be cleaned off before it 'sets,' which it has done here.

Picture 7. The sensible place to start cleaning your caravan is the roof. I wasn't sensible, and ended up washing dirt from the roof off the sides after I'd cleaned them. Fortunately, it only took a few minutes with the hose.

Picture 8. I used the pump dispenser to spray Würth Primary Vehicle Cleaner onto all the stained, mould-encrusted areas of the caravan.

Picture 9. I also attacked the bird-dropping-splattered panels with the same stuff, giving it a good dose and leaving it to soak in well.

Picture 10. Next, I used some Würth Car Shampoo to wash all the side-walls. The Primary Vehicle Cleaner did a wonderful job on the bird lime and on the mould, though vertical black streaks were still evident.

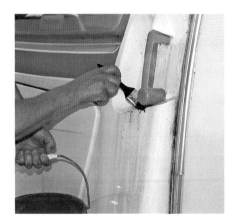

Picture 11. Nooks and crannies are best reached with a small brush, such as a paintbrush, and this also works well on alloy wheels. I don't know how else I could have got into the handle recesses.

Picture 12. I also used the hose on a gentle setting, and a soft hand brush to remove stubborn dirt and spiders' webs.

TOP TIP!
• *It might seem tempting, but you must never use a pressure washer on the body of your caravan. The power of the washer could force water through window and door seals, and into the caravan's interior. Worse still, there is a real risk of removing sealant and allowing water to penetrate the structure in future.*

Picture 13. When you're towing at motorway speeds, and flies and bugs hit your caravan – and worse still, your tow vehicle – they can be difficult to remove. Würth Insect Remover is incredibly effective at shifting the little blighters. I applied it using the same pump dispenser I'd used earlier.

Picture 14. You need to spray a good amount onto bug-studded areas, such as the front of the tow car's bonnet, grille, and side mirrors – as well as any areas of the caravan that have been 'attacked.'

TOP TIP!

Picture 15. Use soapy water with a cotton cloth, rather than a sponge, after the Insect Remover has had a good soak. Cloth is usually more abrasive than sponge, and will help remove any persistent insects much more quickly.

Picture 16. Having removed the mould, bugs, and settled dirt, it was time to turn my attention to the vertical stains from the roof. Of all the marks, these were the most difficult to remove.

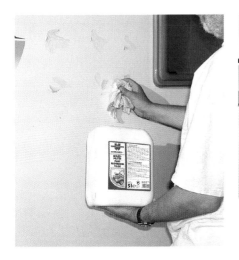

Picture 17. There are several grades and makes of abrasive bodywork polish to choose from, and I selected Würth New Paint Polish because it's the least abrasive of those available. You want to polish off just enough of the paint's surface to make it look like new, but not so much that you thin the paint film appreciably or – horror of horrors – cut right through the paint. I suspect that the paint on many caravans is not applied as heavily as it is on cars, so there's probably less leeway.

Picture 18. I used a cheap 12V power polisher. It's preferable to an air-powered or 230V machine, because you apply only very light pressure over a small area. Here, I'm splashing a few drops of water onto the foam polishing pad to thin the polish, making it a little less abrasive.

Picture 19. Work on a fairly small, controllable area at a time, whether polishing by hand or with a polisher. I placed a few dabs of polish onto the area I wanted to work on, and concentrated on that area alone.

Picture 20. You can see the staining coming off onto the polishing foam. This means you have to stop regularly, and wash the foam to remove excessive dirt.

Picture 21. This isn't a problem you have when working by hand, of course – you just turn the cloth to a clean part. Be warned: unless you polish with a clean cloth, you'll leave smears on the surface. I bought and used an entire roll of scrim cloth on this cleaning session!

Picture 22. If you ignore the dark areas just above the trim rail (they are the reflections of trees), you can clearly see the difference between the polished area on the right, and the unpolished paint on the left.

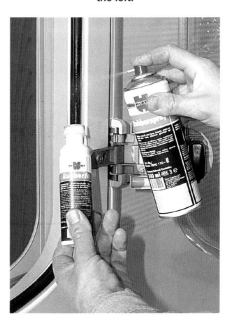

Picture 23. This is an essential adjunct to cleaning and polishing. When I opened the window in the door, the plastic stuck to the rubber seal, and had to be carefully squeezed away. This sticking can be so severe that the bacl tear. Würth Rubber Lubricant, available either in 'roll-on' or aerosol containers, prevents this from happening, and also extends the life of rubber seals by preventing them from drying out.

Würth products are available from many motor trade Motor Factors all around the country, though not from many caravan outlets. Find them in Yellow Pages, or online.

CARAVAN BODYWORK VALETING

All caravans attract dirt and mould in a way that cars rarely do, mainly because they spend most of their lives in one spot. Flat roofs allow pollution in air and rain to gather, and mould grows happily. It takes a lot of shifting.

Here, I'll explain how Paul Asserati, of Tourershine, undertakes what I describe as 'the ultimate in caravan bodywork valeting' – a 10-stage plan that can turn your caravan into a just-like-new stunner, and at a remarkably low cost.

Paul offers three levels of valet service: a 'Standard' valet (only offered within 35 miles of Stamford, Lincolnshire, unless three or more caravans are to be cleaned at the same time), a 'Superior' valet, and a 'Restoration' valet, that can take up to two full days, and has to be priced individually.

Picture 3. Next, he pressure washes the bodywork with his special lower pressure jet (regular pressure washers can cause damage), removing cleaner and degreasing the body in preparation for the rest of the process.

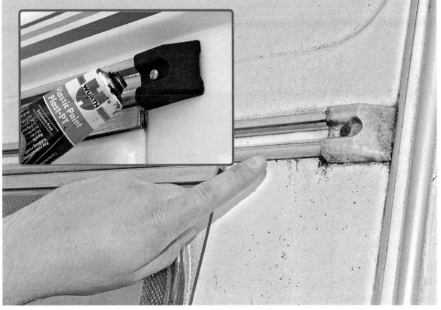

Picture 1. Typical mould and black staining. We replaced trim screws, and coloured some plastic trims with Würth's Plastic Dye. Old screws tend to shear if corroded, requiring fresh holes and sealant.

Picture 4. The whole roof is then brushed with a shampoo, and pressure washed off. Paul offers a roof wax service, and I'd strongly recommend it – after all, it's where most dirt initially lands.

Picture 2. First in his 10-stage plan, Paul applies an 'advanced' multi-purpose cleaner to the whole caravan body, including the roof, to loosen grime, moss, black streaks, and general dirt.

Picture 5. If the surface isn't too bad, brushing replaces power washing. After washing, Paul goes over the entire caravan with a fresh microfibre drying cloth, removing all water from the surface.

Picture 6. Paul then carries out a process that most owners can't do: he machine mops all of the caravan side-walls, using different grade compounds, to restore the factory colour.

Picture 9. ... and on top of that, a coat of liquid 'hardwax' is applied, left for up to an hour, then buffed to an intense shine, providing a high level of protection.

Picture 7. Paul also likes to remove any faded stripes, decals, and stickers, replacing with new, more modern ones, if wanted. Ours were a nightmare to remove!

Picture 8. There are also hours of hand work with fine abrasives, and a coat of super resin polish, that includes a sealer to protect the surface and give a brilliant glossy shine ...

Picture 10. Paul polished all the windows, inside and out, to a clear shine. Then, after 12 hours of work on two caravans, took a well-deserved nap ... The finished caravans looked amazing!

Paul spends ages on detailing, including cleaning rubber seals, removing tarnishing from lockers and handles, and removing surplus sealer.

He says, "I hate to see this, as it traps grime and ruins the finished look of the caravan." He also cleans and polishes the wheels, and applies a subtle tyre shine.

I was honestly gobsmacked at the difference that Tourershine made. The Bürstner had a deeper shine than it had from new, and the fibreglass Freedom model was taken from 'shabby chic' to sparkling brightness in a way that I wouldn't have believed possible.

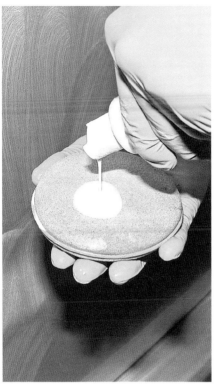

TREATING PAINTWORK

Caravans are notable for collecting black streaks and green mould. However, caravan paint is notoriously poor: too much rubbing down, and you'll go through the paint. Sealing the paint surface is the answer: a surface treatment with a Teflon coating that prevents black streaks from sticking.

Picture 3. This is the Paintseal product, a mix containing DuPont Teflon – aka polytetrafluoroethylene, but known to friends as PTFE. It's so good, the product is guaranteed for five years, if applied to caravans under six months old.

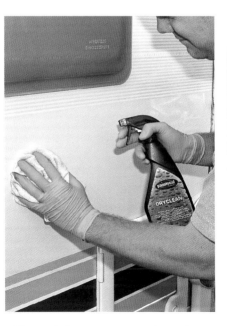

Picture 1. Paintseal fitter Mark displays the kit he'll be using. I was pleased that all the company's fitters are employed and paid by the day, NOT by the job. No cutting corners!

Picture 2. Our caravan was cleaned not long ago, so Mark used a spray-on 'dry clean' to ensure the surface was perfect. He also used T-Cut to polish out a couple of scratches.

Picture 4. Mark applies a coating of Paintseal over all the caravan's surfaces; aluminium, ABS, fibreglass, and all. When dry, he polishes it off.

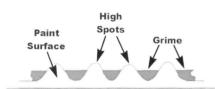

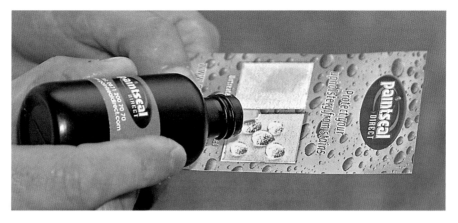

Picture 5. Abrasive polish, like T-Cut, cuts the microscopic peaks off the paint's surface, and removes the grime, too. However, it leaves the paint thinner each time it's used; Paintseal fills the troughs.

Picture 8. Paintseal Fabric Protection has been applied to the cloth on the lower part of the card, but not the upper one. Both have been wetted with the same amount of water drops.

Picture 6. The treatment also works well on alloy wheels, making it much easier to remove the unavoidable layer of slightly sticky brake dust that attaches to their surface.

Picture 9. Mark uses a battery-powered sprayer to treat the caravan's fabric upholstery. With open-weave cloth, spilled liquids may not 'perch' on the surface, but they won't soak into the fibres, either.

Picture 10. Paintseal's MD, Andy Bradbury, displays the range of after-care products available (by phone and online), including cleaner specifically for acrylic windows. A starter pack is supplied when the caravan is treated.

Picture 7. You can have an attractive Paintseal sticker attached, then look out for other users. You'll spot their caravans on site, anyway: it's amazing how rain 'beads' on the paint's new surface.

Our three year old Bürstner actually looks better than when it was new, and I'm confident it won't need its annual paint cleaning exercise for quite a while! Wax-based treatments don't compare with this stuff, and you can feel the difference with your hand.

It's important not to clean the Paintseal treated surface with wax or wax shampoo, because it can cause blooming. Instead, there's special Paintseal detergent. The dirt just floats off anyway, along with those pesky black streaks!

Provided it lasts (the guarantee is reassuring), this is the finest paint surface product I've yet come across.

PROTECT UPHOLSTERY

If you, or the kids, drop curry, coffee, or Coca-Cola on the upholstery, you could be in for a large re-upholstery bill. Here, I'll show you how you can remove some upholstery stains, and block others before they happen.

This all started when UltraShield sent me some of its upholstery protector to try. Before I got around to using it, I managed to get an oily stain on the driver's seat of our Volkswagen tow-vehicle; a perfect opportunity for a test.

Picture 3. This was followed up with Würth upholstery cleaner, applied in a thick layer of foam from the can, before being rubbed vigorously with a clean cloth.

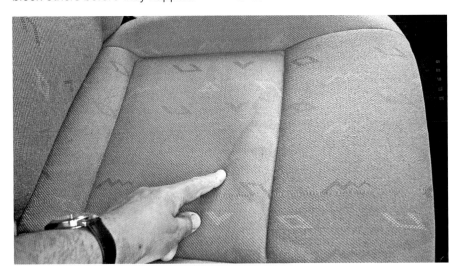

Picture 1. Our Volkswagen T5 Transporter is one of the best tow-vehicles I've ever driven, but it does get used for lugging car parts around, too. It was after sitting on something oily, then getting into the vehicle, that I managed to stain the new upholstery. A wash-off with soap and water only managed to leave a bad tide mark.

Picture 4. Another clean cloth was used to dry the fabric as much as possible, and then the seat was left to dry thoroughly. In winter, you may need to leave the door open in a heated garage.

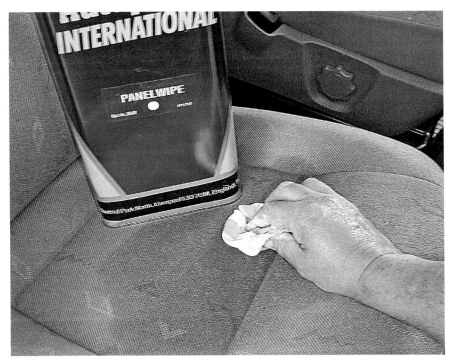

Picture 2. The first step in removing an oily stain is to dissolve it as much as you can. Panel wipe, used in car bodywork repairs, did the job well, without damaging the fabric.

Picture 5. Once the upholstery was dry, I applied UltraShield fabric protector. It's expensive, but goes a long way. Here, I'm using the pump-up spray you can buy from UltraShield, and it's fine for smaller areas such as the seats of your tow-vehicle. The manufacturer says; "UltraShield Fabric Protection penetrates deep into the fabric, forming an invisible shield around each and every fibre. This protective coating inhibits the penetration of frustrating spills such as coffee, tea, milk and fizzy drinks – without affecting the fabric's natural texture."

SAFETY FIRST!

• The liquid and vapour are flammable, and must only be used away from all sources of ignition.
• Keep it out of your eyes. If you do get some in your eyes, wash them with plenty of clean water.
• Wear a breathing mask suitable for organic vapours when spraying.

Picture 7. I also applied UltraShield to all of our caravan's upholstery. It was removed from the caravan, and spread out in our garage on an assortment of boxes, to keep it off the ground.

Picture 6. It's highly recommended that you apply the material only in a well-ventilated area, and you should wear an adequate air-fed breathing mask, such as this Würth disposable item, rather than the simpler types that don't protect against vapours. The producer says, "UltraShield Fabric Protection is non-toxic and is CFC-free," but in my view, it's not sensible to breathe in the vapourised liquid.

Picture 8. I used a spray gun with a compressor, because the pump-up applicator would have taken ages, and required many breaks to pump up the container. The cheapest spray gun from Machine Mart would do the job. I'm lucky enough to have a Clarke workshop compressor, but you could hire one, or buy a small, cheap one. They're also handy for inflating caravan tyres without the hassle of manoeuvring in a garage forecourt.

I sprayed each cushion top in overlapping patterns, horizontally then vertically. Then, I turned my attention to the edges and sprayed those as well. The manufacturer says that the finer the mist, the more effective the application, so set your sprayer accordingly.

If you work methodically, you won't forget which cushions you have or haven't sprayed. The UltraShield smells slightly when applied, but has no odour at all when dry. The application took about 40 minutes, but it would have taken much longer with a hand-pumped applicator. The upholstery was left overnight to dry and to lose its odour, before being replaced in the caravan.

UltraShield Fabric Protection is backed by a seven year warranty from the date of application, so I think it's well worth using. Just remember not to sit on the upholstery with an oily bottom before you've used it, like some people we know ...

One container of UltraShield Fabric Protection provided two coats on all the caravan upholstery shown in this section, though coverage will obviously depend on how much you apply. The UltraShield Hand-Pump Sprayer enables a very fine mist to be applied.

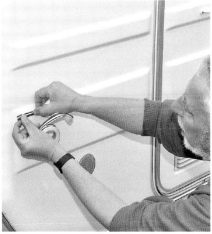

Picture 2. I find it easiest to line up against an existing trim or moulding. If there isn't one, use washable felt pen or masking tape to make a perfectly level line to work against.

STRIPES AND STICKERS

Subtle use of graphics can improve your caravan's appearance no end. Sticking vinyl graphics on your caravan isn't rocket science, but it will look awful unless you do it properly.

Existing graphics can be damaged in an accident, even just scraping past tree branches can be enough. Or you might want to personalise your caravan to suit your own tastes. You can even have a copy of original graphics made for you, if they're not available new.

Picture 3. Having firmly stuck down the first few millimetres, pull the strip lightly, and check the level by looking along it. Get down level with the stripe, and if necessary, have a second pair of eyes double-check ...

Picture 1. This styling stripe has backing paper on its self-adhesive surface. Cut the end off square before you start. Don't peel too much off to start with, or it'll stick together!

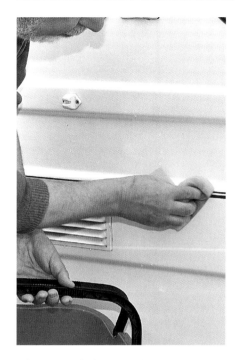

Picture 4. ... before pressing down lightly. Do one or two metres at a time, and don't press down TOO hard until you're sure it's positioned correctly. Use a wet sponge for the final smoothing.

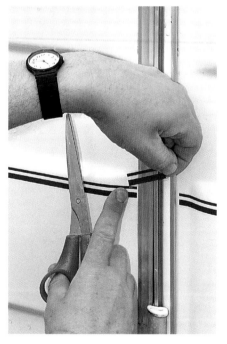

Picture 5. As you saw earlier, you go right over door and access hatch openings, then go back later and carefully cut to fit. Some favour a sharp knife – but don't scratch the paint.

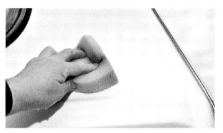

Picture 6. Fitting a graphic is a similar process. Because of its size, it's much more likely you'll trap air bubbles. So sponge some soapy water onto the panel. While still wet ...

Picture 7. ... and after peeling the vinyl graphic off the backing paper, get ready to place it on the panel. It's best to wet the graphic before peeling: it will inevitably wrap around on itself ...

Picture 8. ... and wetting the graphic prevents the self-adhesive layer on the back of the graphic sticking to itself. Slide the graphic (which often consists of separate parts) onto the paintwork. Don't worry, it WILL stick when the water dries.

Picture 9. The main section of this particular graphic is being placed on the panel. It will slide around very easily, but keep your fingers wet, too – it makes it much easier to handle!

Picture 10. It's vital that you spend time aligning the graphic correctly, AND that you squeeze all air bubbles out. For larger graphics, use a squeegee, removing air gently from the centre, outwards.

To have graphics made, most graphics printers will need you to take a good quality photograph, taken straight on to avoid distortion, and without any shadows or reflections visible. You'll also need to specify the exact overall dimensions of the finished graphic.

Then, subject to the photograph being good enough quality, Eco-Nomical will be able to make you as many copies of the graphic as you want.

Note that if you've seen a graphic you like, and wish to use it, don't assume that you can simply copy it: it's almost certainly protected by copyright. Renewing existing graphics on your own caravan is probably okay, but copying someone else's design is illegal.

FIT MINI-HEKI ROOF LIGHT

Clear plastic rooflights can be damaged by impact, and often craze with age. You could replace the plastic, or even cut a fresh hole and fit an entire new unit. Alternatively, you could upgrade to the more sophisticated Seitz Mini-Heki unit from Dometic, shown here. It opens like full-sized units, has three vent positions, and an integral blind.

You'll need a roll of butyl sealant, too. Dometic's engineer, Ian Walker, of Chase Caravans, fitted our rooflight, and you might be looking at two to four hours' labour, on average, if you have one professionally fitted.

Picture 3. If you're not replacing an existing rooflight of the same size, you'll need to cut a hole in the roof.

Picture 1. The Seitz Mini-Heki consists of these three major components. The top two clamp together from each side of the roof.

Picture 4. If you do need to cut a hole, it's essential to avoid any supports or wiring. Ian measured the roof thickness, and selected from the screws provided.

Picture 2. Ian removed the old unit – there's always a struggle to 'unstick' old sealant (best to wear gloves).

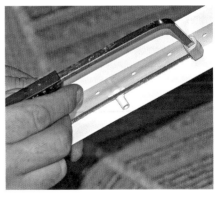

Picture 5. Using figures supplied on the chart that comes with the instructions, Ian trimmed the plastic lugs on the unit.

Picture 6. This centre section is also fitted with spring clips, allowing the fitting of the lower panel incorporating the blind.

Picture 7. Butyl sealer never sets, but sticks tenaciously. The easiest type to use is this tape with peel-off backing strip.

Picture 8. The extremely resilient polycarbonate domed rooflight was lowered, accurately, into its correct position, on the top of the caravan roof.

Picture 9. The screws passed through the centre panel, into the domed top section, and were tightened using a small torque wrench, to 1.5Nm.

Picture 10. Finally, Ian clipped the lower trim panel, with integral roller blind, onto the spring clips.

The Seitz Mini-Heki is made to fit the standard 400mm square opening in many caravan roofs (provided they're between 25mm and 60mm thick), and has superior features compared with many, more basic units. In many ways, it's a small version of the full-sized Heki rooflight.

Replacing an existing unit should be within the powers of most DIYers, but cutting a fresh hole could be disastrous. Make sure you know where any wiring or other hidden features are located in the roof space, before starting to cut (if you don't know, ask your local caravan dealer to find out for you).

FIT A MANOEUVRING HANDLE

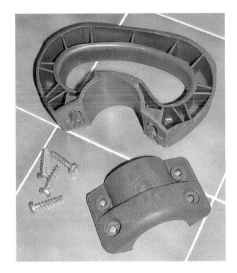

Picture 1. The AL-KO Manoeuvring Handle kit is simple, yet very useful. The handle, clamp plate, and screws comprise the entire contents of the kit. They are for use on caravans' standard 48mm jockey wheel posts, but check before buying, as some trailer jockey wheels have narrower posts.

Picture 2. Fit the handle at the top of the post so that you retain the maximum amount of adjustment in the A-frame. Don't worry if the handle appears too small – it's not. It pulls tightly to shape, and grips hard as the screws are evenly tightened.

Picture 2. Viewed from underneath the overrun, the A-frame cover and hitch cover both pass over a bolt fixed to the chassis. Remove the plastic wing nut (inset, arrowed), before levering the end of the cover over the bolt.

Picture 3. Tipped upside-down, this is the hole in the end of the cover. Be wary: depending on the length of the bolt, there's a very real risk of cracking the plastic. A lot of levering is called for!

OVERRUN COVER REPLACEMENT

Picture 1. This is the AL-KO chrome overrun cover, alongside the dull plastic one it replaces. Even if you're not going for a chrome version, it's useful to see how to remove this item on an AL-KO chassis.

Picture 4. I used a power mini-grinder to cut a slot in the end of the cover. Note how the slot is tapered, helping it to locate onto the bolt as you push the cover home. You can't cut the chrome cover with a hack saw, the chrome plating is much too hard.

Picture 5. With the jockey wheel handle facing forward, and the handbrake lever in the 'on' position, the cover is easily fitted. It grips at the front by friction, and at the rear by refitting the nut you removed earlier.

Picture 6. Personally, I think it brightens the appearance of the front of the caravan no end.

CORNER STEADY FEET

Many years ago, my father-in-law (who got my wife started on caravanning in the '60s, when she was still a girl) cut a set of circular corner steady pads from thick aluminium sheet. When he stopped caravanning, we inherited them, and very useful they were, too ... as long as we remembered to take them!

Corner steady pads that are permanently fixed to the corner steadies, and which fold themselves back as the corner steadies are retracted, make life so much simpler.

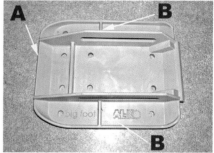

Picture 1. The foot of the AL-KO Big Foot must be fitted with the rounded end (A) facing the outside of the caravan, so that it 'toes' the ground as the steady is lowered. There are two spring mounting points (B), one on each side.

Picture 2. All the steel parts are rust-proof stainless-steel, not bright zinc plated. The first job, is to spring the split-pin open with a screwdriver, and slide on the loop at one end of the spring.

Picture 3. I found it useful to cut off part of one of the split-pin's legs ...

Picture 4. ... because the hole into which the split-pin is placed is close to the side of the support on the foot. Alternatively, you could bend it over the top of the plastic bar through which it passes. Stainless steel is less malleable than mild steel, so bending is quite difficult.

Picture 6. The nut is tightened on the bolt, but only to the point where the foot can slide readily between the large washers – don't over tighten.

Picture 5. Using the long stainless steel bolts, washers, and lock-nuts supplied, the foot is bolted to the corner steady leg. Later AL-KO corner steadies already have a hole for the bolt; earlier ones might need to have new holes drilled, using the paper template provided as a guide.

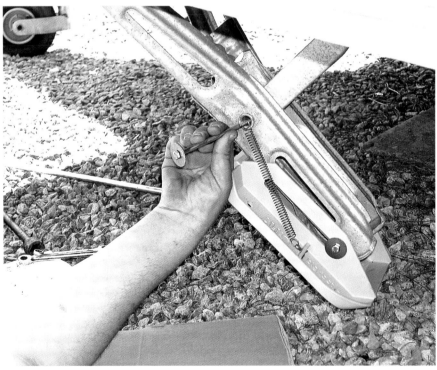

Picture 7. Another large washer, and the other bolt, is slipped through the eye in the other end of the spring, and pushed through the swivel bush hole in the leg, before another washer and lock-nut are fitted from the other side. I replaced the stainless steel washers provided with smaller ones, from Screwfix. They fit much more neatly on the eye of the spring, instead of bearing on the side of the coils.

Picture 8. If the foot is sliding correctly, it will fold itself back against the leg when it is retracted. The foot twists to one side a little, because of the offset pull of the spring, but it works fine.

Picture 9. If you frequently park on a steep slope, these Big Foot Adapters (extension plates) could be useful. They are 'insteps' that fit between foot and leg, and provide an extra 45mm on the inside leg measurement.

Picture 10. As the corner steady is wound down, the Big Foot slides along the end of the leg and provides a wide, stable pad, capable of coping with undulations in the ground. Incidentally, as I discovered – but only after fitting the front feet – the appearance is slightly better if you fit the spring to the inside, as shown here.

Picture 3. Life is never straightforward, is it! AL-KO recommend cutting the side wall of the caravan if necessary, and in some installations that could be a good idea. Our Bürstner is complex in this area, so I made a pair of wooden blocks, tapered at the rear, to lift the tube away from the bodywork.

CORNER STEADY TUBES

Kneeling down on wet grass to try to locate the corner steady hexagons can be a pain – in more ways than one if you suffer from a bad back. AL-KO's Comfort Kit helps make corner steady winding much more comfortable.

Picture 1. The Comfort Kit consists of four lengths of plastic tube, and a pair of extensions with articulated joints.

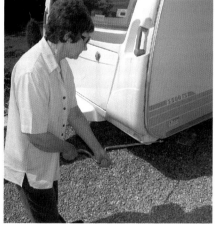

Picture 2. The tubes, which must be cut to length, allow you to locate the extension bars without kneeling on the ground. The extension bars allow you stand at normal height while winding the corner steadies.

TOP TIP!

• Use a rot-proof timber, such as cedar or tanalised (rot-resistant) timber. Ordinary softwood will rapidly deteriorate.

IMPORTANT NOTE:
Don't assume steadies are symmetrical, and that you can cut both tubes to the same length (the front ones on ours weren't).

Picture 4. My Screwfix stainless steel assortment came in handy, as I searched it for suitable stainless steel screws (to avoid corrosion), before drilling clearance holes in the plastic tube's base-plate and screwing it in place.

Picture 5. On our caravan, the rear tubes were much shorter. Note that there may be wires unavoidably in the way, front or rear. If so, cut part of the base plate away. It'll be okay because most of the strength is in the tubular section.

FLIP-UP TOWBALL COVER
Despite the initial expense, flip-up towball covers have the advantage of looking smart, being very easy to use, and helping to prevent loss or theft. However, they can't, at the time of writing, be used with the extended neck AL-KO-type towball.

Picture 1. All modern AL-KO hitches demand the use of a special long-neck towball. The standard towball won't do, because the hitch will foul on it. If you're using your existing tow vehicle, but switching to a new AL-KO hitch, you MUST change the towball.

When using an AL-KO stabiliser, all paint must be removed from the ball of the towball, otherwise the friction linings in the stabiliser will be ruined. At the time of writing, the over-centre type of chrome towball cover, shown here, isn't available for use with the long-neck towball.

Picture 2. AL-KO's own towball cover is made to fit, needless to say.

PROTECT YOUR SHINS

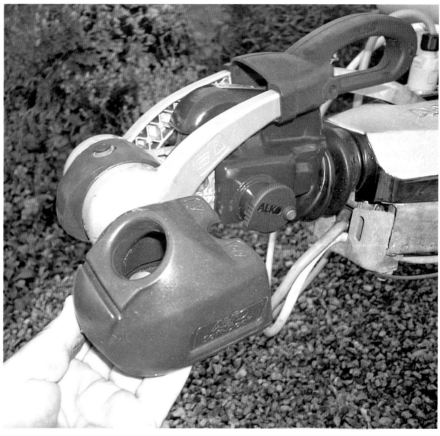

Picture 1. A more universal alternative to a flip-up cover, is to fit an AL-KO Soft Ball. AL-KO claims that it's to prevent reversing damage, but it also hurts less if you accidentally walk into it!

Picture 2. This is version mainly for trailer owners whose trailer is fitted with model couplings from AK7, AK10/2, AK160/300 and AK252. The Soft Dock helps prevent damage if you reverse your car a little too close to the trailer, and is similar to the rubber 'cushion' fitted as standard to modern AL-KO caravan hitches.

FIT A 13-PIN PLUG AND SOCKET

You can convert your 12N and 12S 'black'- and 'white'-type sockets into a single, superior, 13-pin 'Euro' connection, using parts from MCL Ltd. New cars and caravans normally come with the newer, 13-pin socket, unless you specify otherwise: they're a much better, longer-lasting design. Also, MCL's parts are said to be 'original equipment' quality.

Picture 1. MCL has several different types of adapter available (detailed at the end of this section) but, of course, it makes life simpler if all your plugs and sockets can be of the same, 13-pin type.

Picture 2. Tim Consolante, from MCL, demonstrated the 'innards' of the newer 13-pin socket. In essence, 2 x 7-pin sockets make a 13-pin socket, because you don't need two separate vehicle earth connections.

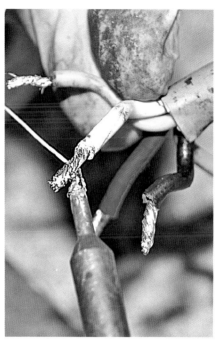

Picture 4. ... which wire was which. In theory, the colour code should tell you, but it's best to check. He twisted and soldered each cable end, before inserting each cable into its relevant hole ...

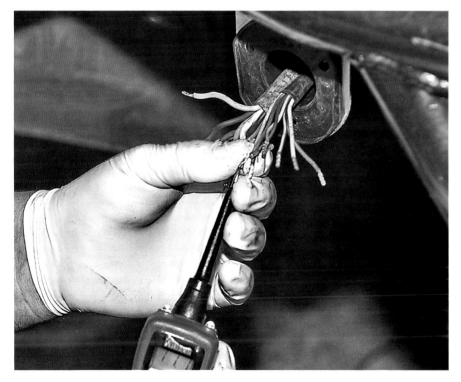

Picture 3. Before getting this far, you must make sure the vehicle battery has been disconnected (note alarm and ICE settings etc, first). Tim used his tester to make certain he knew ...

Picture 5. ... in the 13-pin socket. (He'd previously slackened each of the screws.) The downside with these plugs, is that there are almost twice as many wires to fit ...

Picture 6. ... into almost the same amount of space, so care is needed. MCL can also supply this wonderful, shrink-fit sleeving that shrinks as it's heated, and has sealant built in.

Picture 8. If your caravan has two 7-core cables, MCL can supply this clever 13-pin adapter plug that has two holes in the cable grommet (inset), allowing sealed entry for both cables.

Picture 7. The sealant melts, solidifying again as it cools. Tim used stainless steel bolts and locknuts to attach the socket to the stainless steel bracket, available from Extreme 4x4.

Picture 9. But what if you also tow a small trailer with single, 7-pin wiring? You simply purchase an inexpensive 13-to-7-pin adapter, fit the adapter to the socket, and fit the trailer plug to the adapter.

Picture 10. This is a caravan-mounted 13-pin socket, allowing you to remove the cable completely when parked up. You can also see how a pair of cables enter the twin-cable 13-pin plug.

What's so good about 13-pin?
• Pins and sockets are stronger, and made from superior materials (at least, MCL's are).
• The plug is positively engaged, so it can't be wobbled, preventing pin deformation.

• The plug locks, and the flap on the socket clips over the disc on the plug only when correctly inserted.
• 13-core cable has larger earth conductors than 7-core cable, reducing voltage drop.

Picture 1 (page 34) shows some of MCL's products: A and B are male/female adapters; C and D are a 13-pin plug and socket; E, a stainless bracket; and F cleverly allows a conventional tow-vehicle to power LED lights on a caravan.

STAINLESS STEEL GAS HOSES

Failed, blocked gas regulators can be a pain, but preventing failure is simpler than you might think.

Here are some solutions from Gaslow, fitted by top, Gas Safe registered caravan engineer, Rob Sheasby.

Replacing rubber hoses with stainless steel while upgrading other, ancillary components

Rubber hoses are believed to cause regulator blockage, and require replacement after five years. Stainless steel hoses last for 20 years and don't leak 'oil' into the regulator. We added spanner-free adapters, and a guaranteed Gaslow regulator for convenience and reliability.

Picture 1. The Gaslow 300 30mbar regulator (left) comes with 750mm stainless steel hose (for Gaslow refillable cylinders) and a propane adapter. Rob also refitted my Gaslow auto-changeover valve and gauges.

Picture 2. Work on the caravan-side of the regulator must be carried by a qualified engineer. Because the new Gaslow regulator is taller than the old one, Rob cut a length ...

Picture 3. ... of copper pipe, and fitted the nut and olive. This is a Wade Couplings nut and olive set: only use them as sets, because the Wade olive has parallel sides.

Picture 4. Rob connected the new length of pipe to the Gaslow regulator using a pair of spanners. Under-tightening or over-tightening will cause a leak.

Picture 5. Caravan gas engineers use a Truma pressure tester to check for leaks. For about £12, Gaslow will provide your engineer with an adapter that goes onto the Gaslow regulator.

Picture 6. Here you can see why; with the extra height of the automatic changeover valve and gauges, Rob needed to make a specific length and shape of copper connection pipe (arrowed).

Picture 7. The Gaslow regulator comes attached to its own mounting bracket. Rob carefully drilled pilot holes in the caravan bulkhead, and used self tapping screws to attach the bracket.

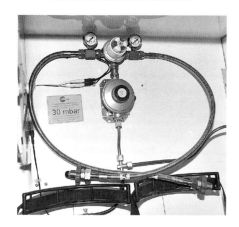

Picture 8. Before fitting the hand-tightened propane connector (right) to the stainless hose, Rob checked the rubber seal (top inset). The stainless steel hose's inner eliminates plasticiser extraction, which can cause regulator failure.

Picture 9. Finally, our caravan's twin-hose system was installed and ready for its cylinders. There is still a slim chance of re-condensed gas draining back into the regulator. However, this is easily prevented ...

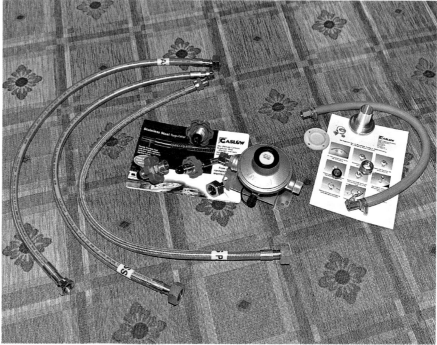

Picture 10. ... by making sure the stainless steel hose is long enough to fall slightly lower than the inlet, before it connects to the regulator. This is a typical single-hose installation.

Listed here are some of the major differences between old-style rubber hoses, and Gaslow's stainless steel gas hoses:

Rubber hose
• Should be changed every five years.
• Uses crimped end fittings.
• Is gas permeable, so it will smell of gas.

Stainless steel hose
• Should be changed every 20 years.
• Uses welded end fittings.
• Has zero permeation, so does not smell of gas.

There's a huge amount of technical and background information on Gaslow's website. If you download the appropriate .pdf files, you'll be able to print out and absorb the information at your leisure. There are many differences between pre- and post-2004 systems, and they're explained on the website.

GAS CHANGEOVER SYSTEM

If your gas runs out while its raining, in very cold weather, or in the middle of the night, changing the gas cylinder ranks with emptying the chemical toilet as a 'Job We All Hate.' However, installing a Gaslow 500 Automatic Changeover System, along with spanner-free cylinder connectors, will help. Plus, anyone who owns at least two adjustable spanners can carry out this job – provided there's room in the gas locker.

There are several different types if changeover system, the two main types being the Gaslow 500, which uses its own regulator in place of your old one, or a head unit only, for systems with an existing, bulkhead-mounted regulator.

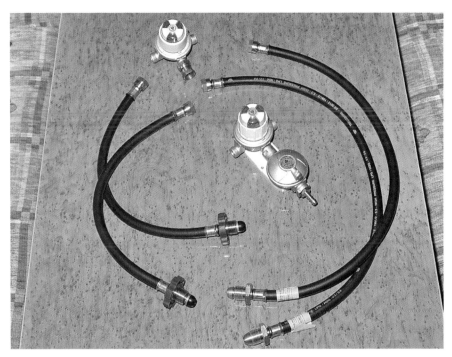

Picture 1. On our Bürstner, the gas cylinders were on opposite sides of the locker, until I resited them. You may need to reposition your cylinder clamps if they aren't close together.

Picture 2. This is the Gaslow 500, with its own regulator. Its inlet is for a rubber hose, secured with a jubilee clip. It must be securely mounted inside the gas locker.

Picture 3. Caravans from 2004 model year have a 30mbar regulator permanently fixed in place. The 'tail' (rubber hose) is removed by locking the fixed hexagon and unscrewing the union nut.

Picture 4. Before fitting new connectors, ensure that the seals (arrowed) are undamaged and in position. Buy new ones from Gaslow, Calor, or your caravan shop if they're needed.

Picture 5. The Gaslow 500 head unit is best connected to the two 'tails' while you have good access. Use a spanner to lock the body while tightening the union on the hose.

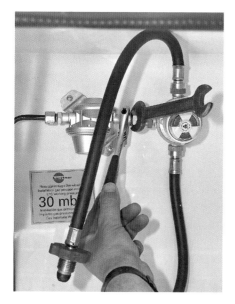

Picture 6. There was just enough room for the new unit. If the regulator needs repositioning, it's a job for a qualified installer, not a DIY task. Tighten well, but don't over-tighten.

Picture 7. Gaslow's Easy-Fit hoses (left) can be used even if you don't fit the changeover valve. The rubber seal makes it possible to hand-tighten, unlike the traditional brass dome.

Picture 8. The knurled red plastic knob pushes the seal into the cylinder valve (as usual, first check that it's clear), and is tightened with surprising ease.

You shouldn't use sealant on gas connections. Clean running threads and new seals are essential, but sealant could temporarily conceal a problem.

You'll need ½in Whitworth spanners for these connectors – not found in the vast majority of tool boxes. It's better to use two correctly adjusted adjustable spanners than

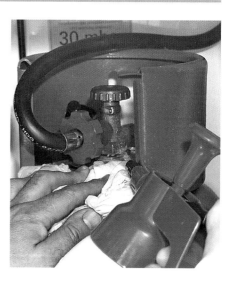

Picture 9. After completion, you must check for leaks with a proprietary leak check solution or washing-up liquid solution. The former does a much better job.

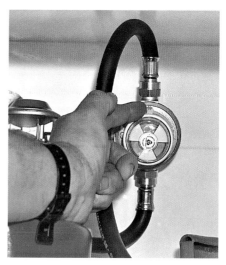

Picture 10. When connected, and with gas turned on, the valve switches to Green. You turn the knob until the indicator points to the cylinder you want to use first.

risk the near certainty of damaging the hexagons with over-sized AF or Metric spanners.

The downside? It's possible that both cylinders could run out without your noticing. You could always leave number two cylinder turned off until number one expires. A quick turn on at the valve, and you'll be cooking with gas!

FITTING A FRIDGE VENT

In hot summers, Dometic can receive record numbers of call-outs from caravanners whose fridges aren't cooling properly. The reason? High ambient temperatures leading to a lack of air circulation behind the fridge. The answer? Fit an electric fan, using nothing more sophisticated than an electric drill.

Provided you have an electrician make the electrical connections, you can fit your own thermostatically operated fridge vent fan. Here we show how to fit one of the two CAK fridge vent fans, as presented here by CAK's MD, Jonathan Frost.

The CAK FFT1 fridge vent fan uses a single fan and is suitable for use in the UK and short visits to southern Europe with 80-litre or smaller fridges. The FFT2 has two fans, and is intended for longer stays in southern Europe, and for much larger fridges and freezers in the UK.

Picture 1. On a standard Dometic caravan fridge vent, the tags are pushed down with a screwdriver, and the exhaust trim lifted off. The oval pipe cover is then unclipped from underneath (inset).

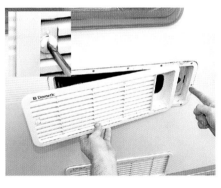

Picture 2. The main vent cover is detached after turning the turnbuckle anti-clockwise (inset), then lifting away from the left. When refitting, push the slotted hole onto the long peg shown here.

Picture 3. Inside the caravan, you need to access the Dometic fridge top. Pull off the three knobs, unscrew the catch, and then remove the two screws (arrowed) to remove the cover.

Picture 4. On some caravans, removing the sink will expose the fridge-top wiring. The plug hole (a) was unscrewed from the trap (b), the sink unscrewed, and removed. Some have replaceable sealant.

Picture 5. Back outside again, Dave, who was carrying out the work, marked the fixing positions on the fridge vent, and drilled holes for the screws provided with the kit.

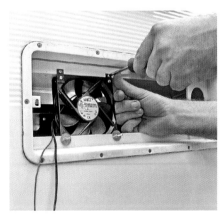

Picture 6. The 'Meccano'-style strips supplied were cut to size, to fit the fan to the aluminium deflector with self-tapping screws. The lower part, bolted to the plastic, was reinforced with washers.

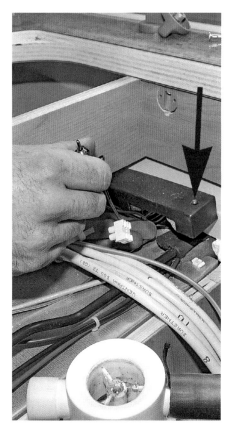

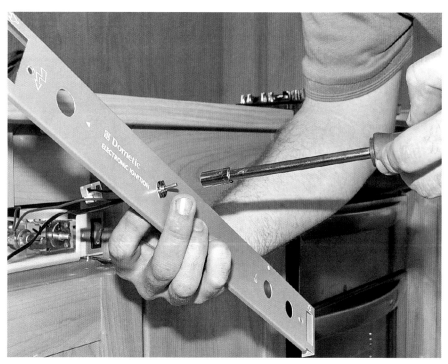

Picture 9. The fridge front trim panel, removed earlier, should be covered in masking tape, carefully measured, marked out, centre punched, drilled, and the new switch screwed carefully into place.

Picture 7. Dave unscrewed the trunking (arrowed), passed the wiring along the existing wiring route into the space atop the fridge, and used the existing foam sealant to guard against draughts.

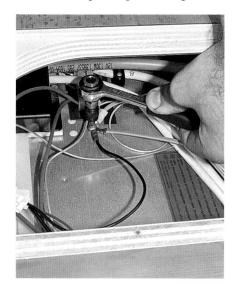

Picture 10. The switch allows OFF, permanent running, or thermostat. In thermostat mode, the built in air temperature sensor switches on the fan automatically when the temperature behind the fridge reaches 30-35 degrees Celsius.

Picture 8. You'll need to have a qualified electrician fabricate an earth cable to fix to the fridge's earth strap, and a 'positive' feed to a fused, permanent feed on the fridge.

If, in hot weather, you feel the fridge isn't as cold as usual, there's probably overheating in the space behind the fridge. If so, you need a fridge vent fan.

Quoting CAK's Jonathan Frost, "A fridge fan will improve the cooling performance of any make of 3-way gas absorption fridge. The fan pushes hot air out of the top vent, allowing more cooler air to enter the lower vent. The improved airflow reduces the overheating of the absorption unit, allowing a more efficient process of cooling the fridge's interior."

Fridge fans are not suitable for DC compressor-based fridges and freezers.

REPLACING BLOWN AIR TRUNKING

Replacing or extending blown air heater trunking is easy, provided you know what parts are available, and it is something anyone capable of using kitchen scissors can do themselves.

Each connector used here cost around £3-£4, while the hose cost me over £20 on eBay. Truma have excellent online catalogues and price lists. See trumauk.com for details of all the parts used here, and the very many alternatives available from Truma.

Picture 3. ... with a special narrow blade for sharp corners. Start by drilling access holes for the blade. If you want to try this yourself, practice on scrap plywood first.

Picture 1. You can see the crush damage caused to the original heater trunking (arrowed). The new Webasto aluminium motorhome-type trunking is stronger – albeit expensive, even on eBay.

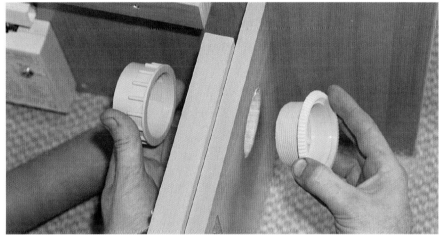

Picture 4. The masking tape was effective in preventing the foot of the jigsaw from marking the veneer. The Truma vent has an 'outer' vent flap and an 'inner', threaded fixing ring.

Picture 2. I wanted a new outlet, so I covered the underbed panel with masking tape, and marked out the area to be cut. A hole saw is easiest; I used a jigsaw ...

Picture 5. It's difficult to trim trunking to give a squared-off end. Both the card-type and this aluminium-type can be cut with a craft knife, then trimmed level with household scissors.

Picture 6. The inside of the Truma outlet has a ribbed gripper inside (see inset). You fully push in the trunking, keeping it level, and the gripper does the rest.

Picture 7. This is Truma's inline joining section. It uses the same gripper system, and has a diverter to spread a little warm air under the bed box. Note the directional arrow.

Picture 8. Trunking must be supported higher up, to protect it. These self-adhesive clips from Würth allow a cable tie to pass through, before wrapping it around the trunking for support.

Picture 9. TIP ONE: Before sticking on the clips, clean the surface with methylated spirit or similar.
TIP TWO: 'Flame' the cut end of the cable tie to prevent the sharp end from drawing blood if you catch yourself on it.

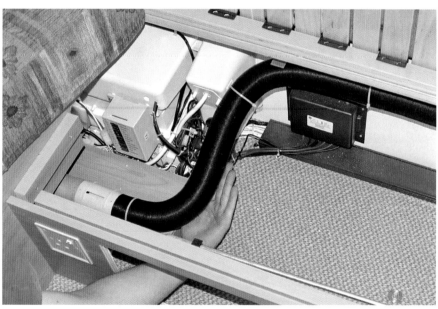

Picture 10. The new trunking is stronger, more securely located, and less likely to be damaged than the old. It's also provided us with another blown air outlet. Result!

The original Truma trunking, found in the vast majority of caravans with Truma blown air heating, is okay – provided you don't squash it (like I did!). I replaced ours with the stronger, aluminium trunking seen here.

It's worth remembering that the original trunking has slits at intervals along its length. When the side of the slit furthest from the heater is pushed in, it diverts a small part of the air in the pipe out into the surrounding area. If installing this type of trunking, where clothes or bedding are likely to be stored, it's worth remembering to push in the tabs!

FIT A BETTER BATTERY CHARGER

The latest battery chargers, such as the better car battery chargers, can be left permanently connected, and prolong the life of your liquid or gel-filled battery. Here's how the latest technology can be applied to your caravan. You do most of this job yourself – but you'll need a registered electrician to make the final connection.

Standard caravan battery chargers are relatively crude. Left on permanently, there's a likelihood of over-charging and damaging the battery. The CB500 series, from CAK, have electronic controls to ensure the battery can be kept permanently charged without harming it.

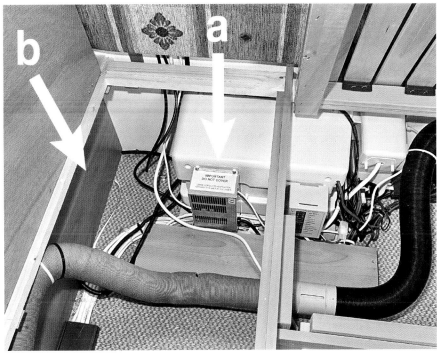

Picture 1. The 'old' charger (a) is almost always on, or next to, the battery box. I decided to fit the CAK electronic battery charger to the adjacent bulkhead panel (b).

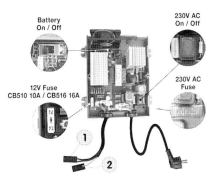

Picture 2. This shows the 'innards' of the charger with the cover removed. Socket 1 (red and black wires) is used. Socket 2, for motorhomes only, wasn't used here.

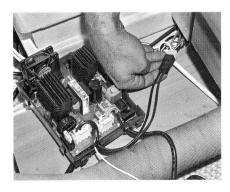

Picture 4. If the caravan's existing 12V plug is of the standard type, all you need to do is plug it into Socket 1. If not, have an electrician fit a new one.

Picture 3. After disconnecting the mains cable and the battery terminals, the charger was unplugged and unscrewed. The 2-pin continental plug was cut off the new charger's mains cable.

Picture 5. In our case, the 12V cable on the charger wasn't long enough, so we extended it using soldered connections (another electrician's job), and protected the joint with Würth heat-shrink tubing.

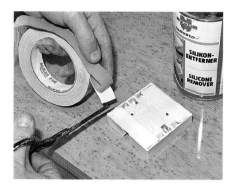

Picture 6. We added a switched fuse so that power to the charger could be turned off. The backplate was fitted with double-sided tape and screws, after first degreasing with Würth Silicone Remover.

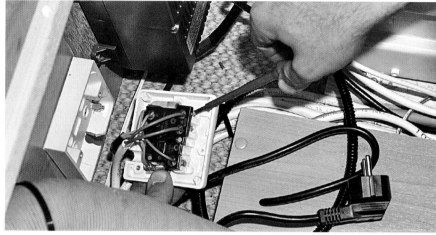

Picture 9. Connecting the mains cables to the switched fuse is an electrician's job. I've never understood why caravan battery chargers aren't always fitted with their own isolator switches: this one now is.

Picture 7. Our caravan's bulkhead consists of insulation sandwiched between thin sheets. These sheets are too thin for screws, but the charger must be screwed down, so plywood reinforcing was taped and screwed in place.

Picture 10. Each CAK CB500 series battery charger has its own built-in switch, a clear indicator light, a four-stage processor (including stand-by), and is both compact and light.

Picture 8. The charger's integral brackets were slotted home before refitting the cover. When fastened, there's an air gap behind the charger, and there must be clear space all around it, too.

Permanently connected, a CB battery charger from CAK could extend the life of your leisure battery by years. Given the price of these chargers, compared with the price of a new, quality leisure battery, they soon pay for themselves!

The charger has either a 15 amp (CB510) or 25 amp (CB516) output, sufficient for also supplying 12V items such as Truma's power-hungry combination water/air heater, or a 12V TV, when on site.

The integral cooling fan is an excellent feature, running only when needed. If it annoys you when you're in bed, you can simply turn off the charger.

SWITCH TO REMISMART BLINDS

Look at how much of the inside of your caravan is taken up by the windows. When the blinds are drawn, they dominate the appearance of your décor, and fitting more attractive blinds can 'lift' the look of the whole interior.

Picture 1. It doesn't take long to work out how to remove the old blinds. Dave, who came along to help, checks out the jamming and wrinkling in the old blind.

Picture 2. Most roller blind's side rails are attached by a single screw, at the base. Sometimes, depending on the model, it's recessed into the base of the moulding.

Picture 3. With the bottom screw removed, side rails may pull out of their locations in the top rail. Each end of the top rail is also screwed on, with an easily visible screw.

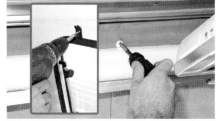

Picture 4. The blinds that we removed had two different types of fixing for the inboard sections of the top rail. One (inset) was only visible after the top rail had been lifted away.

Picture 5. Here's one of the six new blinds that we fitted to two different caravans. Note the way they're ready-assembled, apart from the corner covers. This blind has been turned through 90 degrees.

Picture 6. One disadvantage of ready-assembled blinds, is that the frame has to be manoeuvred carefully into position. This, of course, was slightly trickier for the larger front-window blind.

Picture 7. To get the height exact, we used two thin wooden packing pieces, one at each end, to ensure that the blind frame was parallel with the shelf.

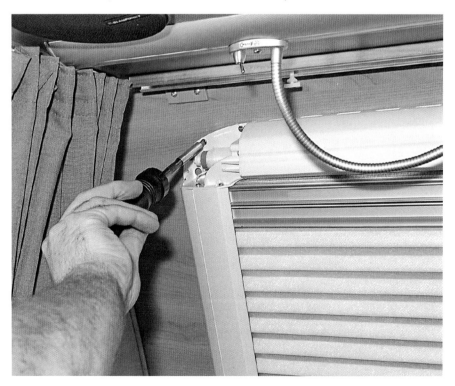

Picture 8. Once the horizontal dimensions had been measured and checked, wood screws were used to attach each corner in turn. There are four attachment holes in each corner.

Picture 9. No screws were supplied by Remis, so we used Screwfix 'Turbo Gold' – especially suitable for plywood. Corner covers simply clicked into place, starting with each inside corner.

Picture 10. The fly screen slides down from the top; the pleated screen slides up from below. You can vary positions by clipping them together at top, bottom, or any point in between.

I found Remis REMIsmart blinds to be ideal from several points of view:
• First, appearance. The smooth, one-piece frame has an integrated feel to it, and the pleated blinds are especially classy-looking.
• Second, function. There is absolutely no jamming whatsoever, from either the fly screen or pleated blind, even on the widest window that covered almost the full width of the caravan. And, because the blinds roll from opposite directions, they can't 'fall over' each other when being opened and closed, unlike some where both pull down from the top.
• Third, ease of fitting.

RE-LINING SHOWER ROOM WALLS

Showers, especially in caravans, must be watertight, so here we show you how we fitted a frame, and installed Proclad wall panels to a caravan that didn't have a shower compartment.

Many caravan shower compartments use a shower curtain to keep water off the walls (the walls aren't waterproof). Proclad is a closed-cell, rigid, lightweight foam PVC sheet, with a high gloss surface (Class 1Y fire rated), that you can use to repair or replace existing shower compartment walls.

Picture 1. We fitted the sheeting to a Freedom caravan made from fibreglass, so, in that respect, it's not typical. Having removed the old washroom interior, we screwed and bonded the timber battens to the caravan's structure.

Picture 2. Conventional aluminium caravans already have these battens in place. We used sheets of thin card to meticulously create patterns for the side panel. It's vitally important to get the exact shape.

Picture 3. Sections of 6mm ply were cut to make a jigsaw puzzle and, when all the pieces fitted, they were screwed and glued to the battens. All screw heads were carefully countersunk.

Picture 4. Here's the biggest section of Proclad sheet we used. After shaping and cutting the window aperture, I used a contact adhesive with 'shuffling time,' to allow movement before it finally set.

Picture 5. Using adhesive with 'shuffling time' was essential, to enable lining the panel up with the position of the shower tray (still to be fitted), wall, and window aperture. I used EVO-STIK Timebond.

Picture 6. Then, I lined the ceiling with hardboard, because of its ability to flex and follow the line of the roof. It was screwed, where possible, and bonded with Würth Bond+Seal.

Picture 7. The same Würth polyurethane adhesive was used to bond battens, lining and Proclad sheet in place. If you're using this in cold weather, heat the cartridge first.

Picture 8. Of course, polyurethane adhesive doesn't work like contact adhesive, and had to be held in place while it set. I clamped two strips of timber to adjust the height.

Picture 9. There had previously been a vent in the wall. We used a hole cutter and, when the drill in the centre broke through, drilled from the inside, neatly completing the hole.

Picture 10. This is the finished job, viewed from low down, after peeling off the protective plastic film, and fitting the Remis blind and the vent cover. It all looks factory fitted!

Industrial Plastic Solutions Ltd, distributors of Proclad, also supply various edging strips. Our ceiling panels were fitted with edging strips, left free so they can slide outwards, making a perfect fit with the walls on each side.

Fitting the wall linings took longer than expected, but the advantages of waterproof, almost break-proof, wipe-down shower wall linings make it worthwhile.

FITTING A PROPEX MALAGA WATER HEATER

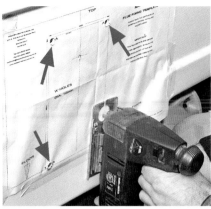

Picture 3. With four 10mm holes drilled (one in each corner) a jigsaw must be used to cut the section of side wall away. Make sure the blade is cutting a 90 degree angle ...

The Propex Malaga 3E is a compact water heater that runs off gas, or gas-plus-electricity, and fits inside the bed box, with a flue through the sidewall of the caravan. As a self-build or replacement unit, it's easy to fit and use.

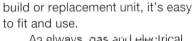

As always, gas and electrical connections MUST be carried out by certificated professionals.

Picture 4. ... so that it goes through inner and outer skins evenly. You WILL have checked for any wiring or pipework first, won't you? The flue cover fit was checked ...

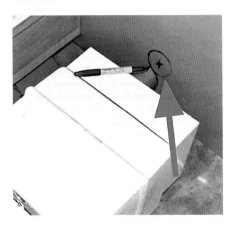

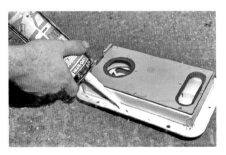

Picture 1. Allowing room for water pipes, and for a professional to fit the gas pipe, we calculated the flue outlet's position. Flammable trim MUST be removed from the area.

Picture 2. After drilling a small pilot hole through the caravan wall, Dave attached the paper template supplied with the kit with masking tape, levelling it with the moulding on the caravan wall.

Picture 5. ... and the pilot holes drilled for the fixing screws. Next, a bead of white silicone was gunned around the edge. Drill holes in the side walls before applying the silicone ...

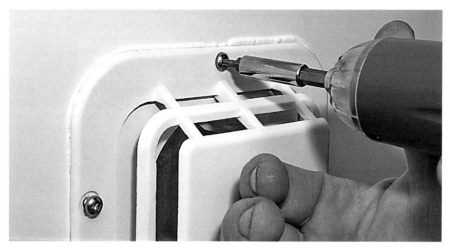

Picture 6. ... or you'll trap swarf in it. We used stainless steel screws from Screwfix. The heads were slightly too high to allow the plastic caps supplied to fit, but they look fine.

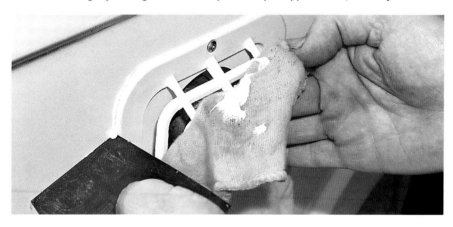

Picture 7. The screws must be tightened evenly, so the silicone doesn't get squeezed out of one side and leave a gap when fully down. A plastic scraper and cloth was used to remove the excess.

Picture 8. Inside, the on-off switch and indicator light were fitted, after drilling the side of the wardrobe. I don't like having these switches at ankle-height: it's lazy manufacturing.

Picture 9. There must be a gas 'drop-out' point near the gas connection. CAK sell different lengths for different floor types. Drill with a hole cutter, seal with silicone, screw down – job done!

Picture 10. We used Whale push-fit connectors, and semi-rigid pipes, also from CAK, to fit the water supply. We'll show how to fit the plumbing in the next section.

The Propex Malaga 3E has a switch panel with a three-position switch, for selecting gas only, gas plus 230V, or off. The 12V supply is for operation and ignition.

Features
• You can use gas on its own, or with the 750W electric element for even faster heating.
• The small flue terminal gives a neat appearance outside the caravan.
• There's an optional flue adapter plate, so you can fit a Malaga in place of an old Carver Cascade unit.
• A gas-only model – the Malaga 3 – is available.
• Water capacity: 13.5L. Dimensions: H:250mm, W:325mm, D:445mm. Weight (dry): 9.3Kg.

INSTALLING WATER PIPES

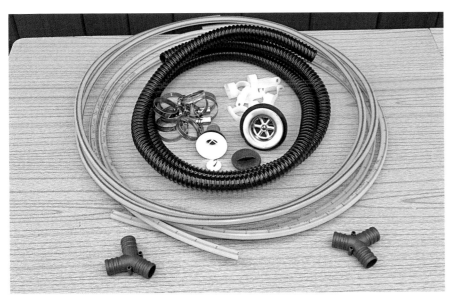

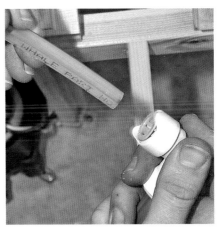

Picture 2. The pipe is held tight after pushing in firmly. To remove the pipe, push the grey collar away from the pipe, while pulling the pipe itself.

There are better methods of connecting caravan pipes than pushing-on and clamping. Water pipes can be connected using best building practice, and you need very few special tools to do it.
Caravan water pipe connections have, traditionally, been hit-and-miss, but products, such as those from Whale, bring your pipework up to date. Modern systems are far less leak-prone, and far easier to connect and disconnect when necessary.

Picture 3. This is a piece of 20mm pipe, used in houses for water storage tank overflows. Here's what happens when you cut using a hacksaw – a frayed finish.

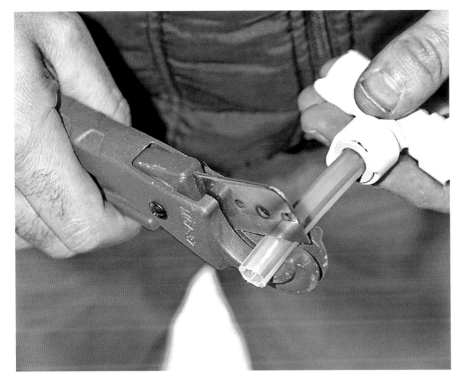

Picture 1. For caravans, 12mm is the optimum pipe size. You could cut the pipe with a sharp craft knife, pushing down on a cutting board, but a square cut would be difficult.

Picture 4. You can buy an inexpensive pipe cutter suitable for all of your caravan's plastic pipes. Ensure you hold it square to the pipe before starting to cut.

Picture 5. Cut right through, in one smooth movement. It pays to look after the blade, because it's easily damaged if used for levering, or cutting inappropriate materials.

Picture 6. You can see that the cut pipe, whether a drain or a water pipe, is smooth and ready. On some cutters, a blunt blade can be reversed, but new ones are easily fitted.

Picture 7. Rigid PVC pipes are best welded together, though it does mean you can't separate the joints later. Plastic weld can permanently damage many non-PVC plastics if it comes into contact with them.

Picture 8. You need to brush a continuous layer of plastic weld around the outside of the pipe and the inside of the pipe fitting. Solvent weld actually melts the surface of the plastic ...

Whale pipe connectors might seem expensive, but you probably won't need many of them, and they have big advantages.

CAK make an important point:

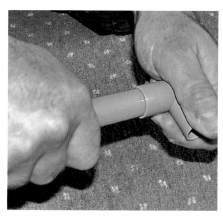

Picture 9. ... so don't let it harden before twisting the pipe into the fitting, until you feel it start to grip. BEWARE! The joint can briefly heat up enough to burn your skin.

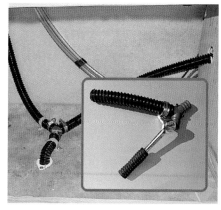

Picture 10. CAK supplied our convoluted flexible drain pipe and fittings, including stainless steel clips. A quarter-inch drive ratchet is far better (and much safer) than a screwdriver for tightening.

before buying flexible drain pipe, you should check that it's the smooth bore type, otherwise there is a real risk of food particles becoming stuck in the pipe.

REPLACING A SHOWER TAP

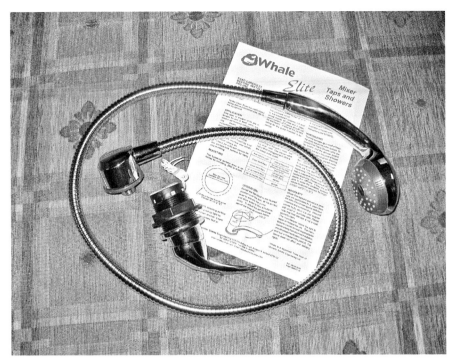

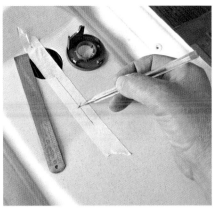

Picture 3. ... until the Whale Elite tap unit was a nice, sliding fit from the front of the panel. Seen here from behind, the fixing nut is added. Note the colour-coded blanking plugs.

Here's how to fit a Whale Elite mixer-type shower tap, with two separate pipe fittings.

If you're replacing an existing Whale tap, because of frost damage for instance, you won't need these detailed fitting instructions: these instructions are for when you're moving from a single point tap. However, it's still useful to see how everything goes together.

Picture 4. Back to the front, and I marked out the panel (removed it from the shower room, as you can see) to accurately drill a hole for the remote connector.

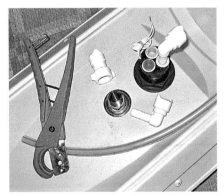

Picture 1. The supplied shower head is very good quality, as is the flexible hose. The tap has three push-fit connectors, allowing it to be connected to the remote fitting.

Picture 2. The old, frost-damaged shower tap had the hose connector built in, so there was only one hole – which was too small. After marking out, I sanded the plastic ...

Picture 5. I needed a 20mm hole, and these hole cutters often cut over-size. And so it proved here, because this 19mm cutter made a perfect sized hole. Slow cutting speeds are essential.

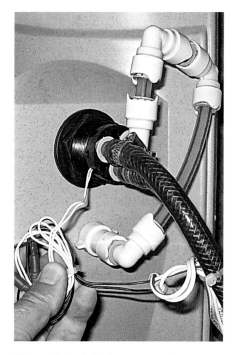

Picture 6. Back in the caravan, I started to plumb the pipework using Whale push-fit connectors. The Whale 12mm semi-rigid pipe pushes straight into the tap connectors, with no adapters required.

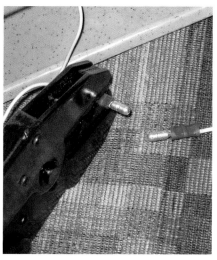

Picture 8. Rather than fixed wiring, I used male/female crimped-on electrical connectors. The male connectors go on the pump wiring; the shielded female connectors MUST go on the power-side.

Picture 9. My hoses were ½in flexible plastic.

NOTE:
To make fitting easier, I often use the following process:
• Soften the pipe in hot water
• Select the correct sized Whale adapters for the hose
• Tighten (while still warm) with a 7mm socket – NOT a screwdriver

Picture 7. I realised that this plate had to be screwed on (stainless steel screws), the elbow being held by the plate and its cover. The ½in BSP adapter had been fitted first.

Picture 10. The semi-rigid hose had to take a circuitous route from tap to remote adapter, because of inlet hose positions. Everything was tidied up with cable ties before testing then refitting.

I was surprised by how long this job took, mainly due to lack of instructions. Perhaps the manufacturers assume these will either be fitted in the factory, or by professionals who've fitted them before.

Another reason was the difficulty I had in satisfactorily mounting the remote hose connector. The first method I tried, using a conventional ½in BSP nut didn't work, because the elbow had nothing to tighten against. But using the plastic fitting to support the elbow didn't 'feel' right, either. Either way, it's a cracking shower, and comes with a two year warranty.

INSTALLING A TIP-UP WASH BASIN

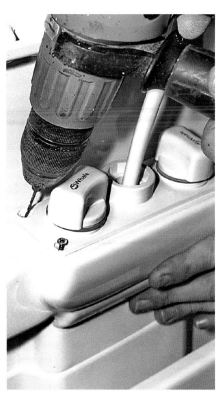

Picture 3. Positioning the tap is crucial because of all that goes on behind it – see picture 5. Sealant beneath the tap, and stainless steel screws (inexpensive, from Screwfix) are essential.

A tip-up wash basin provides extra washroom space, and a CAK WRT2500 Combo Mixer Tap and Shower unit sets the job off nicely.

Our tiny 'project' Freedom caravan had a washroom, but no shower or WC. This tip-up wash basin, from Cirencester Plastics, released room for the Thetford cassette loo that we will be fitting later (see page 61), and can be combined with a shower head for further space-saving.

Picture 1. The Cleo tip-up wash basin is made of lightweight moulded plastic. Ours was fractionally too wide for the space available, but the plastic is easily trimmed with a fine-blade jigsaw.

Picture 2. We used another power saw for the tap hole – we made a cardboard template first – but a hacksaw blade in a padsaw handle would have worked.

Picture 4. CAK can supply the appropriate ¾in waste fitting for the basin drain, but you have to drill your own hole. With seals and sealant in place, it screws on hand-tight.

Picture 5. The smooth-bore waste pipe was held on with a pipe clip. Whale push-fit hot and cold pipes and pipe connectors – adjusted to provide clearance – were and fitted to the unit ...

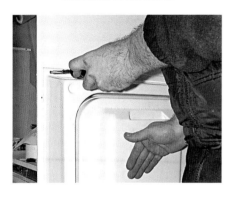

Picture 6. ... before screwing it in place on the caravan wall. Not shown is the large amount of offering-up and trial fitting that took place before the position was finally selected.

Picture 7. Where there's just a small amount of sealant to apply, it's usually easiest to do it by hand. For extensive jobs, you can buy a compressor-caulking gun from Screwfix.

Picture 8. The installed tip-up wash basin is a fantastic space-saver. It drains as you tip it up, and the tap simply swivels to one side. (The WC, fitted on page 61, had already been fitted in this photo.)

Picture 9. Rigid 22mm pipe (the same as domestic water overflow pipes) clipped to the chassis, carries waste water to the CAK 25-litre Waste Water Taxi, with its 1m flexible hose.

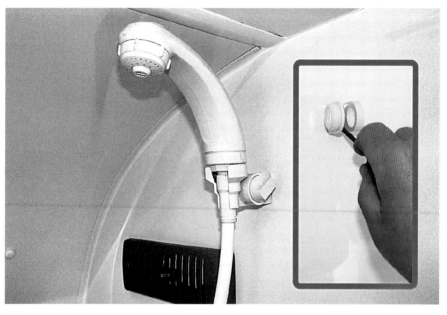

Picture 10. The tap shown in picture 8 can be pulled out and clipped to a wall bracket. Positioning the bracket is important, of course. More stainless steel screws used here.

Fitting your own tip-up wash basin isn't a job for beginners, but shouldn't be beyond the more competent DIYer – if for no other reason than that there are no gas or electrical connections to make. Even so, if you use taps with pressure switches, you should have an electrician make the terminal ends.

In our case, the old washroom was completely stripped out, but if you're building into an existing room, you'll have to make certain you won't leave an unsightly mess where old units have been removed.

Both the basin and taps are of superb quality.

FITTING A SHOWER TRAY

Whether you have a damaged shower tray, you're planning on changing the layout of your caravan, you need to repair damp ingress, or you're fitting a shower tray where no shower tray has gone before, it helps to know how it all fits.

We fitted a CAK shower tray to a caravan that had never had one fitted. The work required as much 'thinking' as 'doing' ...

Picture 4. The floor flexed, too, so we made a steel sheet to reinforce it. Not yet knowing which side the drain would have to go, we used a plasma cutter to cut an access hole on each side.

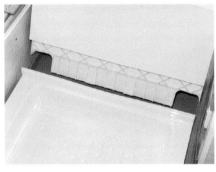

Picture 2. There's an upstand moulded into the back of the CAK shower tray, and a recess in the front panel of the Thetford WC unit slots neatly over the upstand.

Picture 1. The last thing you want from a shower tray is a leak. This one is made to complement the shape of the commonly fitted Thetford C400 WC unit.

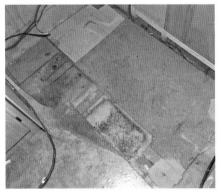

Picture 3. This had been a cloakroom, but the floor was a peculiar shape and had to be made level. This was done by fitting appropriately-shaped pieces of marine plywood.

Picture 5. The steel sheet was fixed with Würth Bond+Seal, and held down with screws while the sealant set.

Picture 6. We were fortunate in having the use of a Clarke hydraulic car hoist to raise the caravan off the ground. Otherwise, you must jack onto axle stands.

Picture 7. Now we could see that the drain had to be fitted to the inboard-side of the shower tray, so we used the hole cutter from above ...

Picture 8. ... until the drill centre just appeared below, then transferred the cutter to the underfloor area. The cutter size is determined by the size of the waste outlet, again from CAK.

Picture 9. The waste outlet, with stub for attaching the drain hose, is held from beneath, while the grille and seal are fitted above, and tightened together with the central fixing screw.

Picture 10. CAK's proprietor, Jonathan Frost, demonstrates some of the pipes available from stock, and also the new, lightweight, CAK Water Taxis, each containing 25 litres of fresh or waste water.

CAK's Universal C400 Shower Tray (in white) is one of about a dozen shower trays in the CAK range.

When installing a shower tray where there hasn't been one before, you have to be prepared to cut-and-shut the shower tray to make it fit. Cutting vacuum-formed plastic is fairly easy with a jigsaw, but you must support it well to eliminate any risk of cracking, and protect the surface so you don't scratch it.

INSTALLING A NEW CASSETTE TOILET

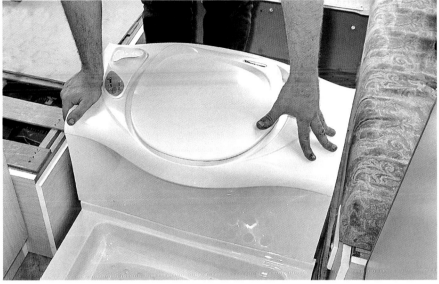

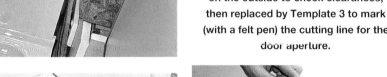

Picture 3. ... Template 2 is positioned on the outside to check clearances, then replaced by Template 3 to mark (with a felt pen) the cutting line for the door aperture.

Not many people need to fit a WC from scratch, and not many caravans come without a cassette toilet.

In the WC compartment of our little caravan was a Porta-Potti, but we wanted a proper, fitted unit, so we opted for a new Thetford C400 cassette loo, from CAK Tanks.

Thetford's instructions were good, but every installation is individual, so we measured, checked, scratched our heads, test-fitted, and finally installed our new loo. Here's how ...

Picture 2. The shape was marked against the side wall, the toilet removed, and Template 1 (supplied) was used to position two 3mm holes, drilled from inside. Using the drilled holes ...

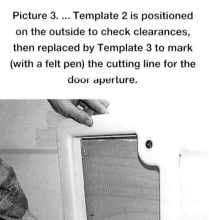

Picture 4. The door frame was checked for fit. Usually, the outer wall cut-out is used in the door panel, so don't make extra cuts in it! Our shaped, fibreglass cut-out was discarded.

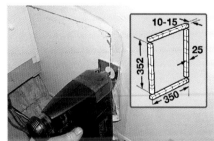

Picture 5. We needed to jigsaw the inner wall panels separately. With conventional aluminium caravans, a wooden frame (inset) must be glued to the wall around the door aperture to take fixing screws.

Picture 1. The toilet is best fitted with a shower with flange, to avoid shower leakage. Some trimming may be needed; in our case it was to fit the curve of the compartment wall.

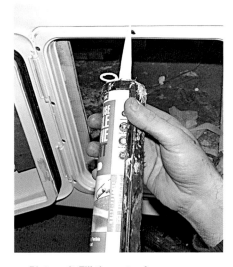

Picture 6. Fill the outer frame groove with sealant before fitting. We sealed the shaped gap on our caravan with Würth Bond+Seal. You should use a good butyl or polyurethane sealant.

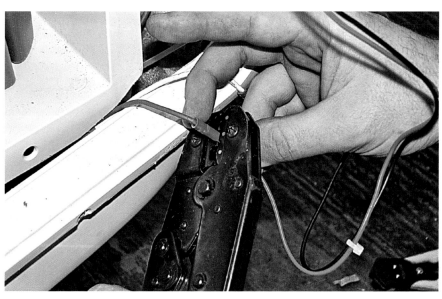

Picture 8. Before the WC is fitted, water connections are tightened (for model C403 and caravans with internal water tanks), and 12V connections made by a qualified electrician (the wiring diagram is supplied with the toilet).

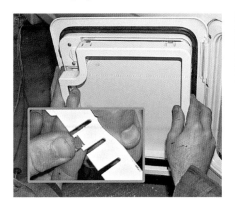

Picture 7. We cut a new door panel from flat plastic sheet. It's held in place with an internal frame, fitted with spring clips. Door hinges should face towards the direction of travel.

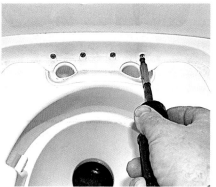

Picture 9. If necessary, install the shower tray first. You can see the necessarily strong fixing points that must be available in the wall structure. Some versions use mounting brackets.

Picture 10. Fixings are beneath the slot-in seat. Finally, seal from the outside, between door and toilet. Our unit was fixed throughout with Screwfix stainless steel screws in place of those provided.

Thetford toilets are available either right- or left-handed, depending on which side the cassette (waste tank) has to slide out. There's a removable panel opposite the cassette door, to access free space beneath the toilet for 85x70mm ducting.

Minimum space requirements:
- Width: 670mm wide (+2mm with the wall seal).
- Floor space to back wall: 270mm.
- Height: 820mm.

Before carrying out any cutting, check with your caravan dealer to avoid damaging vital parts. The distance from the cassette door frame to the rear wall (or wheelarch) should be 20mm minimum for fitting of the door frame.

INSTALLING A PRESSURISED PUMP SYSTEM

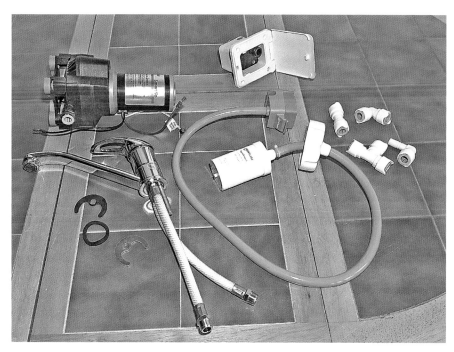

Picture 3. ... there were no obstructions on the inside of the caravan. You can, of course, get away with drilling just two holes in diagonal corners.

Here we present a less common approach to caravan water systems – a Whale onboard water pump.

Instead of a pump on the end of the pipe dangling in your water tank, you can fit a permanent, onboard water pump. It's an uncommon approach to caravan water systems; onboard pumps are invariably fitted to boats and camper vans, but not so often to caravans. However, you get better water pressure from the permanently pressurised system (when the pump is turned on), and greater reliability, albeit with slightly greater weight.

Picture 4. The inlet – no wiring, of course – was fitted using stainless steel screws, and sealant to prevent the ingress of water. Don't over tighten – caravan bodywork is thin!

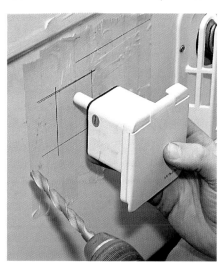

Picture 1. You can use the existing inlet, but we fitted a new one from scratch. We protected the surface of the bodywork with masking tape before marking out the hole size.

Picture 2. Following the excellent instructions that came with the Whale inlet, we drilled a hole in each corner, large enough to take the jigsaw blade – and making sure ...

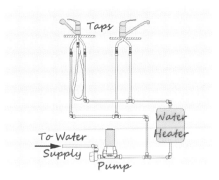

Picture 5. Here you can see that the pump is fitted at the start of the pipe run, and pushes cold water straight to the taps, and hot water through the water heater first.

Picture 6. The Whale pump is screwed down to the floor via anti-vibration feet. You should fit a filter on the inlet side, so make sure there is access for checking and changing.

Picture 7. Whale push-fit pipework and pipe connectors make the plumbing easy, (as we showed on page 53). There's even a push-fit connector built into the pump itself.

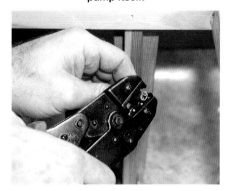

Picture 8. As we've said before, wiring MUST be carried out only by a qualified technician. Because the pump is permanently pressurised, the pipework also needs expert checking after installation.

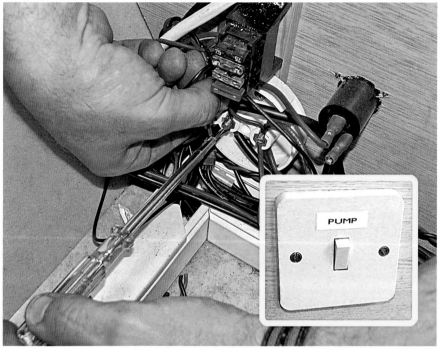

Picture 9. In addition to the wiring being fused, there needs to be an isolator switch to the pump, installed within easy reach on the inside of the caravan. We also fitted a top quality ...

Picture 10. ... 'Elite' tap, from CAK (without microswitches) and, after the inevitable splashing as air was cleared from the system, water delivery was much more impressive than the previous dribble!

This was a fresh installation, but it should be relatively simple to adapt an existing installation. Wiring would need changing so that the pump's electrical feed becomes supplied from a main switch instead of tap microswitches.

The advantages include greater pressure – especially valuable in a larger caravan where more than one set of taps might be used at once – and much less of a chance of damaging a pump, compared with the conventional type. There are also no microswitches on the taps to go wrong.

The downsides include a small weight increase, and some might not want permanently pressurised hoses inside the caravan.

FITTING A HOOK N'LOCK TABLE

Inspired by motor caravan tables, here's how you can take your original caravan table, and convert it to accept the more versatile 'hook n'lock' technology.

We always felt that our caravan table was in the way. It seemed too wide for access but, if made narrower, would have been awkward at meal times. So why not make it clip-on, clip-off, and slide from side-to-side?

Picture 1. The Bi-fold leg from CAK is sturdy, but slightly too beefy for our storage space. When on the table, it wouldn't fit the allotted space.

Picture 2. So instead, cabinet maker Matt test-fitted a CAK Swing n'Lock Folding Leg to a piece of scrap chipboard used as a test template. This would be an essential step ...

Picture 3. ... if you were making an all-new top, to check size and fit. Matt carefully levelled the table, so that he could measure the exact height that the hook n'lock slide bar...

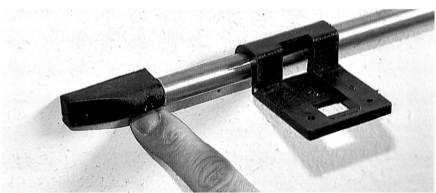

Picture 4. ... would be screwed to the caravan side wall. First, we experimented on the shed wall, because it wasn't immediately clear how it would all go together.

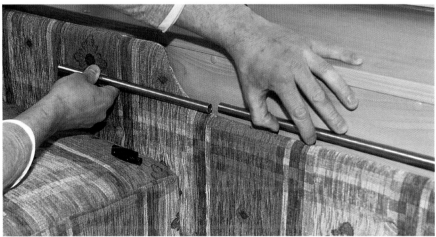

Picture 5. The slide bar was longer than we had room for, but that's no problem. After measuring, it's easily cut with a hacksaw, before filing the burrs on the end.

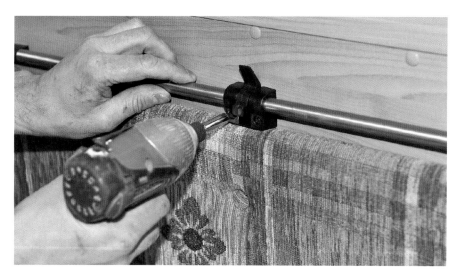

Picture 6. The centre catch is pushed along the slide bar, and the centre measured, before loosely fitting the first screw. The slide bar must be levelled by taking measurements ...

Picture 9. ... before each plastic clip is screwed to the table. The steel plates are held by detents, or dimples in the plastic, when in the open or closed positions.

Picture 7. ... from inside the caravan. You can't use a spirit level – the caravan almost certainly won't be level. End caps are pushed onto the tube and screwed in place.

Picture 10. Here, the table top is still upside-down. This steel catch locates on the centre catch (inset), which holds the table in place when in the centre position on the slide rail.

Picture 8. After a bit of head-scratching, and a call to CAK, we established that these steel retaining plates have to be inserted into the table clips this way up ...

We're really pleased with our sliding, hook n'lock table. Fixed tables have the disadvantage that, not to put too fine a point on it, they're fixed! Sideways movement improves access considerably.

A free-standing table can too easily be knocked – embarrassing with full glasses on it – and must be put away when travelling. They also suffer from the extra weight of having two sets of legs instead, of the one used here.

We re-used our existing table, and have gained versatility and a small weight reduction. And the downsides? None so far.

FOLDING WORK SURFACE EXTENSION

Fold-out work surfaces have always been a popular and often applied mod. But these days, a fold-out work surface really needs to look the part.

We used a pair of CAK's Folding Flap Shelf Supports, and a recycled piece of caravan, to create an original-looking accessory. If you need to know why this job appeals, you must be a Continental-style caravanner who doesn't cook or wash-up indoors. It's incredibly rare to find a caravan with sufficient work surface, as there's never enough space – but this mod ensures none is wasted.

Picture 3. ... enough to be wrapped around a corner of the board. When cool, move on to the next corner. Cabinet maker Matt superglued and clamped the lipping into position.

Picture 1. Because each support would be screwed against a highly finished surface, I glued a rubber gasket, made from old inner tube cut with scissors, to the back.

Picture 2. I chose plastic lipping to finish the board (available from DIY outlets), and a heat gun was used to soften each corner of the plastic in turn, until it became floppy ...

Picture 4. Matt and I spent some time working out the best position for the board. Once established, Matt measured and marked in pencil where the top of the board would go.

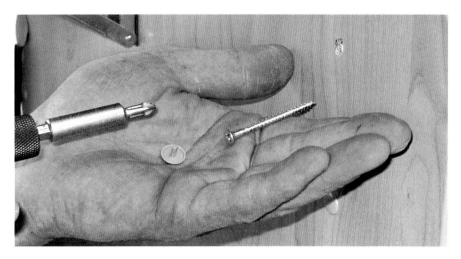

Picture 5. This was partly determined by the positions of large screws holding the sink unit together, which we decided to remove temporarily and reuse for the shelf support's top fixing points.

Picture 9. The shelf was attached to the brackets using short countersunk-head screws and nuts. The board was carefully countersunk so that each screw remained flush with the top of the board.

Picture 6. Both of these screws were refitted. Incidentally, note that the shelf has the same finish as the sink unit. That's because it's the recycled (never used) sink cover.

Picture 10. Matching screw caps finish off beautifully. We now have to move the backrest cushion to raise or lower the extension, but it's a small price to pay for the extra work space.

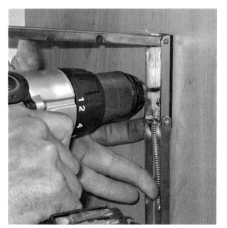

Picture 7. After checking everything was upright by measuring, a second hole was drilled to match the lower one in each bracket ...

Picture 8. ... this time, right through into the drawer space so that a nut and bolt could be used – much stronger than driving a wood screw into lightweight, caravan composite panelling.

These shelf supports might seem expensive, but each one is a really nice piece of engineering, and they work perfectly. When the shelf is folded down, its weight holds the hinge flat against the vertical panel. When lifted up, it simply clicks into place. To release it, there is a lever in the outer end of each support: press this lever and the support folds easily – it would be almost impossible to release accidentally.

There are several lengths of support available, from the 250mm length seen here, up to 445mm.

FIT A PUSH-IN DOOR CATCH

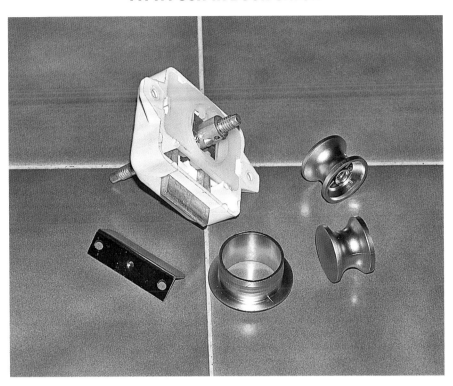

WC or shower room door catches are often made of plastic, and break as the plastic ages and becomes brittle. Some doors are fitted with magnetic catches that can fly open when you're on the move. With some straightforward DIY skills, you can fit your own new or replacement lockable shower or toilet room door catch.

Picture 3. Next, after making sure the drill was held perfectly level and at a right angle to the surface of the door, a pilot hole was drilled right through the door.

Picture 1. When, as in this case, the door doesn't fit flush with its surround, you can't use the striker plate provided. We applied masking tape before marking out or cutting.

Picture 2. After marking the position of the doorpost on the door, we took a measurement from the catch for the position of where the shaft has to pass through the door.

Picture 4. You could use a whole cutter of the exact size, but an alternative is to use a stepped sheet metal cutter like the one shown here ...

Picture 5. ... being offered up to the bezel to establish the correct size. We had to drill first from one side and then the other, to the depth of the step ...

Picture 8. After pushing in the bezel from the other side to ensure accurate centring, the lock body was pushed in to mate with it, and screwed to the door.

Picture 10. The new catch works well. From the inside, it's held shut by pulling the knob towards you. From the outside, you push the button in to latch or release.

Picture 6. ... before completing the inner part of the hole (the part that the narrower sections of the stepped cutter couldn't reach) using a coarse round file, taking care not to damage door surfaces.

Picture 9. The striker plate couldn't be fitted so we cut a slot in the door pillar using the Dremel once again. Ideally, a slotted metal plate should be screwed on top.

This is a double sided button for toilet or shower compartment, where the lock needs to be able to be operated from both sides. This kit includes: lock case, two coloured knobs, a bezel, and a striker plate. The inner knob is supplied in the same colour as the outer one.

If you are fitting this catch to a recessed door, you will need to fit the striker plate to the door post. It's designed to wrap around the edge of the post. You'd need to establish the correct height for the lock latch, and use a couple of countersunk head screws (not supplied) to fix it in place.

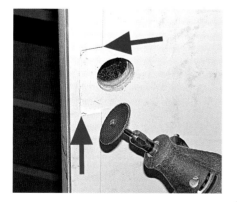

Picture 7. Some plastic edge trim got in the way and, after accurate marking out, this was carefully cut away with a Dremel fitted with a cutting disc.

FIT A DRAIN OUTLET SOCKET

Some caravans have two separate waste water outlets, requiring two separate flexible pipes. This modification simplifies matters considerably (as attested by Roger Ellaway, Site Warden at the Broad Park Caravan Club Site), combining the two outlet pipes into a neat, single connector with its own closing flap.

Picture 1. Here you can see the 28mm outlet hose socket (left), and the Y-piece for joining two waste outlet pipes into one waste container. Fixing them together ...

Picture 2. ... proved trickier than expected. The difference in sizes meant I couldn't use hose, so I inserted the Y-piece into the socket, after softening with heat, then used plastic adhesive and a jubilee clip to secure it.

Picture 3. Our caravan has an aluminium skirt all the way around, and I needed the socket to be mounted just beneath it. The rigid waste pipes on the caravan ...

Picture 4. ... were mounted too low for me to cut the skirt and pass through it, even if I'd wanted to, so I made this bracket out of a piece of aluminium channel.

Picture 5. Some small stainless steel nuts, bolts, and spring washers were used to attach the socket and Y-piece assembly to the bracket. As usual with a job like this ...

Picture 6. ... more thinking time than doing time was involved. The assembly was screwed to the underside of the caravan floor using stainless steel wood screws.

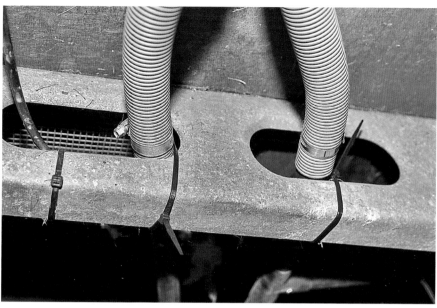

Picture 9. It's essential to keep a steady fall on waste pipes, so that grey water can flow away without pooling in low spots. These cable ties ...

Picture 7. I bought this tool from a plumbers' suppliers. The cheaper versions are not expensive and are ideal for cutting plastic caravan hose.

Picture 10. ... keep the rigid pipes at the correct height while preventing them from flapping around. There's almost no sign of the mod from outside the caravan, which is just the way you want it.

Picture 8. The Y-piece stubs were slightly too small for the hose, so I built them up with self-amalgamating tape, as used by electricians, and for hose repairs.

In almost every case where you want to combine two pipes into one, there will be unique and different minor challenges to overcome. Your main priority is to ensure the steady flow of grey water, unimpeded, through the waste pipes, and that means making sure that the outlet pipes are well supported and have no sags in them.

If you wish, you can cut into decorative trims, such as the aluminium skirt on our caravan, but it's usually best not to: it's extremely difficult to make a neat job, and it could be impossible to revert back, should you want to do so.

Part 3
Comfort

REPLACING CARAVAN CUSHIONS

Picture 1. Selwyn, co-owner of Tockfield, explained that typical coil-sprung caravan cushions are ineffectual: springs can't work properly with such little depth, and they invariably rapidly collapse.

Cushions in the majority of caravans have notoriously short lives before the foam sags, or the springs collapse – or both – leading to uncomfortable seating and a broken night's sleep.

However, caravan cushions simply need refilling to give them a greatly extended lease of life – and you get a better night's sleep!

Take your cushions, or post your covers, to the helpful folk at Tockfield, and they'll make your seats and beds better-than-new.

Picture 2. Visitors to Tockfield can try each grade of foam, as Angie demonstrated, and even test the 'bed' which has been made from different strips.

Picture 5. ... before cutting off the surplus material at the sides, as well as along the fabric's length. Without the 'bump,' the fabric doesn't have to be as long as before.

Picture 8. If you do need to cut the underlining, Tockfield include the fitting of new ones as part of the cost. Joe prepared the buttons with new twines, and with the hook back-buttons on standby ...

Picture 3. If you're sending just your covers to Tockfield, remove all buttons by cutting through the twine, then unzip the cover or cut through the underlining to remove old foam or springs.

Picture 6. Annie had now received the trimmed covers, and sewed up the seams, on one of the many industrial grade sewing machines in Tockfield's impressive workshop.

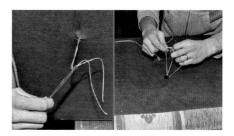

Picture 9. ... used his upholsterer's needle to push the twine right through the seat, tied it with one knot to the back button, before pushing the button down, pulling tighter, then tying off.

Picture 4. We wanted the raised fronts levelled off: Tockfield make no extra charge for this. After receiving the covers, its skilled upholsterers carefully cut through the stitching at each seam ...

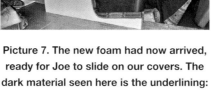

Picture 7. The new foam had now arrived, ready for Joe to slide on our covers. The dark material seen here is the underlining: you'll need to cut through it if there are no zips.

Picture 10. Our seats look great, feel great, and, as beds, are far more comfortable than before (the old foam felt too hard). There's even a seven year guarantee.

Note that good quality foam is fairly expensive. Poor quality foam can be made cheaply, but the honeycomb soon pops open in use. Tockfield, who've been established since 1982, say its foams can be expected to last 12-20 years.

It usually takes less than two hours to re-fill, re-line, and re-button your existing cushions with Tockfield Comfort System (TCS) fillings. While-you-wait is by appointment.

TCS400 foam is for people weighing up to 14 stone, and feels luxuriously springy. TCS600 Medium is for people weighing up to 25 stone, or if you prefer a firmer, but still springy foam, while TCS600 Very Firm is just what it says!

RESHAPE AND TRANSFORM A FIXED BED MATTRESS

After my wife, Shan, noticed the mattress on our fixed bed had a superfluous overhang, we decided to get it reshaped.

Removing 75mm would significantly increase dressing space, and give us an opportunity to fit

Tockfield's wonderfully comfortable bed foam.

So, at Tockfield's Derbyshire workshop our mattress was stripped and rebuilt while we waited and watched.

Picture 3. After trimming the underlining (to the line I had marked back at home), workshop foreman Kevin helped with transferring the markings to the main cover.

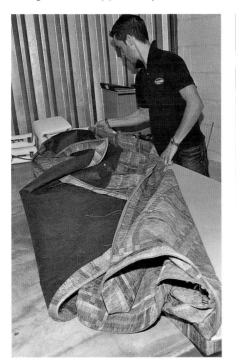

Picture 1. Tockfield's Lee started by unzipping the cover from the old foam. The foam itself wasn't showing signs of wear, but was to prove inferior to Tockfield's new foam.

Picture 2. The underlining needed to be detached from the main cover – although only part of the way round in this case – by unpicking and cutting through each of the threads.

Picture 4. The cover top, having been unpicked from the side panel, was cut to match the underlining. You can see how much superfluous overhang we were able to remove.

Picture 5. That piece of underlining was used to mark out and cut the original piece of foam to the correct shape: it made a perfect template.

Picture 6. Next, in Tockfield's workshop, two jobs were being carried out on my cushion simultaneously. Pam sewed the fabric cushion panels together in their new shape ...

Picture 7. ... while Lee used our old piece of foam to mark a section of Tockfield's admittedly expensive, but vastly superior cushion foam, to suit the new mattress' dimensions.

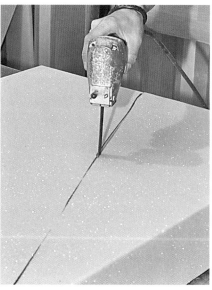

Picture 8. Large sheets of foam are cut with a bandsaw, but small cuts can be made with this jigsaw-like device. The two reciprocating blades slice through foam but won't damage skin.

Picture 9. Lee sprayed adhesive, the fumes drawn away by a powerful extractor fan, and glued a thin layer of wadding to provide that extra luxurious feeling to the top of the mattress.

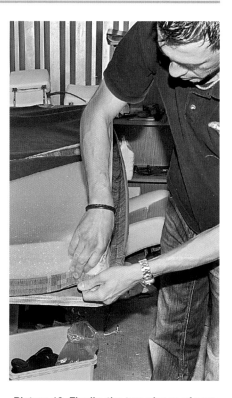

Picture 10. Finally, the two pieces of new foam were inserted into the reshaped cover. It's important to ease the foam into position, pulling the cover evenly and avoiding creases.

If you're unable to visit in person, all you need to do is remove the covers and post them to Tockfield for refilling. Easy for zip-up cushions, but how do you remove the covers from cushions without zips? Simple: just follow the four simple steps shown on Tockfield's website (www.foam. co.uk).

Tockfield's guarantee states, "We guarantee that your new Tockfield foam filling will provide consistent comfort for at least seven years. However, the actual life expectancy of our products is 12 to 20 years. Also, if your underlining has split or worn, we will replace it free on cushions being refilled."

FITTING BLINDS AND FLY SCREENS

One thing that anyone new to caravanning often finds on their first night away, is that caravan curtains can have a vital flaw: when closed, they often leave a gap in the middle that interrupts your privacy – and that can be far too generous in letting in the early rays of the morning sun when you're trying to have a holiday lie-in.

Another problem is that, when you're away in your caravan during hot weather, and particularly if you're by a river or lake, flies and insects seem to be drawn to the lights in your caravan: the invitation of an open window is simply too much for them to bear.

Because of this, many caravans are fitted with blinds and fly screens. For those that aren't, fitting is certainly one of the simpler DIY jobs. But, before starting this job, make sure that there's enough room around your caravan's windows to fit them. If the top of the window is too close to a roof-locker or overhead shelf, there may not be enough room to attach the cassette that contains the blinds and fly screens.

Picture 1. Measure the width and depth of the windows that are going to be equipped with the blinds and fly screens. Then add an extra 10mm each side – but check that a blind unit of this width will actually fit. Use these measurements to make sure that you buy suitable blinds and fly screens.

Picture 2. Offer up the blind and fly screen unit, hold it in place above the window, and, preferably after using a cordless drill to drill small pilot holes, screw it into place.

Picture 3. Next, position the side guide rails and, depending on the model, either screw or clip them into place. Take care that the guide rails are parallel to the sides of the windows. Guide rails can be cut to length, but ensure that they are cut squarely and equally.

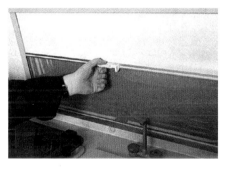

Picture 4. Pull the blind and fly screen down, first separately and then together, to make sure that they work properly. Then screw the retaining catch into place, if fitted.

MAKE YOUR OWN SHOWER CURTAIN RAIL

What's wrong with the shower compartment shown above? Would you see this in the caravan dealership and think something was wrong with it? Neither would we. But when we came to use it, it turned out to be a very silly shower indeed.

We're still delighted with the Bürstner caravan we bought in 2004: it's lived up to the marque's legendary reputation for solid build quality, and it tows with wonderful stability (possibly due to the shock absorbers that German manufacturers tend to fit). But it wouldn't let you take a shower. Yet, the hot water and drainage systems work perfectly, and the shower curtain draws smoothly with a decent amount of overlap. The shower compartment seems fine – so what's the problem?

The shower compartment walls and fixtures aren't sealed against water ingress (we'll put that right on page 81). That's not forgetfulness: Bürstner simply assumes that the shower curtain will always be used, and will prevent the compartment walls from getting wet. However, we found that the shower curtain wasn't able to make a seal while you have a shower, because the curtain overlap didn't coincide with the position of the shower head.

The curtain fits tight up against the ceiling, so you can't poke the shower head over the top of the rail – unless you want to cut a hole in the roof. To introduce the shower head inside the curtain enclosure, you had to open the curtain to pass it through, exposing the door and surrounding area to spray. It's possible they fitted the wrong curtain track at the factory, perhaps one designed for the left-hand drive models.

The easiest solution would have been to take the caravan back to Chelston Caravans, in Somerset, from where it was purchased. They have provided excellent after-sales service, and would have replaced the shower rail without a quibble. However, the trip would have been inconvenient, plus I wanted to enlarge the usable area in the shower compartment at the same time.

My initial thought was to reshape the existing track, but that isn't feasible, as it's factory-formed using equipment that curves the aluminium without affecting its profile. If you tried reshaping it by hand, the track would kink or fold in on itself.

So, first we visited all of the DIY outlets looking for suitable curtain track, but none stocked anything we could use. We then popped into our local caravan dealer and bought a length of, what turned out to be, Swish curtain track, along with the relevant fittings. (We still haven't seen any of this type in DIY centres, although you might be more fortunate.)

Picture 1. The shower head is neatly tucked into the corner of the shower compartment, but the overlap on the shower curtain is well away from the shower head. Taking a shower meant threading the head around the curtain, holding it in one hand, while operating the tap with extreme difficulty, and trying to prevent too much overspray from running down the door. Basically, impractical.

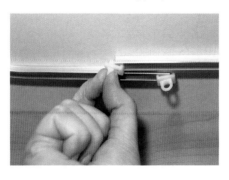

Picture 2. To remove the curtain from this type of track, take the ring on the end-stop between thumb and finger and twist the ring through ninety degrees. This frees the end-stop from the track, so you can simply slide it off.

Picture 3. You can now slide the curtain runners along and off the track.

Picture 4. With the curtain out of the way, you can clearly see the shower rail overlap is in the wrong place. You can also see another problem that I decided to rectify. All shower curtains tend to cling to you, the cheaper plastic ones being far worse than the coated fabric curtains. Our caravan has a good quality curtain, but the track was further in from the compartment walls than needed, reducing the space available inside, and adding to that claustrophobic feeling.

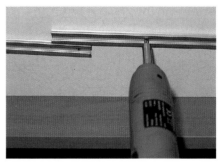

Picture 5. Removing the old track was easy, simply a matter of removing the screws holding it to the ceiling. I used an inexpensive electric screwdriver for speed. It's important to select the correct screwdriver bit: Pozidriv and Philips types don't match well, and there's a risk of rounding off the screw.

Picture 6. The old aluminium track was simply removed from the ceiling. It's a good idea to leave two or three evenly spaced screws in the track while you remove all the others, then you don't need to support the floppy track with one hand, while removing lots of fiddly screws with the other.

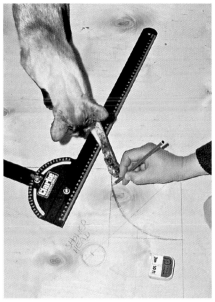

Picture 9. As you can see, I had a little assistance when transferring the shape of the shower head pillar onto my template. A helping paw is always welcome, don't you think?

Picture 7. I decided to make a replica shower compartment 'ceiling' out of plywood, and make the new track fit that, rather than having to go in and out of the caravan, and work holding the new track above my head in a restricted space. I measured the ceiling ...

Picture 8. ... and transferred the measurements onto a piece of plywood, using this large square to ensure the angles were correct.

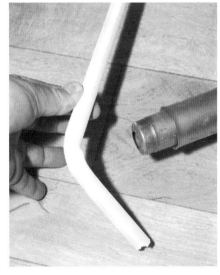

Picture 10. With my feline assistant safely out of the way, I experimented with softening the plastic track using a heat gun, so that it could be bent. I'd found that hot water and a hair dryer were both insufficient to heat the plastic to bending point. I also discovered that the rail still kinked slightly as it was bent, which may have prevented the runners from passing over the rail. Also, the rail became very hot – certainly hot enough to burn skin.

Picture 11. Once I was satisfied that I had mastered the process, I used my plywood template and marked the point at which I wanted the first bend to be made, putting a pencil mark on both the template and the curtain track.

Picture 12. I then heated a sufficient length of the plastic rail to complete the bend, passing the heat gun back and forth until the plastic became floppy. Note the use of oven gloves.
Be aware that you can singe the plastic, leaving a brown mark, or even set fire to it. Have a fire extinguisher handy, and work outside if the weather is dry.

Picture 13. Shan's great idea for preventing the track from kinking was to use a former of the right diameter (in this case a plastic tub) to bend the track around. The marks on template and track were lined up, so that the bend was made in the right place.

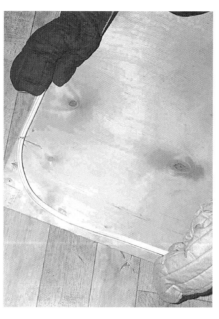

Picture 14. Here, the tub has been lifted away and the track is held in alignment with the marks on the template while the plastic cools. Cooling can take several minutes, so we used the hair dryer set to cold to speed up the process.

Picture 15. If all goes according to plan, you should have a length of curtain track that fits on the marks you made on your template. You can see that the track has been set just a little way in from the outer edges of the 'ceiling,' allowing for folds in the curtain, and so that there is no risk of the runners fouling on the shower compartment walls. You may also need to consider the fixing positions of the curtain track supports, depending on the type you use.

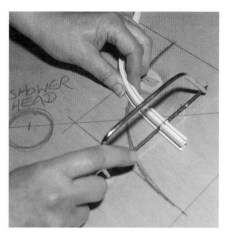

Picture 16. When all the bends are in place, cutting the track to length is simply a matter of cutting through it with a junior hack saw.

Picture 17. Plastic swarf looks unsightly and can make it difficult to get the runners on, but it's easy to remove with a piece of abrasive paper.

Picture 18. When we placed the old track inside the new, the extra space available could clearly be seen.

Picture 19. Back inside the caravan, I now had to mask the holes left after removing the old track. Each hole was injected with sealant ...

Picture 20. ... and a stainless steel screw and cap fitted. I reused the stainless steel screws used to hold the original track in place.

Picture 21. I used a more powerful rechargeable Erbauer drill, from Screwfix, to drive the screws holding the new curtain track fixing clips to the ceiling. I also had an assortment box of stainless steel screws, also from Screwfix, so I was able to find the right size for the job. Mild steel screws, even plated ones, would eventually rust in this environment.

Picture 22. Looking up at the new track from beneath you can see how it has made much more sensible use of the space in the shower compartment. However, one problem we didn't foresee was that the shower curtain was now too short to go all the way round the track.

Picture 23. We looked everywhere for a larger curtain, but they were all no larger than the one we already had. Ever resourceful, Shan decided to cut the existing curtain down the centre, and sew in a piece from another shower curtain to extend its length. The domestic sewing machine coped easily with the shower curtain material. Here, she starts to thread the new runners onto the shower track.

Picture 24. Now what's wrong with this shower compartment?
Answer: absolutely nothing.

Picture 11. I had black butyl to hand, and since it wasn't going to show, the colour didn't matter. I placed it all the way around the inner face of the shower head unit. To use it, peel off the protective paper immediately before use, and position the unit as accurately as you can. You can move it slightly, pushing against the butyl, but it's best not to unless absolutely necessary.

Picture 12. Before screwing the panel back into place, I placed a blob of silicone sealant in the hole, so that the screw would seal when fitted.

Picture 13. Note how the butyl spread as the screws were tightened. This was unintentional: I positioned it too close to the edge, and the excess had to be carefully cut away with the craft knife.

Picture 14. The surplus silicone was wiped away before starting to set.

Picture 15. It's extremely difficult to apply silicone without making a mess.

TOP TIP!

• Apply masking tape down the edges of where you want the silicone to finish, as shown here.
• Have rags and plenty of panel wipe handy. If your first attempts go wrong, stop, wipe off the silicone you've applied with rags and panel wipe, and start again.
• Cut the end of the nozzle at an angle, to improve the appearance of the finished bead.
• Apply silicone with the nozzle facing away from the direction of travel, to prevent a build-up at the end of the nozzle.

Picture 16. Peel off the masking tape before the silicone has set, otherwise it won't come off. Have plastic bags ready for disposal of the old tape: remember that it's coated with sticky silicone, so keep it away from the sides of the shower compartment.

Picture 17. I extended the application of silicone away from the shower head unit, to cover any areas into which water might run, including this one between the shower tray and the shower compartment wall.

SMOOTH TIPS

One way to achieve a decent finish to a bead of silicone, is to wet your finger in soapy water, and run it carefully along the bead.

Another, if you want to keep your fingers cleaner, is to use an 'artificial finger' spreader tool, available from Screwfix Direct. In practice, it's easy to make a mess if you're not experienced.

Don't forget those rags, bags, and panel wipe, should you need to wipe off and start again.

FITTING A SHOWER CURTAIN AND RAIL

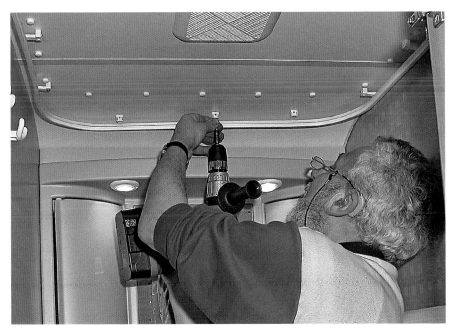

Picture 2. You can sew shower curtains with a machine, but you must use polyester thread, because cotton can rot. You'll need to measure to establish what length of track you need.

You can easily and cheaply fit a new shower rail and curtain without using more expensive caravan-specific parts.

Perhaps you need to replace a broken shower rail, or you might want to extend your existing curtain cover. In some caravans, the loo gets soaked every time you use the shower, and a second curtain could stop that happening.

Picture 3. Plastic curtain track cuts very easily with a hacksaw. Cut longer than needed to start with, as it's difficult to establish where any curve in the track will have to come.

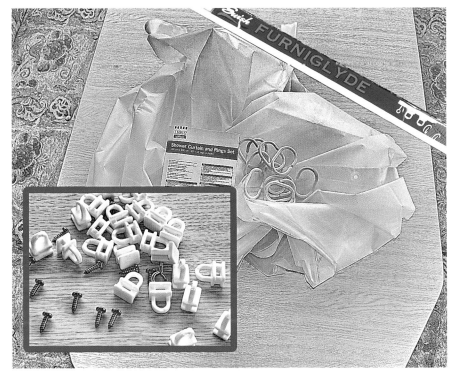

Picture 1. There's a vast range of shower curtains available, but we opted for cheap and cheerful. You might need to turn-up the ends if the curtain is too long.

Picture 4. You'll need a heat gun or hair dryer to soften the plastic. It takes a while to heat up, but then softens quickly. Use a piece of surplus curtain track to practice on first.

Picture 5. The open U-shape will tend to fold or kink, so try packing the gap with strips of hardboard just before starting to bend it. If necessary ...

Picture 6. ... open the gap, later, using a file or Dremel power tool, or the runners will bind. You can now measure, offer up, and cut to the exact lengths needed.

Picture 7. You'll need to drill holes in the curtain track. It's a good idea to use stainless steel screws in an environment that's both damp, and likely to be unused for long periods.

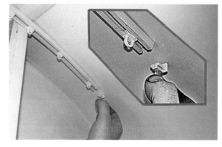

Picture 8. Use very short screws, or be certain there are no wires or obstacles behind the panel. After fitting the curtain runners, fit the end caps provided to stop them sliding off.

Picture 9. If you're worried about screwing through the panel and into something important, use double-sided tape from a car accessory store for fixing external trim to bodywork; it withstands both heat and water.

Picture 10. This is a cheap and simple way of adding extra shower room protection, or replacing old curtain track, and there are several advantages in using ceiling-mounted track.

Ceiling-mounted track looks neat, and the fixing screws will be partly hidden. More importantly, most domestic curtain track hangs down, leaving a gap between the ceiling and the top of the shower curtain. You will be showering in quite a confined space, with a shower head mounted close to the ceiling, so the less chance you have of water spraying over the top of the shower curtain, the better.

TOP TIP!

• *I always keep a pack of stainless steel self tapping screws from Screwfix handy. A pack of 725 screws is fairly inexpensive and lasts me a good couple of years of DIY.*

INSTALLING A WASHROOM EXTRACTOR FAN

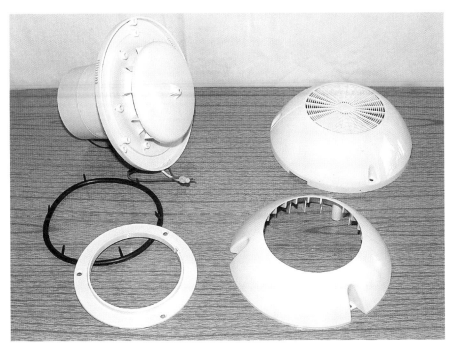

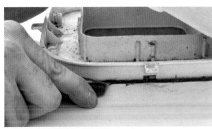

Picture 2. The vent was bonded down securely. After cutting through with a knife, I resorted to a wood chisel, driven carefully between roof and vent without damaging the former.

Putting a Dometic extractor fan in your shower and WC can solve one of winter caravanning's biggest problems: getting rid of steam and fumes without letting in cold air.

Fitting the fan can be the most time-consuming part of the installation, but – as always – the wiring must be carried out by an electrician.

Picture 3. If there are no obvious or hidden screws, careful levering of the inner vent may be the only way to remove it. This one clipped in place, so was carefully pulled out.

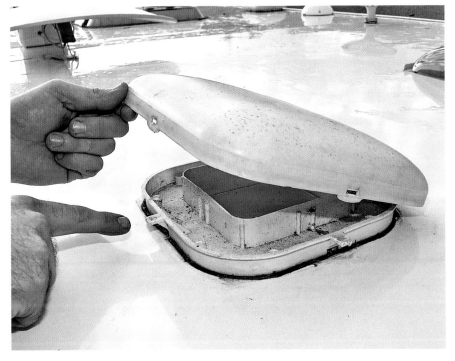

Picture 1. We decided to fit the extractor at the site of an existing vent. On the roof, the outer cover was removed after pressing in these tabs, revealing fixing screws beneath.

Picture 4. You can't fit a round vent in a square hole, so we made aluminium plates to convert the opening, with a good bead of Würth Bond+Seal.

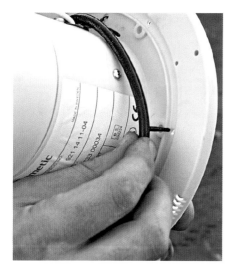

Picture 5. The Dometic vent unit came with its own neoprene seal that had to be fitted in the sealing groove around the base of the top flange on the unit.

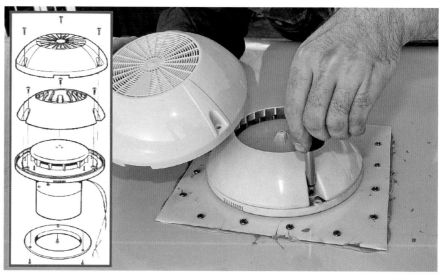

Picture 7. Stainless steel screws were provided by Dometic for each of the three 'layers' to be fixed in place. Our aluminium plate was also screwed down, with excess sealant wiped away later.

Picture 6. Fitter, Dave, added two strips of butyl sealant. Caravan manufacturers use this to seal some joints, and it never sets, allowing removal in future if necessary.

Picture 8. A smaller ceiling plate was fitted, and finished off with the Dometic trim plate. The stainless steel screws we used came from Screwfix Direct – quite inexpensive.

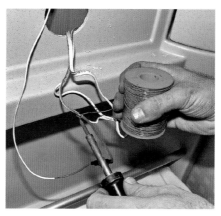

Picture 9. This step must be done by a qualified electrician. A large hole cut in the shower trim allowed access to the cables. The fan positive terminal was given a permanent (fused) connection.

Picture 10. The fan body protruded slightly: if you haven't enough head room, plan to fit it to one side. The wiring was neatly trunked to the ceiling (arrowed).

We had already fitted a Dometic CK155 cooker hood ventilator to our caravan, to deal with smells and steam from the cooking area. Adding the Dometic GY11 roof vent meant that we could now enjoy the shower without steaming up the rest of the caravan.

WHALE WATER HEATER INSTALLATION

Picture 2. Outside, the Truma vent was removed. There's an optional blanking plate for when Carver or Henry water heaters are replaced.

Picture 3. The Whale heater came with a template for creating the new hole in the caravan sidewall. A hole was drilled in each corner ...

You might want to replace your original water heater with a new Whale unit, possibly because it has failed. But, according to Whale, installing one of its heaters will increase the availability of hot water by up to 50 per cent for regular shower users.

Picture 1. After making sure there was room for the new heater, Whale's Richard Kee started by removing the existing Truma unit.

Picture 4. ... then a jigsaw was used, with template still in place to prevent scratching. We extended the original hole position, making it neater.

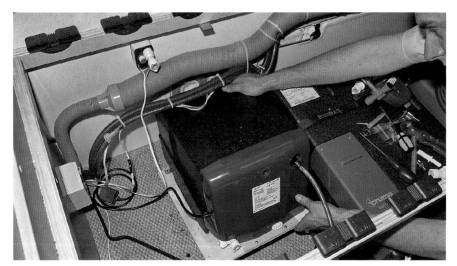

Picture 5. Richard re-routed pipes and wiring where necessary. The standard raised baseboard allows them to pass beneath the unit when required.

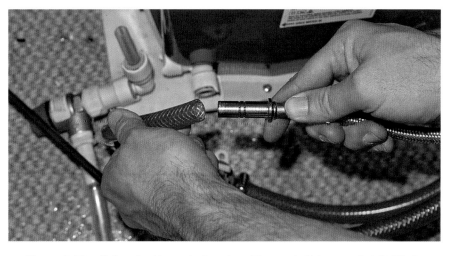

Picture 6. Pipe fittings had been designed to either push-fit into semi-rigid Whale pipework, or fit into flexible hose with hose clip.

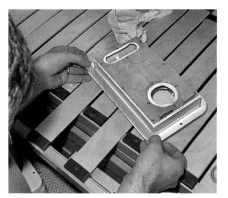

Picture 7. Before fitting the new flue, Richard applied sealant – non-setting butyl tape is ideal. There must be no gaps in the sealant.

Picture 8. The flue was tightened evenly using stainless screws. You won't have to remember to remove/refit the cover as there isn't one.

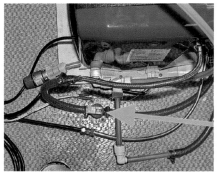

Picture 9. The drain tap (arrowed) exits through a hole in the floor. If a 13 amp socket is available, simply plug it in – no electrician required.

Picture 10. You'll need a Gas Safe Register qualified fitter for the gas connections. The Whale switch is a direct replacement for the Truma one.

Here's a few more of the Whale unit's advantages:
• The control switch is designed to be simple to use.
• It makes 13 litres of hot water available.
• It's micro-processor controlled, so if it's accidentally turned on when empty, it won't burn out the element.
• It heats water faster: it takes 22 minutes from cold, then supplies hot water for two five minute showers, with ten minute intervals, on the highest setting.
• There are five heat settings: 600W electric, with/without gas; 1200W electric, with/without gas; or gas only.
• There's also a high level of insulation to retain heat, and a braided stainless steel heater hose for enhanced safety.

FITTING A TRUMA ULTRAFLOW FILTER

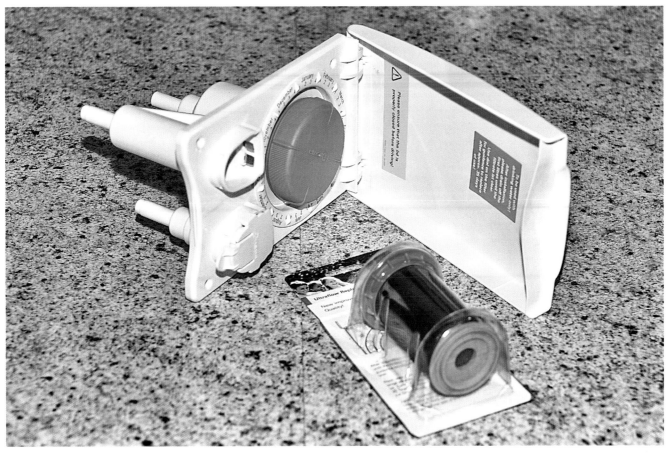

The Truma Ultraflow Filter assembly is designed to filter water as it enters your caravan.

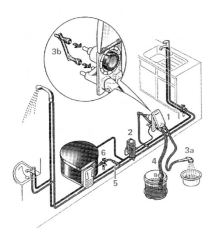

Picture 1. This is a typical installation using the Truma Ultraflow Filter assembly.
1 Filter housing. 2 Surge damper. 3a Shower assembly. 3b Shower connection.
4 Pump assembly. 5 Non-return valve. 6 Ultrastore drain valve.

Tools and accessories

The following tools and accessories may be required:
Jigsaw or padsaw.
Drill with 2mm and 10mm diameter drill bits.
Pozidrive screwdriver.
Non-hardening mastic.

Timber will probably be needed to line the hole (approximately 600mm long by the thickness of the caravan wall). If so, you will also need 20mm-long panel pins.

Selecting the position

Choose a flat vertical wall without interference from trim, etc, if possible, and with the shortest possible route to the plumbing system, without crossing doorways.

The pipework should be concealed in cupboards or under bed lockers etc, but shouldn't be run under the floor of the caravan.

The accessibility of existing electrical and water connections should also be taken into consideration.

Structural sections within the wall of the caravan should be avoided for safety reasons.

After selecting the position proceed as follows:

Inside the caravan

Temporarily fit the template to the inside wall, with the bottom of the template touching the floor. Mark position '0' through the template onto the wall. Remove the template and

FITTING AN ELECTRIC WATER PURIFIER

Here we look at various water supply options, in particular, Dometic's new Water Purifier.

The Dometic Water Purifier works by a three-stage process: UV radiation (the safest way to eliminate harmful microbes), plus particle and carbon block filters to remove particles, bad taste, and odour. The water purifier operates on 12-volts and, while it's always on standby, it consumes very little energy.

The carbon block filter and the UV lamp are easily accessible and can be exchanged easily.

Dometic claim that its water purifier can be discretely installed anywhere in the caravan, but recommend that it's installed close to the water tap in the kitchen.

Picture 2. Dometic's engineer, Ian Walker, screws the mounting bracket in place after working out the correct location.

Picture 3. He also drills the necessary drain hole, after first having checked beneath for obstructions.

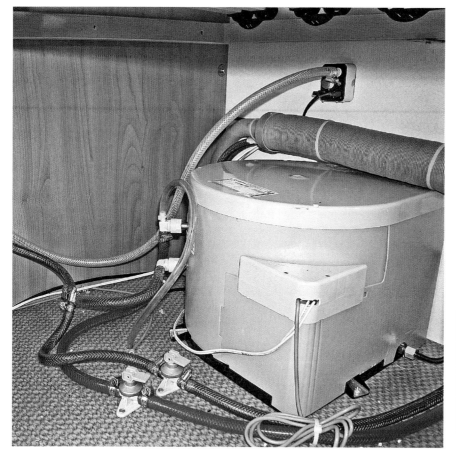

Picture 1. The Dometic filter should go near the tap – under a bed box works well in this instance.

Picture 4. With the drain hose passed through the hole in the floor, he clips the filter in position.

Picture 5. This diagram shows 'before' and 'after' wiring configurations, but all connections should be made by a qualified electrician.

Picture 7. This time-consuming job (he wanted to hide all the wires) terminated in the bed box.

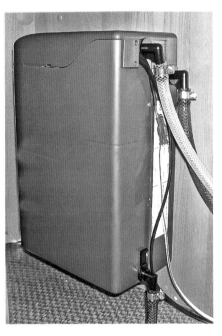

Picture 9. New water quality hoses were used to break into the supply from pump to tap.

Overall

The comprehensive instructions supplied show the user how to prepare and use the unit and change filters.

Drain tap

Winter draining is achieved simply by releasing the clip and pulling on the drain elbow.

Picture 6. Ian runs a cable from the battery box at the other end of the caravan.

Picture 8. After connecting to the relevant terminals, the cable is neatly clipped in place along the unit itself.

Picture 10. An alternative approach is to fit an onboard tank, for which you may need a different pump.

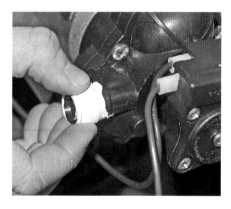

Picture 11. PTFE tape is used to seal water connection threads – ALWAYS wind in the direction of thread-tightening.

Picture 12. This CAK Tank's pump is fitted with its own inline filter, useful to keep out particles.

Picture 13. The filter is screwed to the inlet. If it's not tight or the tape bunches, it'll leak.

Picture 14. A hose clip is used to fix the water hose to the stub on the filter.

Picture 15. Anti-vibration pads are fitted to the fixing bracket beneath the mounting screws on this SHURflow pump.

Picture 16. CAK Tanks also sell this AquaSource filter – far less effective, but cheaper than Dometic's.

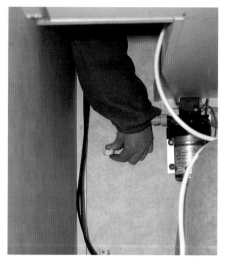

Picture 17. The filter weighs little and is easy to fit. Here, a pair of pipe clips are screwed in place on the bed box wall ...

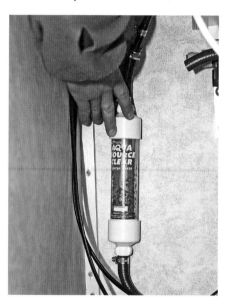

Picture 18. .... before slotting the pipes and filter in place, into the clips.

TOP TIP

- Water supplied by UK or western European caravan sites is highly unlikely to be contaminated. The two instances where water purification will help are where:
- Untreated caravan pipes and storage tanks, which 'grow' their own bacteria.
- Less dependable water supplies, which in some parts of the world may require treatment.

FITTING BLOWN AIR HEATING

As caravanning has increasingly become a year-round pastime, so the heating systems have become more sophisticated. Many older and more basic caravans make do with a simple gas heater, while more modern and higher specified models often have the benefit of blown air distribution systems. These either come with a 1800, 2000, or 3000 series heater, through a Junior Blown Air Heating System, or a 3000 series heater through a Senior Blown Air Heating System.

Also available is an electric back-up heater called the Fanmaster, an automatically controlled fan designed to distribute warm air through ducts, to outlets positioned around the caravan.

Enhancing a basic heater to incorporate the advantages of blown air is one of the best ways of ensuring that you can get the most out of your caravan by being able to use it through the winter months. Easy to install kits are available through caravan dealerships.

Fitting a Junior or Senior Blown Air Heating Kit

Fitting a Junior or Senior Blown Air Heating kit to a caravan's basic heater follows, basically, the same procedure.

The Junior kit uses a less powerful fan, so is only suitable for smaller caravans with up to two blown air outlets. The Senior kit, however, uses a more powerful fan, and can supply up to six blown air outlets. The Senior fan can also be powered by mains electricity.

Picture 1. At the rear of the existing heater casing is a pre-cut hole, plus some pre-drilled screw holes. Remove the pre-cut section.

Picture 2. In the kit is a 12-volt fan unit and some screws. With the Senior kit, use the pre-drilled holes and attach the fan unit to the heater casing. With the Junior kit, however, the fan can be connected, for instance, to the inside wall of a wardrobe, and joined to the back of the heater by a length of piping.

Picture 3. The warm air is directed by the fan around the caravan through lengths of ducting. When you've chosen where you want the ducting to go, you'll need to cut holes through sections of furniture using a 65mm holesaw.

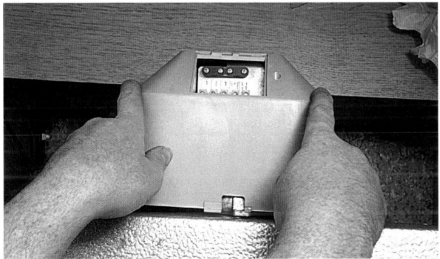

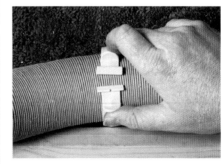

Picture 4. With the route planned and prepared, put the ducting in place and attach it to the wall of the furniture, using the clips provided with the kit.

Picture 5. The warm, blown air enters the caravan through vents in the base of the furniture. Decide where you want the vents to go, and use the 65mm holesaw to cut suitable holes, then mount the vents in place. Push the ducting into place.

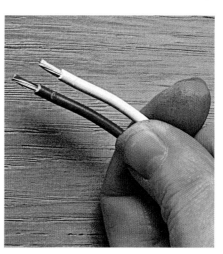

Picture 7. Disconnect the caravan's battery and locate a nearby 12-volt supply, to which you can connect the fan's live and negative supply. For safety, fix an inline 10A fuse.

Picture 6. To operate the system's electric fan, a control unit is supplied with the kit. This is commonly mounted on the side of the wardrobe. Don't forget to drill a hole at the back, for the wiring to reach the fan unit, when fitting.

Picture 8. Back at the fan unit, connect the 12-volt live and negative wires, as per the instructions. Reconnect the caravan's battery, and test the unit.

SAFETY FIRST!

• *It's essential that mains electric installations or connections are checked by a qualified caravan electrician BEFORE the system is used.*

FITTING A BLOWN AIR SPACE HEATER

The Propex Heatsource is a compact LPG-powered unit. Light, and taking up little space, it could make a useful supplementary heater for larger caravans. Mains electricity isn't required, but 12-volt wiring and gas connections must be made by suitable qualified specialists.

We found it fitted easily inside a suitable bed box in our tiny Freedom caravan.

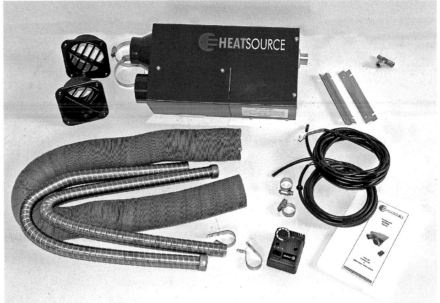

Picture 1. The supplied template shows where to drill the two holes for the inlet and exhaust pipes. It's essential that you avoid pipes, cables, and chassis rails beneath the floor

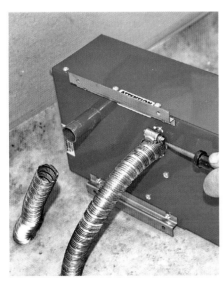

Picture 2. The stainless steel hoses supplied were pushed through the holes, and fixed to the spigots on the base of the unit with the supplied hose clips.

Picture 3. It's essential that a gas drop vent is fitted to the floor wherever a gas appliance is sited. These are available from CAK Tanks, in various lengths.

Picture 4. We raised the Propex Heatsource on strips of plywood to allow for the thickness of the pipe clips. Larger holes in the caravan floor would have been an alternative.

Picture 5. The exhaust pipe must angle backwards from the direction of travel, and exhaust at the edge of the caravan, keeping gases away from any openings leading to the interior.

Picture 6. Back inside the caravan, holes were drilled into which vents could be fitted: one or two for the outlet vents, and one for the inlet hose. A hole cutter does a neater job than a jigsaw.

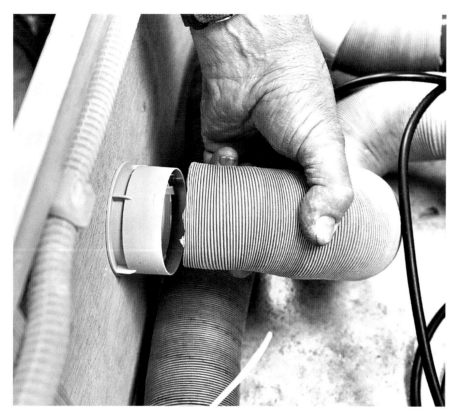

Picture 7. The Truma-type vents were fixed in place (each consists of two parts) and the hose was simply pushed in. It self-gripped onto the grooves inside the vent.

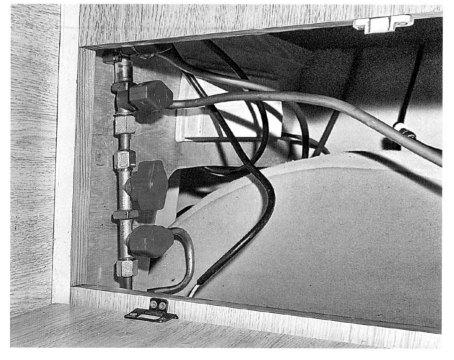

Picture 8. There was now an extra gas appliance to feed, so our gas fitter added an extra tap, once again supplied by CAK Tanks. It was added to the two existing taps in situ.

Picture 9. Although the 12V electrical connections must be made by a qualified electrician, the heater-end of the cables are already fitted with plugs, with matching sockets inside the unit.

Picture 10. The thermostat was fitted to the living area, and the wires connected. Fixing screws are concealed with these buttons, and the adjuster knob was fitted last of all.

The Propex Heatsource provides almost instant heat, and is perfect for those who like to camp away from mains electricity. Ignition, fan, and controls are all operated by 12-volts.

The only downside is that, as with any fan heater, there is some fan noise.

If you have an inadequately heated end bedroom in a large caravan, the Propex Heatsource could be the solution.

Remember that even if you fit all of the trunking, locate the thermostat, and drill holes for the inlet and exhaust hoses yourself, all electrical and LPG-related connections MUST be made by qualified engineers.

TRUMA HEATER SWITCH RELOCATION

The heater switch in our Bürstner was very awkward to access: reaching it required kneeling on the floor and peering beneath the seat.

However, just because a caravan manufacturer has placed the switch in a bad position, you don't have to put up with it. Here, I show how I relocated my Truma heater's control switch. All I needed was a hole cutter of specific size.

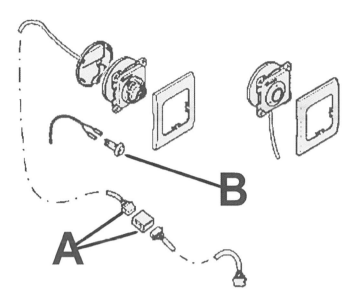

Picture 3. On ours, the cable is permanently fitted to the switch (right), but some aren't. The Truma extension cable (A) push-fits; there's also a remote thermostat (B) available if required.

Picture 1. Here, you can see the original location of the heater switch. Situated above the heat outlet, it wasn't even intelligently positioned as a thermostat: room temperature is best measured higher up.

Picture 2. The Truma switch outer bezel simply unclips (fingers only; no need to lever it), and the switch itself is screwed to the wooden panel in which it sits.

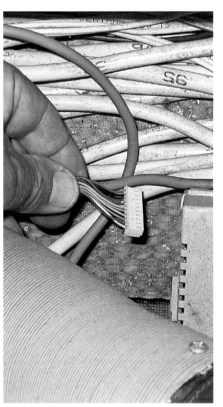

Picture 4. The other end of the cable plugs into the back of the Truma heater unit, often accessed by removing the floor panels from the wardrobe, or other surrounding furniture.

Picture 5. This cable snaked through the back of the bed locker and inside the door step, which contained most of the wiring loom. DON'T damage the plug as you insert it.

Picture 6. After much consideration, I decided to fit the switch to the side of the wardrobe. I used a pencil to mark the position of the switch, and drilled a pilot hole.

Picture 7. Next, a hole cutter was used in a Makita, set at its lowest speed. Taping a piece of card over the panel beforehand will give you some protection against slips.

Picture 8. The hole cutter was nominally 2mm smaller than the switch, as they tend to cut over-size. After a small amount of filing, the switch was screwed on and the bezel refitted.

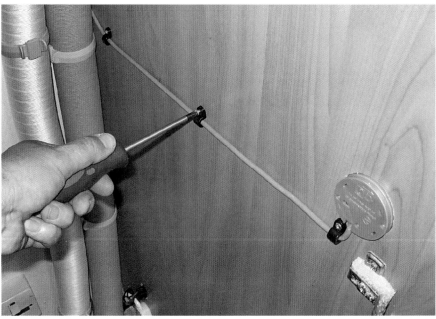

Picture 9. From inside the wardrobe, you can see how the switch fits. Cable clips removed from inside the locker were reused here. Nailed-on cable clips aren't suitable inside a caravan ...

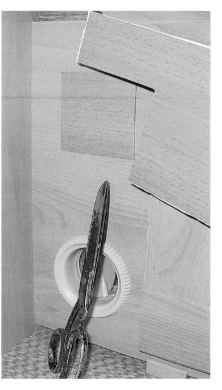

Picture 10. ... because many panels are too flimsy for hammering. The old switch location was originally disguised with a piece of stick-on plastic floor tile cut to size. Some time later, the tile came unstuck, however, so was replaced with a screw-on electrical blanking plate, available from any DIY centre.

The existing, standard-length cable was plenty long enough, and the excess was coiled neatly out of the way, behind the Truma heater unit. However, if you need to extend the cable, you can buy plug-in extension cables, as shown in picture 3. They're a better option than cutting and splicing the wiring (unless you're a qualified electrician).

TRUMA HEATER AUTO-IGNITOR

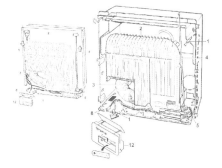

Picture 3. These drawings are for the Trumatic S3002, whereas ours is the S5002 (that has fittings on the opposite side). On the left is the S3002 from '81 to '96, and on the right from '96-on.

Auto-igniters are so common on caravan fridges and some cookers, as well as domestic gas appliances, that we take them for granted. So why they're not fitted to all room heaters is difficult to understand.

A flame failure device cuts off the gas if the heater flame blows out, and they're very unlikely to fail. But if an auto-igniter is also fitted, you've doubled-up on the safety.

I've always found turning on a Truma heater a pain: you have to align your eyesight with the flame window, while pushing the manual ignitor button. With the following kit, all you need do is flick a switch.

I was joined for this project by mobile caravan service engineer Rob Sheasby, to help show how to fit a Truma auto-ignitor.

In theory, this job only involves removing the Truma heater's front cover, and fitting the auto-ignitor parts in accordance with the instructions. However, the instructions were a little confusing ...

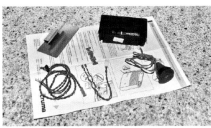

Picture 1. When ordering this kit, you must specify the exact model of your Truma heater (because there are detailed differences), and carefully follow the safety notes in the instructions supplied.

Picture 2. First, Rob removed the front cover, lifting it off the top clips. He disconnected the wiring, and removed the heat-level knob from the casing, and its steel rod (inset).

Picture 4. Rob soon realised that the valve (S5002, on the left) would have to be removed from the heater. The instructions claimed wiring could pass through the cap ...

Picture 5. ... but it couldn't. You must check the direction of the wiring from the contact points to see if the cable can be passed through the cap. If it has to go ...

Picture 6. ... through the body, you'll need to drill a hole, taking great care not to crack the case.

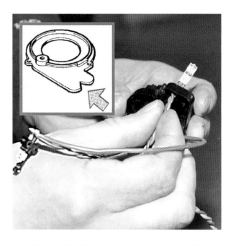

Picture 7. The contact breaker cable could now be passed through the hole in the body. Had the cable been directed upwards, you would have had to cut the lid instead (inset).

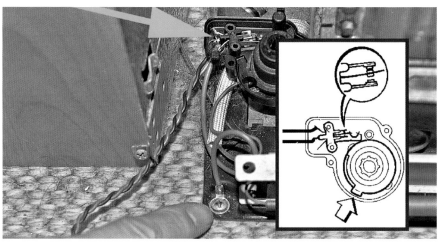

Picture 8. You can see that the contact points simply push down onto the two plastic pins in the casing. Note that Rob has also had to find a suitable earth point for the brown cable.

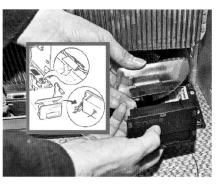

Picture 9. The ignitor unit was fitted, with its clip-on heat shield then clipped into position. Batteries can be changed with the heater cover in position.

Picture 10. Manual ignitor (a) was discarded and replaced with blanking plate (b), removed from the right-hand end of the casing. This, in turn, was replaced with the indicator light.

Although some of the instructions were confusing, Rob soon had it sorted. Overall, the Truma auto-ignitor retrofit kit is both well made and very comprehensive.

Every cable is colour-coded, and all terminals are ready to plug-in. There are even three self adhesive cable clips supplied, to be stuck to the insides of the casing.

Now, to turn the heater on, all you do is turn the heat level control, listen for the clicking, and look for the flashing of the indicator light. When the clicking and flashing stop, the gas fire is alight. You can still check through the flame window should you want to.

INSTALLING A TRUMA AWNING WARMER

Picture 1. The Truma Awning Warmer has been designed to take warm air from the caravan ducted blown air heating system to the awning. Please note that heating the awning reduces the heat output inside the caravan, and it's not intended to fully heat a large awning, or in very cold weather.

The following instructions have been adapted from those for the Truma Awning Warmer kit.

If just the awning is to be heated, Truma recommend that a second duct shut-off is installed, so that warm air to the inside of the caravan can be temporarily turned off. Also, for greater heat output, the manufacturers suggest that a second Truma Awning Warmer could be fitted.

Choice of location

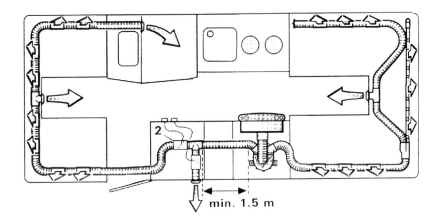

Picture 2. There should be at least 1.5 metres of ducting between the heater fan and the Awning Warmer. Less than this, and the Awning Warmer could overheat.

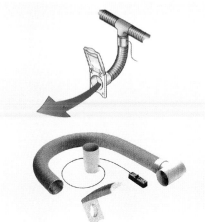

Picture 3. Choose a location on a flat, vertical wall within the area covered by the awning, not too close to the awning fabric, but with the shortest possible route (1.5m min) to the warm air system. Structural parts of the caravan must be avoided for safety reasons, and try to avoid trim.

Cutting the hole

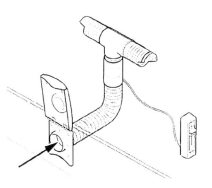

Picture 4. From inside the caravan, drill a 2mm hole horizontally through the side wall, for the housing (position arrowed). From the outside of the caravan, make a 76-80mm cutout around the centre hole. To protect the paintwork during the cutting, work with masking tape: you'll need to cover an area of least 150mm around the pre-drilled hole.
Cut away any trim strips (or similar), or place packing strips so as to make the housing lie flat on the bodywork.
Carefully dress the edge of both the inner and outer walls to remove any sharp edges. Check that the housing will fit into the hole.

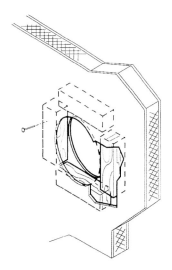

Caravan wall

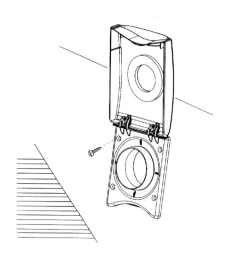

Picture 5. Ideally, the hole should be lined with timber for strength. But before doing so, the insulation around the hole must be removed to the depth of the timber lining. Using a non-hardening plastic sealant – NOT silicone – seal the lining to the inner and outer walls, then secure the timber lining in place with panel pins, and remove any excess sealant from around the hole. It's important to check that all the edges are sealed to prevent water entering the walls.

Warm air system

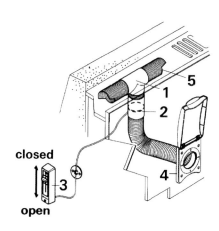

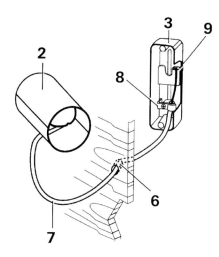

Picture 8. When connections to the warm air system are complete, offer the housing into its position, using the four flange holes as a guide. Remove the outlet flap, and drill mounting holes through the outer wall of the caravan with a 2mm bit. Seal the rear of the outlet flap with plastic anticorrosive sealant – again, DON'T use silicone. Using the four countersunk head screws, secure the housing into position, before removing any excess sealant from the bodywork.

Picture 6. The Truma Awning Warmer is designed for connection to 65mm bore warm air ducts. Fit the T-piece (1) and the duct shut-off (2) into the warm air system as illustrated (don't bend the Bowden cable). To stop water getting in, the feed air duct to the Awning Warmer (4) must be inclined downwards. If necessary, raise the main duct (5).
Select a convenient position for the slide control (3) so the Awning Warmer can be turned on or off from inside the caravan, remembering that the Bowden cable is 80cm long.

Picture 7. Drill a 5mm hole (6) at a 45 degree downward angle. Pass the Bowden cable (7) through the hole (6) from behind. Slacken the fastening clip (8), insert the hook of the Bowden cable into the ring (9). Place the Bowden cable under the fastening clip (8) and screw it down. Fix the control slide with the two 2.9x32 countersunk screws.

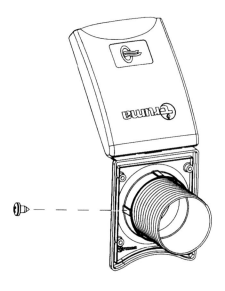

Picture 9. If necessary, secure the air duct with the single 3.5x6.5 screw supplied.

INSTALLING A COOKER HOOD

Dometic, perhaps best known for being the market leader in caravan fridges, also has a huge range of top-quality caravan accessories. Included among them are several types of ventilation system, designed to provide extra ventilation, or extract stale air from toilet or kitchen areas.

There are even two different models of cooker hood: the CK150, which is completely concealed, and the CK155 (shown here), designed to fit beneath a shelf and provide illumination to the cooking area.

Picture 1. The cooker on our Bürstner has a cupboard above it, with lights that are dazzling, rather than illuminating.

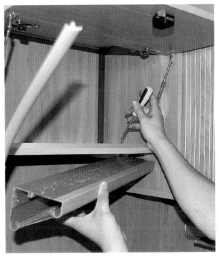

Picture 2. After disconnecting the battery and mains power, Ian Walker, one of Dometic's installers, pulled away the edge trim from the cupboard, and unscrewed the light unit.

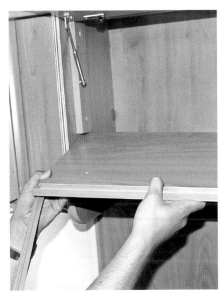

Picture 3. Turnbuckle screws in the base of the shelf were turned anti-clockwise, and the shelf slid out.

Picture 4. Using the drawings supplied in the fitting instructions, Ian worked out where on the underside of the shelf the extractor fan would be fitted.

Picture 5. He cut a 105mm hole in the shelf with his jigsaw. The masking tape was to protect the surface of the shelf from scratches.

Picture 6. He drilled another, much smaller hole for the electrical cable to pass through, then temporarily fitted the extractor hose to calculate where the unit would be located on the shelf.

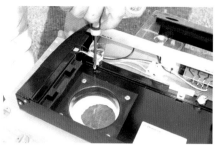

Picture 7. All the screws for fixing the Dometic Cooker Hood to the shelf were lightly fitted, removed again, and the hood taken off once more

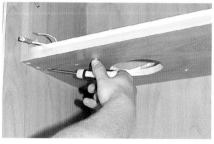

Picture 8. Ian refitted the shelf using the existing special screws. He then ran a new pair of leads for the fan, but reused the lighting cables, seen here, for the new lights. Many caravans would need all new (fused) cables running to this location, though the heavier duty cable needed for the fan could also serve the lower capacity lights.

Picture 9. The position for the roof vent was established, and a small hole drilled right through the centre, bottom-to-top.

IMPORTANT NOTE

• You MUST be certain that there are no wires running through the roof in this location, or you risk having to make wiring repairs in future. Check with your dealer before cutting.

Picture 10. Ian used the central hole to mark and cut the hole in the roof, working from above.

Picture 11. The roof vent has a pair of seals that must be correctly located on its underside before fitting it.

Picture 12. Ian passed the electrical cable through the 105mm hole in the roof, and placed the vent in place. Each screw hole received a coat of non-setting mastic to prevent water ingress.

Picture 13. Using the stainless steel screws provided, the vent inner was screwed to the aluminium roof panel. Be careful – it's easy to strip the threads in the thin aluminium.

Picture 14. With more sealant on the screws, the vent outer cover was fitted next.

Picture 15. Back in the kitchen, Ian offered up the cooker hood with its trunking, to help position it correctly. He then screwed it in place using the screw holes made earlier.

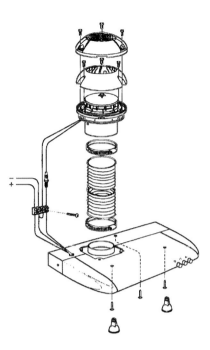

Picture 16. This Dometic diagram shows the simple wiring connections needed, as well as an exploded view of all the individual parts.

Picture 17. Ian connected the wiring using the 'choc block' connectors provided with the kit, then fitted the trunking, tightening it to its spigots using the Jubilee-type clips also provided. Note how it's much easier to tighten the screws with a small ratchet spanner than with a screwdriver.

SAFETY FIRST!

• While it's okay to run the electrical wiring in place yourself, you should have the connections made and the wiring checked and approved by a qualified electrician before reconnecting the electrical supply.

Picture 18. Stephen Hodgson, Dometic's Account Executive, who was on hand throughout, helped by refitting the light bulbs and the washable filter cover to the cooker hood, while Ian tidied up.

Picture 19. In use, the Dometic Cooker Hood is a real boon. It throws light onto a gloomy yet vital part of the kitchen, and is both quiet and efficient in getting rid of cooking fumes and – equally important – steam. You can see more on the range of Dometic extractor fans and other accessories at www.dometic.co.uk.

FIT A BBQ POINT

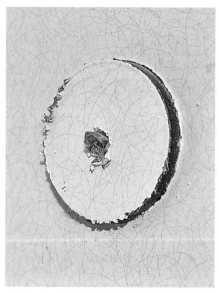

Picture 3. Rob previously drilled a pilot hole because – even after careful measuring – you must be absolutely certain that the hole is going to appear on the inside in the right place.

There's no doubt that the gas barbecue is the cleanest and most controllable way of barbecuing food, although a barbecue with fire might not be allowed on some campsites. A Truma Barbecue Point means you don't have to carry a separate cylinder.

Here's how a gas-qualified caravan engineer can fit a Truma Barbecue Point, enabling you to run your summer barbecue from the contents of your gas locker.

Rob Sheasby, registered with Gas Safe and a leading mobile caravan engineer, shows how he fits one.

Picture 1. As mentioned elsewhere, a spirit level is useless on a caravan, because the caravan itself isn't level. Rob used a square to mark a moulding on the caravan's body.

Picture 2. We made our own template from cardboard. More card was taped to the caravan's panels to protect them. The Makita rechargeable drill has ample power, even for a large hole cutter.

Picture 4. Large hole cutters must be used very slowly, and with plenty of lubricant to prevent overheating. Rob drilled pilot holes for the fixing screws, their positions previously marked on the template.

Picture 5. Aluminium resists corrosion, but isn't immune to it, especially when in contact with mild steel. Würth Cavity Protection Spray was applied because of the clips we would be using (see picture 7)

Picture 8. Rob twisted a strip of butyl tape to form a 'rope,' so it could sit in the slot in the back of the barbecue point, making a seal.

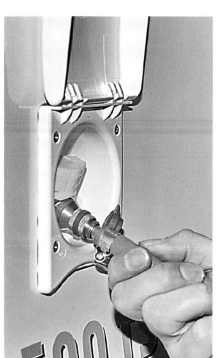

Picture 10. ... that the seal was complete. The connector provided was fitted to the end of the barbecue hose, and is simply plugged in to the external gas socket when needed.

The Truma External Gas Socket (BBQ point) looks very neat when in place, and is easily fitted by an authorised agent. It links into the existing gas pipe in your vehicle caravan.

The only minor downside is that you have to fit the gas plug supplied with the unit to the gas pipe on your barbecue, making it more difficult to use with a stand-alone gas cylinder at home. However, if you want to carry a separate cylinder, a Calor Lite is a great way of doing so.

IMPORTANT NOTE
• The external gas socket is only suitable for extracting gas, and is NOT to be used for feeding gas back into the system.

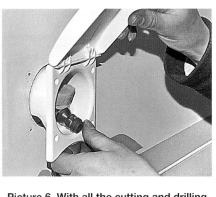

Picture 6. With all the cutting and drilling complete, Rob offered up the external gas socket, made sure that the hole was big enough, and checked that the screw holes were in the correct positions.

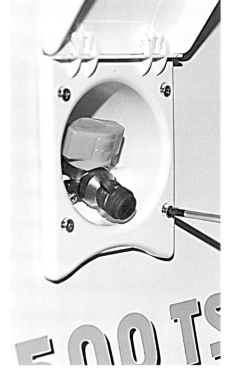

Picture 9. Truma supply stainless steel screws, and these were used to tighten the barbecue point evenly, having first aligned the spire clips with the screw points. Rob checked carefully ...

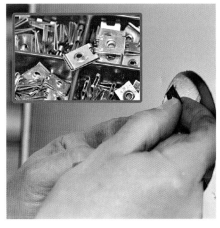

Picture 7. Here's why we needed to protect against corrosion. Thin aluminium is useless for self-tapping screws, so spire clips were pushed over the edges, in line with the screw holes.

ROOF-MOUNTED AIR-CONDITIONING UNIT

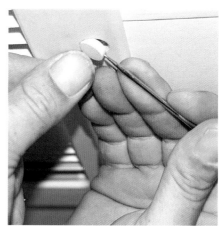

Picture 3. The dimensions (400mm square) mean that it can be fitted in place of a standard vent.

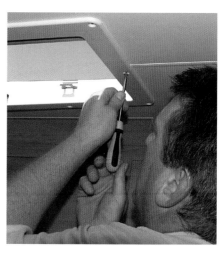

Picture 4. Fixing screws were exposed by levering off the caps, and the eight Allen key screws removed from beneath.

Some people believe that caravanning should be about doing things simply: the idea of air-conditioning in a caravan goes against the grain.

Other people, however, believe it's also about doing things as comfortably as possible, and I prefer to enjoy all the benefits and comforts of modern caravanning – including air-conditioning.

Dometic (formerly Electrolux) has been at the forefront of 'mobile' air-conditioning for many years, and continues to place its units on the caravan roof. This is where it works best – where the air can flow around the heat exchanger. The minor disadvantage is the roof-mounted weight, but air-conditioning is only likely to be fitted to larger caravans, with greater mass lower down maintaining towing stability.

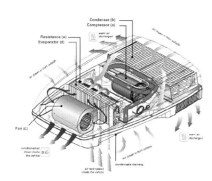

Picture 1. The Dometic unit works well precisely because it's mounted on the roof, cooling the interior from above.

Picture 2. Dometic installer, Ian Walker calculates the best position for the unit using the template supplied.

Picture 5. Outside again, Ian carefully levers away the vent, without damaging or distorting the roof.

Picture 6. Once free from all the sticky butyl sealant, the old vent is lifted away from the roof.

Picture 12. Beneath, the manufacturer had run its own cables, so it was simple to make access for another.

Picture 7. Ian scrapes as much as possible of the old butyl sealant off the roof ...

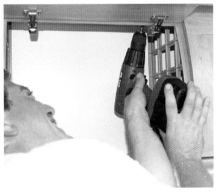

Picture 10. This means carefully drilling holes for electrical cables so that they're completely concealed wherever possible.

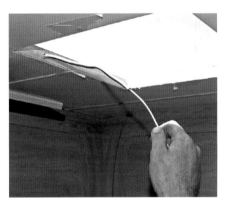

Picture 13. This is a fish wire – a piece of stiff cable used to find a route through difficult locations.

Picture 8. ... so that he can wipe off the residue with solvent (such as white spirit). Disposable gloves keep his fingers clean.

Picture 9. Ian installs units such as this so that they are as close to 'factory' installations as possible.

Picture 11. To pass the cable from the roof lockers down to the sink units, he removes this trunking cover.

Picture 14. Soft electrical cable isn't stiff enough to be pushed through – so it's pulled through by the fish wire!

Picture 15. Ian, with Dometic's Stephen Hodgson, wisely use a trestle when lifting the unit onto the roof.

Picture 16. Most caravans need load supports on the roof itself.

Picture 17. Here's why they need to take care: the user part of the air-conditioner is on the underside.

Picture 18. Ian applies non-setting sealant to the roof before fitting the unit, even though it contains its own seals.

Picture 19. They check for position before lowering the unit into its exact location in the former vent aperture.

Picture 20. Weak roofs could be reinforced by this honeycomb reinforced aluminium plate – as used by Jaguar!

Picture 21. After connecting the electrical wiring to the unit, Ian fits the new plastic trim frame in place.

Picture 24. Along with correct torque, even tightening is essential if the seals fitted to the unit are to work satisfactorily.

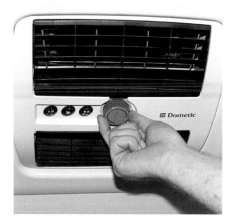

Picture 26. Ian then tests the unit which – very noticeably and refreshingly – cools the hot caravan's interior.

Picture 22. These special bolts pass right through the frame and into the air-conditioner, clamping it onto the roof.

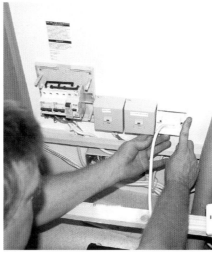

Picture 25. The final job: Ian connects the 230V supply at a new switch unit.

Picture 27. Up on the roof, the Dometic air-conditioning unit is situated where it can work most efficiently.

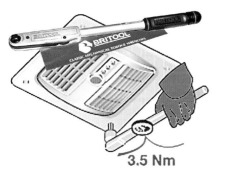

3.5 Nm

Picture 23. Correct torque is critical. This Britool ⅜th drive torque wrench tightens accurately to lower settings than most.

Most British-built caravan roofs aren't capable of taking the weight of an air-conditioner without reinforcement. Honeycomb-reinforced aluminium is immensely strong for its weight, and was used to build the 220mph Jaguar XJ220 supercar. You can buy it in sealed, coated, 10mm-thick panels to the size you need.

UNDERBED MOUNTED AIR-CONDITIONING UNIT

There's no doubt that a caravan can feel hot and confined in the height of summer. If you don't wish to – or can't – fit a roof-mounted unit, Truma's Sapphire air-conditioning units are lightweight and mounted on the caravan's floor.

Here's how Truma can fit air-conditioning in the bed box of your caravan.

Installing the main unit

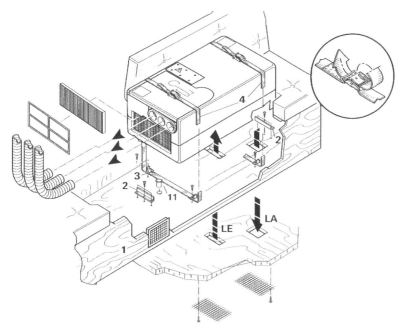

Picture 1. This is the Sapphire Compact unit that, though small, packs quite a punch. Its Expanded Polypropylene housing is sound absorbing and keeps the weight down to 20kg.

Picture 2. Truma's engineer, John, spent a good couple of hours working out where everything would go. The kit included a paper template, but Truma used a plywood version to mark out fixing positions.

Picture 3. It's all very well finding a location inside a bed box, but John also had to be sure that the holes to be cut would miss its wiring, and chassis rails.

Picture 4. After drilling starter holes, John used a jigsaw to cut the rectangular holes for the air supply (already cut, to the right of this shot) and the exhaust.

Picture 5. The template also showed the correct positions for fitting the retaining brackets. John screwed the brackets to the floor and passed the retaining strap through the brackets before offering up ...

Picture 6. ... the air-conditioning unit from inside the caravan. This location beneath the rear bed box is almost ideal, as it's near to the caravan's centre-line. Servicing access is not usually needed.

Picture 7. All air-conditioning units 'dribble' as they extract moisture from the air. A hole had previously been drilled, and John lined up the drain with the outlet on the Sapphire unit.

Picture 8. You can expect to have to make some modifications, but all John needed to do was move a bed support. Make sure that any stowed luggage doesn't interfere with airflow around the AC unit.

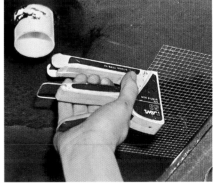

Picture 9. The edges of all cut holes were sealed with underseal, and drains were fitted with mastic. The mesh provided was also fitted to prevent visits from insects and other small animals.

Picture 10. Finally, after tightening the strap fitted earlier, John screwed down the end stops to prevent front-to-rear movement when in transit.

You may see the Sapphire units sold for DIY fitting, but it's not for absolute beginners and, of course, you'd need to have a qualified electrician wire it in.

The Sapphire Compact is intended for caravans up to 5.5m, and the low power consumption makes it ideal for use at most European camp sites. It's also nice not to have an AC unit bouncing around on a fragile roof, making the caravan top-heavy.

Other plus points are: light weight; compact size; standard pollen and dust filter; maintenance free; extra-quiet 'sleep' function; and remote control operation.

COLD AIR DISTRIBUTION

Fitting the air-conditioning unit is only part of a system's installation – finding somewhere to run the air hoses can be a much greater challenge.

Ideally, cold air is distributed high-up in the caravan, so outlets need to be positioned near the ceiling. High-level outlets are far more efficient, but are usually a lot more trouble to fit.

Picture 2. The air hose was sleeved with an outer, stronger hose. This Truma accessory protects against damage and helps to insulate the pipe.

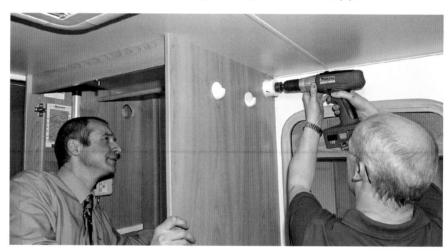

Picture 3. After carefully working out the route, John drilled a hole for an outlet while Service Manager, Richard, watched for break-through. The wardrobe is a good location for a vertical pipe run.

Picture 1. The AC unit was fitted in a bed box to the rear of the axle. Truma's engineer, John, decided to route hoses beneath the caravan, so drilled carefully through the floor.

Picture 4. In our case, the wardrobe provided air outlets into bedroom, kitchen, and sitting areas. From inside the cupboard, the inner part of the connector was pushed into place.

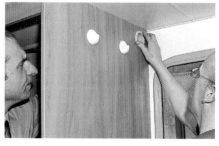

Picture 5. Richard held the inner part of the connector while John slid the outer part in place. Slide them together then twist to tighten.

Picture 6. Another Truma accessory, this rectangular outlet gives directional adjustment. John unscrewed the wardrobe top rail, carefully cut a hole with the jigsaw, and fitted the outlet to it.

Picture 7. John spent longer testing the pipe and vent positions than fitting them. The arrow shows the hole for the bedroom outlet.

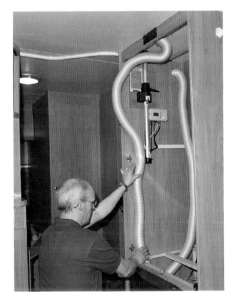

Picture 8. John cleverly clipped the three cold air hoses to the walls so that they followed other protrusions already in the wardrobe, wasting as little wardrobe space as possible.

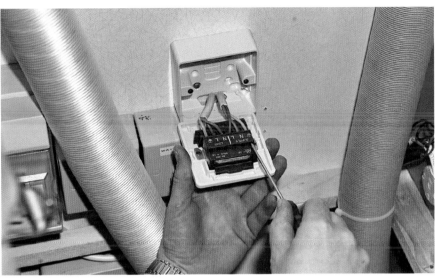

Picture 9. Wiring must be connected only by a qualified electrician. John fitted an isolator switch adjacent to the other mains switches in the wardrobe, and ran cable beneath the caravan.

Picture 10. The infra-red sensor (top left) is operated by the remote control (inset), which has its own bracket. A large air vent is needed, fitted to an under-bed door in this instance.

Truma recommends one of three ventilation systems:

Eco solution: all three vents at floor level. It's rapid and inexpensive, but relatively inefficient, since the hottest air is always at the top of a room.

Comfort solution: the cold air is led upwards, through cold air pipes in a cupboard for example, and evenly distributed around a single room.

Luxury solution: individual for each living area, using a selection from Truma's range of accessories, and a customised air distribution system.

There are also noise suppression accessories available. These could be useful on some continental sites that are said to ban the use of external, noisy air-conditioning units.

CHOOSING AND USING AN AWNING

An awning is often the first major purchase that a caravanner will make after buying the caravan itself. It's an ideal way of gaining extra room for your caravan, or perhaps providing extra sleeping room for visiting friends or grandchildren.

An awning is basically a tent-type structure that attaches to the side of a caravan. Awnings come in a wide variety of shapes, types, makes, and colours. But whichever one you go for, it's extremely important to make sure that it's the correct size to fit your caravan.

While most awning manufacturers will have a list of caravans and their awning sizes, there's always a chance that your caravan is not on their list, particularly if it's an old model. Therefore, it's important to know how to measure your caravan to get the correct awning size.

Using a long piece of string or a tape measure, measure from the ground at the rear nearside corner, up and around the awning rail, and down to the ground at the front nearside corner. This distance is the caravan's awning size, and is generally referred to in centimetres.

Once you know the size, the next job is to decide which type of awning you want. You can have anything from a simple porch awning to a large marquee-type model. While the porch awnings only really act as a storage area for muddy boots and wet clothes, the larger awnings extend to sizes capable of seating up to 20 people in comfort.

Remember that the larger the awning you choose, the heavier it will be, and the more space you'll take up on site. A site warden will not be at all happy if your awning is so big that it spills onto the neighbouring pitch, and you may well have to pay extra for the pleasure of having an awning attached to your caravan.

Type

There's more to choosing an awning than just shape and colour. Choosing the correct type for you and your caravan is essential. Differences in material and frame types will affect its price, weight and durability, and, in turn, the success of your holiday.

Frame

The frame inside an awning is vitally important: without it, you'll be left with a great floppy heap that's good for nothing. In all, there are three types of frame to choose from: IXL glass fibre, aluminium, and steel. Each has its own positive and negative points.

IXL glass fibre has the advantage of being lightweight and strong. It's also impervious to rust and, if treated correctly, should last a long time. However, such qualities don't come cheap, and the unfortunate downside is that IXL frames are generally the most expensive.

Aluminium is the lightest frame material of the three, worthwhile considering when it comes to loading your caravan. It's also cheaper, but it's not quite as strong as IXL glass fibre.

Of the three, steel frames are the cheapest and the strongest. Unfortunately, such benefits are accompanied by weight: steel frames are the heaviest of the trio.

Material

As with frames, there are three types of material commonly used for awnings. This is probably the area that, more than any other, will help you decide which type of awning you will buy, as it affects the awning's price and durability considerably.

Cotton has been used for longer than any other material in the production of awnings, and today it's also the cheapest. In addition, it's breathable, helping to cut down on condensation inside. But cotton is also the heaviest of the fabrics and, if left damp for a long period, it can rot. It also has a habit of fading as it ages.

Acrylic fabric is another popular awning material. There are a number of different types on the market, varying in weight. However, what the different types do have in common is a tendency to last longer than cotton, as well as holding their colour over long periods.

On the down side, acrylic awnings, if stored when damp, are liable to go mouldy. Also, the fabric isn't breathable, allowing a build-up of condensation inside the awning.

Airtex is the least common awning material, and has the big advantage of being the most breathable. It's also slightly more expensive than cotton, but cheaper than acrylic.

ERECTING AN AWNING

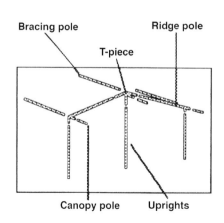

Bracing pole
Ridge pole
T-piece
Canopy pole
Uprights

Picture 1. The process of erecting an awning varies little from model to model, but read the instructions supplied with the awning you purchase, as the process can vary between makes. It's best first attempted slowly and on a still day; windy conditions can make erecting an awning extremely difficult. Having somebody to help, and a small step to assist you in reaching the top of the caravan will also be extremely useful.

Picture 2. Start by laying out the awning frame in front of the caravan, in roughly the same position as the poles will be when you put them together.

Picture 3. Take the awning out of its storage bag and place it towards the rear, on the side that has the awning rail.

Picture 4. Find the point on the awning rail where there's an opening large enough to start threading the awning through. Thread the awning along the awning rail until it reaches the other end, using the step to help you reach the highest parts of the rail.

Picture 5. Position the awning so it hangs squarely on the caravan.

Picture 6. Unzip all the awning's doors and windows.

Picture 7. Inside the awning, connect the ridge pole to the T-pieces, and put them into position inside the fabric, using the guide pins and eye-holes as guides.
Place the ridge poles in position and adjust them so that they're taut.
Put the centre-upright pole into position, and then connect the central bracing pole.
Repeat this procedure with the side-upright and bracing poles, and adjust each one so that they're as taut as possible.

Picture 8. Outside, zip up the doors and windows and, hammer the corner pegs into position. Check that the awning looks neat and square, and then hammer the rest of the pegs into position.

Picture 9. Fix any additional canopy frame poles into place ...

Picture 10. ... and then go back inside and lay out the awning groundsheet, along with any extras such as window blinds.

IMPORTANT NOTE
• The most common mistake when putting up an awning for the first time, is erecting it inside out: ensure you take a good look at what you're doing before you start.

Awning care
As with most things, you must be careful to look after your awning. If it gets dirty, don't use detergents to clean it as this will cause it to lose its waterproofing. Instead, either use plain warm water, or wait for it to dry and use a stiff brush.

Picture 11. If an awning does lose its waterproofing, you'll need to reproof it. There are a number of reproofing products, available from most caravan accessory shops. You simply spray the waterproofing onto the affected area, and leave it to dry.

If you reproof your awning when it's dirty, the reproofer will seal the dirt into the fabric, so spray the affected area from the cleaner, inner side.
When it's time to put the awning away, take care not to store it wet, or it will go mouldy, and cotton awnings may rot. Instead, roll it up, take it home, and spread it out somewhere dry, like a garage, so that it can dry out thoroughly.

Pup tents
A pup tent is one alternative to an awning. These are small frame or dome tents that can be erected near your caravan without actually attaching to it. They are particularly popular with older children wanting some extra space, and who can be trusted to sleep on their own.

FITTING A PORCH AWNING

TOP TIP!

• *Laminate the numbered instruction sheet, and pack it away with the poles so you don't lose it.*

Picture 2. Lie the awning fabric on the ground, so that you can work out which way up it will go. Remember that it's easy to insert it into the awning channel upside-down if you're not careful. Before slipping the awning cord into the end of the channel, remember that any decorative patterns on the roof, and exposed seams in the fabric, will need to end up on the inside (the side facing the centre of the caravan as you thread the awning into position).

This section is intended to be of use no matter what type of porch awning you might choose. Porch awnings of the traditional 'frame tent'-type are inherently heavier and slower to erect than the latest GRP-supported versions, but they have the advantages of usable, almost rectangular space and, perhaps, a touch more solidity.

But, there's no getting away from that fact that they take longer to erect, although we shall try to address that here.

We chose a Pyramid awning on the basis of value-for-money. You do, generally, get what you pay for, but the cost saving over other porch awnings is so great, that we thought we couldn't go far wrong. The poles are made from cheaper, lightweight aluminium, and the quality of the sidewalls and 'draught excluder,' to fill in the gap at the bottom of the caravan, could be better. But the means of attaching the roof poles to the caravan sides are fine, and the lever clips for adjusting the tension of the poles are superb.

Picture 1. The first job is to sort out the supporting poles. No matter which type you have, the poles will be numbered – just remember to take the layout instructions with you when you go away. Assemble the roof poles and lay them on the floor in their correct positions, but without attaching them to each other. That way, you'll be able to go straight to the pole you'll need when you're fitting them in place.

Picture 3. Make sure the awning rail is clear before you start. Using the caravan entry step to give yourself enough height, slide the awning along the rail, without pulling sideways on the fabric.

Picture 4. Awnings all have a method of holding the roof poles at the caravan wall. The method used by Pyramid works well. These pads are prepared by pulling out the two white plastic clips. You can then slide the pad onto the extra cord sewn into the awning fabric just beneath the main awning cord. When in place, push the two clips fully home and they will hold the pad in place.

Picture 5. You'll now need to assemble the two end roof support poles. On this model, the three-way connector is fitted to the outer end, and the adjuster lever is slackened off, allowing the pole lengths to be adjusted at will.

Picture 6. From inside the awning fabric, push the hooked end of the pole into the eye on the pad you fitted earlier.

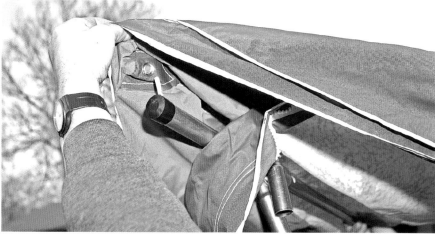

Picture 7. The outer end of the pole (the one with the three-way connector) also has a spike, which is passed through an eyelet sewn into the awning. This allows you to tension the upper corner of the awning.

Picture 8. You can now adjust the pole length, in this case using the catch to clip the adjuster tight. Don't attempt to fully tension the pole at this stage: tighten it just enough to hold everything in place.

Picture 9. After fitting the other roof pole (there's rarely more than two on a porch awning), you can slot the front pole into position. This will be very difficult to do by yourself, it's far better to have a person at each front corner of the awning.

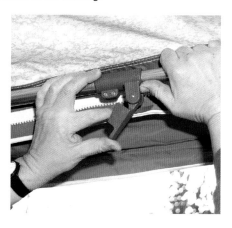

Picture 10. The length of the front pole is also temporarily fixed at this stage.

Picture 11. You can now prepare to fit the corner uprights. Be sure to fit the ferrules at the bases of the uprights BEFORE slotting them into place – otherwise, the weight of the awning may introduce a plug of mud into the end of the tube as it sinks into the ground.

Picture 12. The corner poles will have to be adjusted for height as soon as they are fitted. Don't push too high, because you'll need to judge the correct amount with reference to the lie of the land when everything is in place.

Picture 13. The inner corner poles perform a special purpose: they give support to the height of the awning, so the weight isn't taken on the pad (shown being fitted in picture 4). They also help to hold the side of the awning against the wall of the caravan (something that isn't required with full-length awnings).

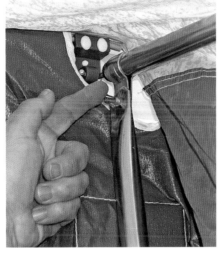

Picture 14. The top of the upright pole must be properly located on the roof rail. This wasn't possible with these uprights, so I dismantled the clips and reassembled them again, so that they gripped the waisted area at the end of the pole without riding over it. This is worth checking before you commence assembly.

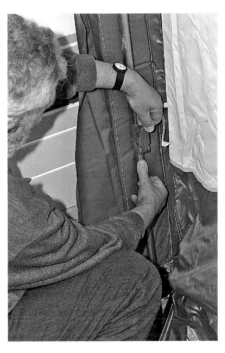

Picture 15. The upright was pushed quite firmly against the foam padded strip down the end of the awning fabric, so that it was pushed tightly against the caravan. You need to ensure that the base of the pole is firmly held in the ground to do this.

Picture 16. You must now ensure that all the zips are closed, and that any removable panels are fitted. The nylon zips on this porch seemed impressively strong, but it's possible to damage any zip through careless handling. Ensure that both pieces of fabric are pretty well aligned before pulling on the zip. You can now adjust the tension on all the poles.

Picture 17. These ladder straps are supplied with the Pyramid awning. I like them because they clip onto the awning sides, and are left permanently in place. They're slightly time-consuming to attach the first time, but you could always fit them at home, before you go away with the awning for the first time. They allow a good range of adjustment for the pegs supplied. Don't forget to take your own mallet and peg extractor if necessary – they're not supplied with this awning.

Picture 18. Your awning should come with a tie-down kit, similar to those used with frame tents. Old-fashioned guy ropes and adjuster toggles are a bit 'retro,' but the ones supplied with this Pyramid kit are simple to use.

Picture 19. After fitting the clips to the straps (the instructions for which are pretty useless), you work out where the spike needs to go, and drive it into the ground, at an angle leaning away from the awning.

Picture 20. The end of the strap with the spring attached is clipped to the spike ...

Picture 21. ... and the upper end is clipped into the buckle sewn into the awning. Fitting and adjustment is a piece of cake.

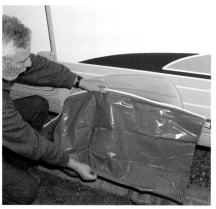

Picture 22. And here's one I should have done earlier. It's best to fit the caravan draught excluders before fitting the awning. I didn't – actually, I couldn't, because our Bürstner caravan comes without rails on the lower sides. Normally, you would slide them into the rails.

Picture 23. After final adjustments for level and tension, it's time to fit the curtains by sliding the plastic clips into the flexible 'rails' sewn into the fabric.

Picture 24. If privacy is important, you may be disappointed: awning curtains often fit together badly. If yours come without Velcro fasteners, you could purchase iron-on Velcro to attach to the curtains. DON'T fit this to the awning walls, however; the glue could cause permanent damage.

FITTING AN OMNISTOR AWNING

Picture 3. The mounting bars are cut to length (the width between mounting screw positions, minus 84mm).

There's a handful of blue-chip companies in the world of caravanning, whose products are watchwords for quality and reliability. Such companies include Dometic, Witter, and AL-KO, among others, and – without a doubt – the well-known awning manufacturer, Omnistor. Omnistor is part of the Thule Group, best known for Its high quality top boxes, and the whole continental-based group of companies, with 2200 employees, is British owned.

When you fit products made by such companies, there's a satisfying sense of permanence about them, and the Omnistor 6002 awning, for roof installation and with retractable arms, is no exception. The following picture sequence shows Omnistor UK's Sales Manager, Mike Dyas, and fitter, Jannick Muylle, (who came over to the UK from Belgium to carry out the work) fitting a unit to a flat-roofed Bürstner caravan. There are several ways of mounting an Omnistor roll-out canopy to a caravan, depending on the type of canopy and caravan model, and different fitting kits are available for caravans with different shaped roofs.

Incidentally, the Omnistor 6002 fits in such as way that the roof rail is unimpeded, so you can still use a traditional type of awning if you're looking to keep out the worst of the weather.

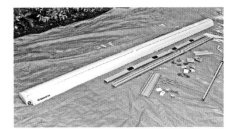

Picture 1. These are the components supplied with the Omnistor 6002 and its separate, roof-specific assembly kit.

Picture 2. Jannick measures the roof width. Note the boards placed on the roof to spread the load.

Picture 4. After cleaning the ends of the rails with a file, the adapter plate mounts were slid on.

Picture 5. Next, the fixing plates, screwed to the rails with the screws provided.

Picture 6. The adapter plates slide onto the mounts along this strong aluminium dovetail, allowing movement for adjustment.

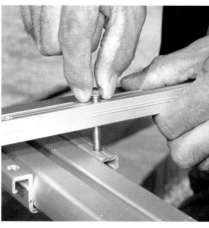

Picture 9. Hexagonal head machine screws are used to fix the two together, but were only fitted loosely at this stage.

Picture 12. After marking the hole positions, Jannick drills 4mm holes so that the screws grip properly.

Picture 7. Jannick is holding the fixing plate he attached earlier, while sliding the adapter plate onto its mount.

Picture 10. A pair of stepped filler pieces are fitted in order to adjust the angle of the awning.

Picture 13. Because leak prevention is a priority, Omnistor instruct that silicone sealant is gunned into each hole.

Picture 8. The adapter plate is held to the sliding mount by inserting zinc plated captive nuts into the aluminium channels.

Picture 11. The strongest point for attaching to the roof is the beading along the top of the sidewall.

Picture 14. As the rail is offered up, you can see how the load is spread across the roof.

Picture 15. More of the 5.5x32mm screws, used earlier, are used to hold the rails down to the roof.

Picture 16. With the screws in place on one side of the roof, Jannick moves to the other.

Picture 17. Note that screws were only fitted to the two outer holes. The centre hole is drilled ...

Picture 18. ... using the 4mm bit as before, then sealed with more silicone sealer to keep water out.

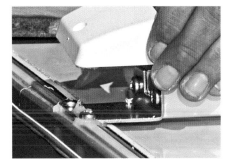

Picture 19. This hole was used for a third screw, holding each end-cap in place.

Picture 20. It takes two people using two ladders to lift the Omnistor awning onto the roof of the caravan.

Picture 21. Note that there is a large piece of foam between the ladder and the caravan, to protect the bodywork.

Picture 22. The awning body fits into these channels (arrowed). Jannick slackens all mounting bolts to allow fitting.

Picture 23. With awning body slotted into place, the fixing bolts are tightened, holding the awning firmly in position.

Picture 24. The angle of the awning, the location, and alignment of the body were all checked and adjusted.

Picture 25. There's two strong front corner legs folded into the front frame, lowered after releasing the catches.

Picture 26. As the awning is wound out, the corner legs are lowered from the frame and locked in position.

Picture 27. On each end of the awning is a hinged, retractable arm providing yet more strength and stability.

Picture 28. Having a person positioned at each leg enables the extending weight to be taken by the legs.

Omnistor awnings are impressively well-engineered, and although fitting one isn't too difficult, I strongly recommend the following:
• Ask your caravan dealer where the strongest attachment points are BEFORE drilling.
• Have an electrician fit the electric motor, if you choose that option.
• Check the weight of the awning before fitting.

FITTING A PDQ AWNING-IN-A-BAG

Picture 2. Thread the leatherette bag into your awning rail, then feed it around the rail. If necessary, clean out the rail first, and lubricate it with soapy water.

It can take ages to fit an awning when you're on site, especially if it's the first time, or fresh out of the bag. Pyramid Products' PDQ awning is a lightweight summer awning, capable of being erected in a fraction of the time – but you have to install it first!

There are two sizes of awning: the standard size, 3.5m long, is said to fit 90% of caravans. The small size, 2.5m long, is said to fit 99% of caravans, and costs a little less than the standard size. In both cases, there will be variation between suppliers.

Picture 3. You must ensure that the tapered end goes first, and that the curtain rail is on the inside, with the label facing you. Standing on the caravan step helps.

Picture 1. Pyramid's Tim Pearce recommends laying out all the poles first, in the order in which they will be fitted.

Picture 4. Tim threads the two horizontal poles through the sleeves, fits them to the end uprights, and joins them together with the shorter centre piece. He set push-button connectors on to the narrowest setting.

Picture 5. There's only one pole between caravan and outer frame. Tim clips this to the caravan end, screws the clamp tight on the outer end, then adjusts for length.

Picture 6. Tim has now fitted the curtains. The PDQ is finally levelled and tensioned using the adjustments on the internal poles and the tent pegs, and the substantial tie-down kit supplied.

Picture 7. To put the PDQ awning away again, Tim removes the centre roof pole, running from caravan to frame, then shortens the legs, using the adjusters, before folding them inwards.

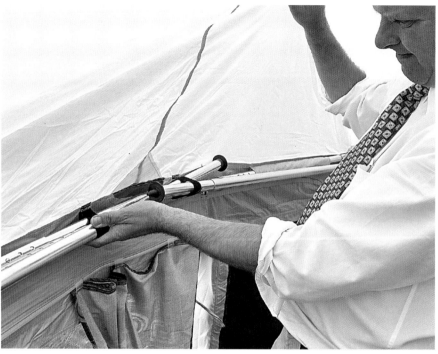

Picture 8. Long Velcro straps, sewn to the awning fabric, are used to tie the legs to the horizontal poles, none of which ever have to be removed.

Picture 9. The sidewalls of the awning are hooked into the bag using the rubber straps and toggles fitted; the whole thing is then rolled-up, towards the bag.

Picture 10. This is possible single handed, but a bit of help holding the rolled-up awning into the bag while the zip is done up, makes the job much easier.

The PDQ awning was developed by Pyramid's in-house engineers in Nottinghamshire. It's both a revelation and a revolution, compared with the chore of erecting traditional awnings. The standard awning measures 3.5m (rear) x 2.5m (front; it's tapererd) x 2.5m (depth), and thanks to its aluminium poles, weighs only 15kg.

The downside? The PDQ isn't intended as a winter awning and would probably need to be taken down in very strong winds, mainly because of the lack of poles at the 'eaves.' But for the vast majority of the time, it's perfect.

FITTING A FIAMMA ROLL-OUT AWNING AND SIDE PANELS

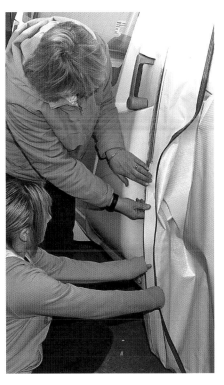

Picture 2. Your caravan's awning channel must be lubricated with silicone spray, available from most caravan shops. With the awning removed from the bag and unfurled, it can be fed into the awning rail ...

We like being able to arrive on site and have the caravan's entrance area protected from the elements quickly and without fuss. Of the many options available, the roll-out Caravanstore awning is among the quickest. Made by AgentFiamma, one of the best brands on the market, this 'awning-in-a-bag' is semi-permanently fitted to the side of the caravan, stowing in a waterproof bag.

Fiamma roll-out awning

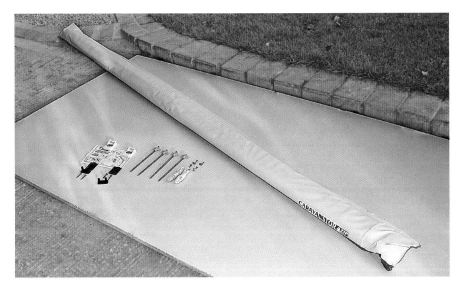

Picture 1. The manual roll-out awning comes with a fully waterproof bag, plus a kit for secure ground fixing and leg mounting brackets.

Picture 3. ... and slid up and along (it's useful to have several helpers). If the awning rail is too tight at the curves, remove the awning and carefully ease it open.

Picture 4. Emily and Dave roll the awning back onto its aluminium tube. It's very easy to do without creasing, but you do need to roll it reasonably evenly. Into the bag ...

Picture 5. ... and the three Velcro ties are used to hold it in place. The bag is only 15cm high, so it's well above the door top. This is the normal putting-away procedure.

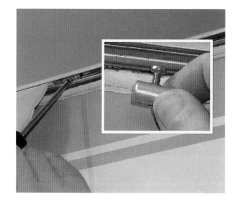

Picture 6. The threaded end-stops and screws appear to be stainless steel (those supplied with cheaper makes rust). After positioning the bag, they're slid in and screwed tight at each end.

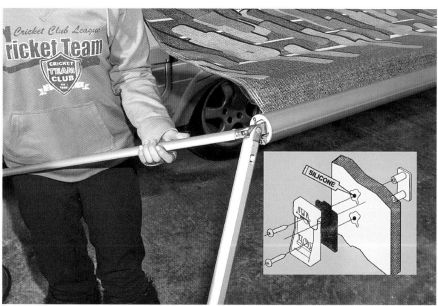

Picture 7. When erecting the awning, each leg and bracing bar slides out of the aluminium tube and swivels into position. There are also leg clips (inset) for fitting the caravan side.

Picture 8. When fitting the supports, be careful not to force them, or you could damage them. Emily fits the telescopic roof bar, while Dave supports the leg which, alternatively, can fit into the caravan plate.

Picture 9. One of the upright leg's sections slides out and clips into place, while the telescopic section is set by closing the plastic clamp, shown here. All very nicely engineered.

Picture 10. Guy ropes are permanently tied to these pop-in, shouldered aluminium pins, and the pins can then be fitted to, or removed from, the tops of the uprights as required.

Perhaps you've tried a conventional awning, and found it too bulky and time-consuming to erect. Or maybe you've tried a fold-out porch awning, and found it too flimsy and leaky. You might have tried a wind-out awning – nice, but very heavy! We think a Fiamma roll-out awning is the best compromise for us.

But what if you want an awning with sides and a door? Well, the Caravanstore can be turned into a 'proper' awning, with zip-in panels and extra aluminium support frame for when the weather is less than perfect ...

FITTING FIAMMA CARAVANSTORE ENCLOSURE

AgentFiamma's Caravanstore Zip and Privacy Room is an effective alternative to traditional awnings when added to Fiamma roll-out awnings. When you arrive on site, you roll out the Caravanstore awning for instant cover, and then fill-in the front and sides at your leisure.

It takes about 20 minutes to turn a Fiamma roll-out awning into a high class zip-on room – just like this ...

Picture 1. The Caravanstore Zip Privacy Room kit is comprehensive and includes a carry bag. With all except the largest Zip models, the Rafter and Tie-Down Kit are extras. The kit is fitted to the already-erected awning roof.

Picture 2. First, assemble one set of poles and push the vertical section through the loop in the top of the side wall. Poles are 'handed' – clip on the inside.

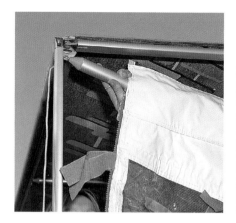

Picture 3. The outer end of the horizontal pole has a point on the end, and this has to be located in a hole near the top of the awning's support leg.

Picture 6. The side wall is now held at the caravan end, and has to be pulled snug while being tensioned, and held to the frame with a number of Velcro fasteners.

Picture 9. The front panel simply slides into a slot in the roof of the awning. We found it best to raise one of the legs while sliding it into the slot.

Picture 4. The side wall and horizontal pole (it's spring-loaded) are raised, and the inner end of the pole slotted into a cup on the inner face of the awning.

Picture 7. Along the sides of the roof, the side walls are finally zipped into place (using the built-in zips). It's a good idea to regularly lubricate zips with tent zip lube.

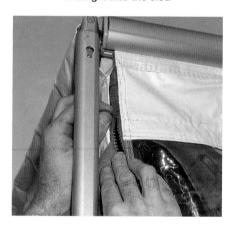

Picture 10. Again, integral zips are used to make a draughtproof joint between each front and side panel. Guy ropes (supplied) and the optional tie-down kit would help greatly in windy weather.

Picture 5. The inner edge of the fabric has a padded panel, sealing between the aluminium upright and caravan body. The upright is slid along the horizontal pole, then locked in position.

Picture 8. Rainwater gathering in an awning roof can be a nuisance. The Fiamma Rafter (which comes as standard with the largest Zip models, but available as an optional extra for the others) helps prevent sag.

I estimate it takes only a couple of minutes to erect the Caravanstore Zip 'roof,' and around another 20 minutes to erect the Enclosure (also referred to as the Privacy Room).

There are several things about this system I really like. The caravan-mounted section is far lighter than a wind-out awning, but far cheaper and almost as quick to erect. The Zip panels make the awning good enough to use as a summer bedroom, and the whole thing is impressively well built.

FITTING AN AWNING LIGHT

Most caravans have a 12-volt awning light fitted above the entrance door, on the outside of the caravan. This serves two purposes: first, it acts as a guide to help you find the way back to your caravan when it's dark. Second, it provides some illumination for the inside of an awning attached to the side of your caravan.

For caravans that aren't equipped with an awning light, fitting one to your caravan is a pretty basic procedure, although the method will alter slightly between types. The model shown here is by Britax.

Disconnect the caravan's 12-volt battery before commencing.

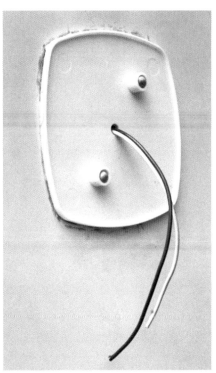

Picture 4. Push the awning light's backplate firmly into position on the caravan wall, feed the wires through the hole in the wall and through the backplate, and screw it into place.

Picture 1. Position the awning light on the side of the caravan, where you want it fixed. Make sure that it's not going to get in the way of the door opening and closing. Using the backplate of the light as a guide, mark the shape of the light on the wall and drill an 8mm hole towards the middle.

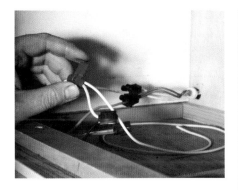

Picture 2. Feed the awning light's wires through the hole, and attach them to a suitable 12-volt power source. Don't forget to include a 5 amp fuse inline.

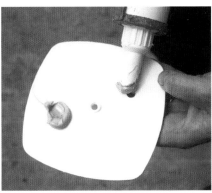

Picture 3. Apply some non-drying silicone mastic sealant to the back of the awning light.

Picture 5. Fit the light unit to the backplate. Connect the wiring: the white live wire to the switch, and the green earth wire to the bulb holder. Reconnect the caravan's battery.

INSTALL AN OUTDOOR SHOWER

Picture 2. Locate the shower outside the awning and away from internal obstructions, but within reach of internal water pipes. I drilled a pilot hole from the inside before Dave used the template ...

A Whale shower is ideal for washing a muddy dog, muddy boots, or for rinsing away the sand and salt after a trip to the beach.

Fitting involves three main elements: cutting into the side wall; adding to the water system; and adapting the 12V electrics – a professional's job. Here's how it's done ...

Picture 1. This is the Whale Swim 'N' Rinse kit, along with all the parts we needed. Originally designed for boats and campers with pressurised water systems, minor modifications are required for caravan use.

Picture 3. ... supplied with the kit to mark out. Then, 10mm corner holes were drilled, and an Erbauer rechargeable jigsaw, from Screwfix, was used to cut the hole. Note the masking tape ...

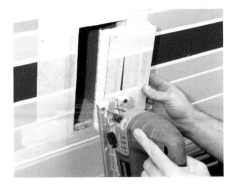

Picture 4. ... on the caravan's paintwork and on the plate of the jigsaw: without this the vibration will scratch the surface. This is a composite wall panel, but many constructions have three separate elements.

Picture 5. Small grooves were filed in the plastic surround, so it sat smoothly over the bodywork's raised ribs. Pilot holes were drilled, sealant applied, and stainless steel screws fixed, followed by trim caps.

Picture 6. Dave removed the skirting board and drilled through the base of the cupboard, before feeding water hoses through to the wash basin area. The loose shower hose sits in the cupboard.

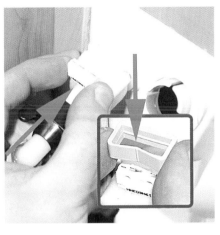

Picture 7. To fit the microswitches needed for conventional caravans (not supplied with the standard kit), simply push onto the two pegs then slide the plastic clip over the top.

Picture 8. You'll also need a pair of tap connectors (90 degree to save space), and small spade terminals for the microswitch connections. Wiring is not supplied. NEVER use mains-type cable.

Installation was straightforward, though it's important to check carefully for leaks. We found one at the wash basin tap, and had to disconnect and remake the joint. You MUST have electrical connections made by a qualified electrician.

You also need to think carefully before cutting the hole in the sidewall.

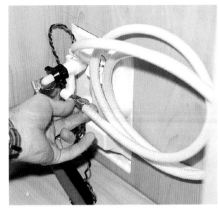

Picture 9. Dave had twisted the two strands of 12V cable, gripping one in the vice and twisting the other with a slow-moving electric drill. You must use the sealing washers when connecting the shower hose.

Picture 10. The water supply was plumbed into the wash basin hoses. Dave used a heat gun to soften the plastic, so it could be pushed onto the T stubs.

The cutting isn't tricky, but you must be absolutely sure that you're cutting in the right place: you won't get a second chance!

Now, keeping boots (or paws) clean after a walk is easy   although for wet-weather cleaning, we'll use a tray to stop the ground getting muddy.

Part 4
Convenience

TAILOR-MADE CARAVAN COVER

Picture 1. The Cover Company is the only company I've come across who requires a template of the shape of the roof corners, but it seems a really good idea to me.

Picture 2. Proprietor Chris Dash used the back of some surplus wallpaper, held on with Blu-Tack. When the paper had been made horizontal, he marked the roof curve with a felt-tip pen.

If you want a tailor-made caravan cover, you're going to have to measure up – and it's vital that you get it right.

Make a mistake in your measurements, and you'll end up with a misshapen bundle on your caravan's roof. However, there are techniques to help ensure that your caravan's new cover fits properly.

Picture 3. He then used a metre ruler to draw a clear, vertical line anywhere on the paper. It's important that the line is vertical, so Chris levelled the ruler ...

Picture 6. All the dimensions you need to supply are set out clearly on the Cover Company's comprehensive and thorough order form.

Picture 9. You'll also need to measure the maximum height of each projection. Fitted pockets will be made for taller items, while lower ones can fall within the sweep of the cloth.

Picture 4. ... with the edge of one of the windows. Where this isn't possible, you must use a spirit level. A vertical line drawn at each end provides vitally important datum points.

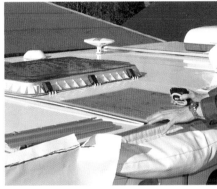

Picture 7. For roof-mounted items, it's essential to measure from imaginary lines drawn at right-angles to the caravan sides. In the absence of a giant tri-square, place a machine-cut rectangle ...

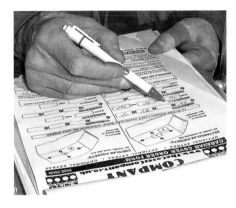

Pioture 10. After you've filled in The Cover Company's form, or written out your dimensions on your own sketch plans, check them against each other. And don't be surprised if there are discrepancies!

Picture 5. The first measurement is the distance between the two lines, for which you'll need a helping hand. Measure top and bottom. If they're not the same, your lines aren't vertical.

Picture 8. ... of MDF board against the caravan edge, and use a long strip of plastic or timber to establish positions. It's easier when you're measuring close to the edge.

A tailored caravan cover will not only look better, but should also chafe less, causing less scratch damage to plastic windows, especially if it's well tightened down. But I cannot overstate the importance of checking that your measurements are accurate. The best way of confirming accuracy, is to check all the measurements against each other. For example, if front-to-door + door-to-back doesn't equal overall length, there's an error somewhere in your measurements or calculations.

There's an old woodworker's saying: "Measure twice and cut once."

CARAVAN COVERS

A caravan cover keeps dirt at bay, but with so many choices available, how do you choose between those on offer? Let's see what the differences are:

BUDGE INDUSTRIES

Light & low-cost

Budge is a large, US-based cover manufacturer, and has been producing covers since 1948. This prototype cover is made to the company's lightest, least-expensive spec. and is very easy and undemanding to fit. The material doesn't appear robust, but there's a reassuring two-year guarantee and other, more expensive grades of fabric are available as higher-priced options.
Supplying Company: Budge Industries
Model: Budge Lite®
Material: Lightweight spun-bonded polypropylene
Weight (kg): 5.4
Door opening: Velcro
Type: Not individually fitted
Guarantee: 2 years
Phone: 001 267 263 0600 (USA)
Website: www.budgeindustries.com

COVER SYSTEMS

Excellent all-rounder

Medium weight, 'slippery' material makes this cover easier to fit than the heavier covers, yet seems robustly made. Available in green or grey. Made to the owner's dimensions – but very carefully cross-checked by Cover Systems. Top-class service. Caravan profile isn't considered, so it could be a little baggy around the top corners, as ours turned out to be. Lots of fitted pockets in the roof, providing an excellent fit but making the cover more difficult to position – and accurate measuring is essential.
Supplying Company: Cover Systems
Model: Caravan Cover
Material: 150D woven textile. Aluminised coating on grey covers.
Weight (kg): 8.6
Door opening: Zip
Type: Tailor-made
Guarantee: No time limit on materials/workmanship
Phone: 01933 410851
Website: www.cover-systems.co.uk

PRO-TEC COVERS

Quite tough

Supplied with lots of extras, including telescopic lifting poles and a bag with carrying straps. The long poles were a real boon, though the lock on one of them failed first time. Roof pockets are long and sweeping, so they resist catching when fitting and means measurements aren't so critical. The cover appears very well made. The downside is that it's darned heavy: it takes two men a lot of lugging when a large caravan is involved. Ideal for longer-term storage.
Supplying Company: Pro-Tec Covers
Model: Caravan Cover
Material: Protex 003 Tri-Laminated
Weight (kg): 11.0
Door opening: Velcro
Type: Tailor-made
Guarantee: Unstated
Phone: 01274 780088
Website: www.pro-teccovers.co.uk

PURPLE LINE

Bright & light

The Purple Line cover material is very bright, light, and seems relatively flimsy (though that could be misleading, seeing as this is a top brand). Because of its light weight it's easy to fit, though sizes don't appear generous. There are many straps and they're time-consuming to fit because the adjusters are fiddly, but they help to prevent scratch damage to windows from chaffing. The protective foam collars for roof obstructions are superb.

Supplying Company: Purple Line
Model: Platinum
Material: Du Pont Tyvec: Non-woven polypropylene
Weight (kg): 5.4
Door opening: Velcro. (Complete side only.)
Type: Not individually fitted
Guarantee: 3 years
Phone: 01473 601200
Website: www.purpleline.co.uk

SPECIALISED ACCESSORIES

Built to last

The fabric appears hard-wearing, the cover is very well made, and the slightly matt finish is unobtrusive. While it's not the same as the Pro-Tec (the fit of both main and separate A-frame covers are better), many of the same comments apply: strong, well made, and relatively heavy. Again, ideal for longer-term use because you wouldn't want to be fitting and removing it too frequently. The very comprehensive extras include repair fabric and corner protectors, and an excellent 3-year guarantee.

Supplying Company: Specialised Accessories
Model: Caravan Cover
Material: Webflex-95
Weight (kg): 9.8
Door opening: Velcro
Type: Tailor-made
Guarantee: 3 years (fabric)
Phone: 01274 780088
Website: www.caravancovers.org.uk

THE COVER COMPANY

First among equals

Although made by Cover Systems, there are differences between the two covers tested here. The Cover Company requires that you fill in a comprehensive size checklist, and that you produce a template of the corner profiles. As a result, fit was even better than the one ordered through the manufacturer. This cover lacked the A-frame fixing straps on the Cover Systems' own-brand, but there were fewer detailed pockets, making it even easier to slide this mid-weight cover into position

Supplying Company: The Cover Company
Model: The Caravan Cover
Material: Woven polyester with polyurethane. Aluminised coating on grey covers.
Weight (kg): 8.6
Door opening: Zip
Type: Tailor-made
Guarantee: 1 year ("or longer if relevant")
Phone: 01432 379 357
Website: www.thecovercompany.co.uk

BUILDING A CARAVAN PORT

Picture 3. The first end has to be erected with enormous care to ensure that corners are square and heights correct. If they weren't, then everything else would be wrong, too.

The biggest enemy of any caravan is water ingress. Keep the water off, and it can't get in and rot the timber framework, and you'll also eliminate black streaks, mould, and weather damage to fittings and accessories.

Newbury Metal Products makes, arguably, the best quality caravan ports available. Here's how to put one up.

Picture 4. Uprights, cross-bars, and roof supporting framework were all raised and bolted into position, using the stainless steel fittings that came with the kit.

Picture 5. Optional side panels are best fitted when facing the prevailing wind. Multi-wall plastic sheeting can easily be cut with a jigsaw, but needs supporting at regular intervals while working.

Picture 1. The whole assembly came packed away in one van, and the fitters spent half an hour laying out all the parts in the order in which they would need them.

Picture 2. They started with the frame. This goes up against an existing building, but many installations have a wall plate bolted to a suitable brick wall instead of uprights.

Picture 6. NMP fit edging and closing strips to the edges of the plastic sheeting, so that water can't get in and leave tell-tale green mould.

Picture 7. When it comes to fitting the corrugated roof sheets, it pays to take time getting the first one as square as possible: otherwise the following sheets will run out of alignment.

Picture 8. NMP strongly recommend having two corrugations overlapping at each joint to ensure that the roof will be waterproof. J-bolts and sealing washers, supplied with the kit, hold the sheets down.

Picture 9. The final sheet will almost certainly require cutting down. Believe it or not, the recommended tool for doing this job is a BLUNT handsaw.

Picture 10. The whole process takes three experienced fitters two days, from start to finish, which just goes to show how careful and meticulous they are when carrying out this work.

When you look at the price of a new or replacement caravan, the investment made in a caravan port looks more and more sensible. Not only will your existing caravan last much longer, but you'll reduce the amount of time spent washing your caravan. Plus, the hitch, the electrics, and any roof-mounted accessories will last much longer, too, when protected from the elements.

FITTING A TRUMA CARAVAN MOVER

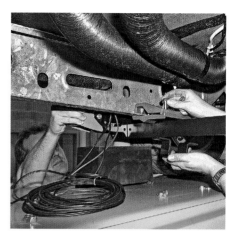

Picture 2. Andy helps to align the dots on the units (arrowed, previous image) with the insides of the tyres, while John fits the chassis clamp and the retaining U-clamp.

As caravans become better equipped and heavier, they become more and more difficult to move. A caravan mover solves this problem, and even reduces the chances of damaging the caravan or tow vehicle when hitching up.

A competent DIYer could certainly fit a Truma caravan mover, but the wiring must be connected by a qualified electrician.

Picture 3. None of the clamp bolts have been tightened yet, allowing the assembly to slide along the chassis when coaxed with a soft hammer. Roller-to-tyre gap is established with the spacer supplied.

Picture 1. Truma's engineer, John, loosely fits the crossbar (with label centred) to the units, and slides them approximately into place. Units can be fitted in front or behind, depending on available space.

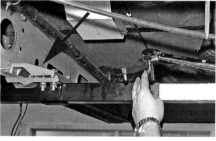

Picture 4. There's a crucial order in tightening the clamp. FIRST, the pinch bolts (arrowed) are tightened to grip the chassis. Only then must the U-clamp bolts and cross-bar bolts be torqued.

Picture 5. It's important that the power cables to each motor are the same lengths, otherwise different voltages will cause the caravan to travel in an arc.

Picture 8. The control unit (here with cover removed) fits beneath a bed box. There are different connections for when the mover is behind or in front of the axle.

Picture 9. Truma is anxious to point out that, even with the unique, purpose-made gearbox (it's said that others are adapted from mobility scooters), there is a lower priced version with manual engagement.

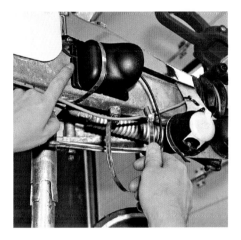

Picture 6. An extra 12N socket must be fitted on electric engagement models. Ingeniously, it clamps on with a pair of stainless steel jubilee clips. There's a slot for wiring at the rear.

Picture 10. John finished off by reconnecting the caravan to the tow vehicle with the mover. The remote is simple to use, and the soft start and stop make precise positioning a doddle.

Picture 7. This safety device means you can't use the mover unless your 12N cable is connected, so it can't be triggered accidently by the remote from inside your towing vehicle whilst you're towing.

This Truma system has a unique, purpose-made gearbox that provides extra clearance under the caravan, which helps makes the Truma 15 per cent lighter than other models.

The electrically-operated engagement is terrific, too: simply hold down two buttons on the remote for a few seconds, and the driving wheels are engaged. When you've finished, apply the handbrake, press two buttons again, and the mover is disengaged.

On twin-axle models, the inner wheels are pulsed when turning, so the tyres don't lock up. On single-axle models, the caravan can even pirouette in its own length.

FITTING A POWRTOUCH CARAVAN MOVER

I was taken by surprise when we came to park our new Bürstner caravan. Having not owned our own caravan for a while, we had tested loan-caravans and bumped smaller, lighter British models up and into our drive without trouble. But, at 1.5 tonne when fully laden, this German luxe-wagen was almost beyond us.

Another problem is that our gateway is so narrow: trying to reverse into it, in the dark, with an offset-step was too risky – especially as the Bürstner was decidedly not cheap. The solution? We had a Powrtouch caravan remote mover fitted.

If you're a competent DIYer, there's no reason why you shouldn't save some money by fitting a Powrtouch yourself. You do need to work with care and a conscientious eye for detail, but there's no welding, cutting, or drilling required in the vast majority of cases. If you don't wish to DIY, Powrwheel, the maker of Powrtouch, has over 40 fitters around the country who'll do it for you.

Each Powrtouch (there are several models) comes with a comprehensive set of fitting instructions. This section sets out to explain how it's done.

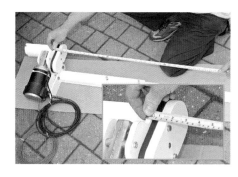

Picture 3. Powrwheels fitter Dave Baxter started by pushing the two drive units onto the crossrail, measuring them to get them roughly symmetrical. Finer adjustment is carried out later.
Establish the approximate dimensions by measuring the distance between the insides of the tyres.
Halve it, deduct 15mm per side, and set this distance from the centre of the crossrail to the outer edge of each roller support (see inset).

Picture 1. Phil Clarke from Powrwheel demonstrates the kit of parts, as they look when they come out of the box. There are two 'handed' drive assemblies, an adjustable crossrail to link them together, brackets for attaching to the chassis, and the simple switch and control unit. There are different motor sizes, wheel sizes, and crossrail lengths, so the vast majority of single- and twin-axle caravans are catered for.

Picture 4. The U-bolts and clamps used to clamp the Powrtouch mover to the caravan chassis.
All main clamp plates have the lip shown here, to take account of the thickness of the caravan's chassis rail.
This is the heavy-duty top plate with threaded holes. Grub screws pass through these holes, providing an extra clamp onto the chassis.

Picture 2. All models have a drive roller, held against the tyre when needed. Each drive roller is driven by an adjacent motor, taking its power from the caravan battery.

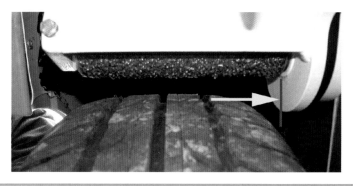

Picture 5. Dave slides the assembly beneath the caravan, using a piece of cardboard packing as a sledge and to prevent damage to the Powrtouch's paintwork.

Picture 6. The Powrtouch wouldn't fit at the front of the wheels (that are recommended to reduce road spray onto the unit) because of the shock absorbers. Fitted behind the wheels, the rollers need to be reversed – easy with DC motors. Dave simply swapped the red- and yellow-tipped wires over at each motor.

Picture 7. The unit is now positioned behind the wheels, and lifted onto suitable supports.

Picture 8. Dave uses a scissor jack to lift first one end, and then the other. The lower clamp plate (a) sits on the Powrtouch tube and 'wraps' around the outer edge of the caravan's chassis rail. A pair of U-bolts clamp the upper plate onto the chassis rail, with the lip (c) mentioned in picture 4, in the position shown.

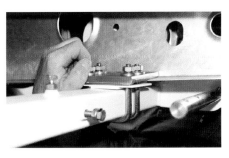

Picture 9. Plain and spring washers, then nuts, are fitted to all the U-bolts. The pinch bolts (out of focus in foreground) holding the crossrail in place are slackened, and only lightly retightened to adjust the distance between drive units.

The drive units are now set so that the distance between the inside of the tyre and the drive unit (see picture 2, arrow) is about 12mm (½in), so that the tyre won't rub as it distorts.

DON'T fully tighten any of the pinch bolts holding the cross tube in place until all are slightly 'nipped' – otherwise they will work loose as the position of the tube settles.

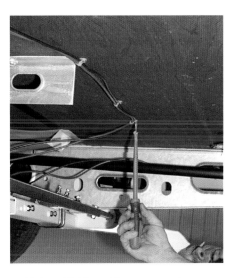

Picture 10. The wiring can now be run across the base of the floor, using the clips provided to route the cables neatly.

Picture 11. You'll need to drill two 12mm holes in the floor, where the wires will pass up into the bed box, and two 6mm holes where the feed wires will pass into the battery box. Drill the floor holes laterally, so that the wires for the left-hand motor pass through the LH hole and those for the rh motor go through the rh hole.

Picture 12. This is the control unit with cover removed, being readied for fitting to the bed box.

149

Picture 13. The wires from the motor are passed through the holes in the floor, and the ready-fitted cable ends are screwed to the control unit (positions are marked on the board). The centre two posts are for the supply cables, from the battery.

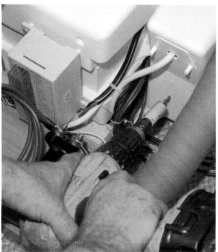

Picture 15. The isolator switch is best fitted to the battery box, in a position that prevents the mains plug being fitted when the removable switch knob is in place. Dave drills a 22mm hole in the casing. There are two main reasons for never using the Powrtouch with the mains cable fitted. 1) The Powrtouch would attempt to draw power from the battery charger damaging it; and 2) the cable might run beneath a caravan wheel, possibly wrecking the battery box, and with a risk of electrocution from bare wires.

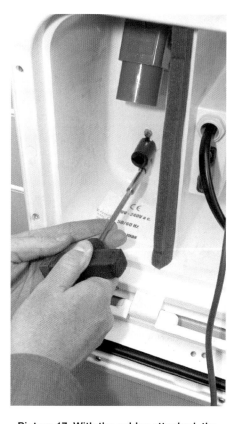

Picture 17. With the cables attached, the switch is held to the battery box with the two screws supplied. Here you can see its position beneath the mains socket.

Picture 14. After motor and battery cables have been screwed on, the unit is fitted to the side-wall of the bed box. You can now refit the cover.
The control unit can become warm when the Powrtouch is in use, so try to position it where luggage won't press against it.

Picture 16. The positive battery cable is supplied in two lengths, and each half is connected to the terminals on the isolator switch.

Picture 18. With isolator switched OFF, the cables can now be connected to the battery. You might need to crimp on new cable ends, depending on the type of battery clamps you are using. Powrwheel say that an 85 ah battery will be sufficient for a single-axle Powrtouch mover, while a 110 ah battery is recommended for a twin-axle model.

I took this opportunity to upgrade to a higher capacity battery. This is an Elecsol 100ah battery, with carbon fibres to prevent plate buckling under heavy load or discharge, and to prevent plate sulphation. These batteries give 20 per cent more power for their size and are guaranteed for five years

Picture 19. Before trying out the Powrtouch unit, you will need to carry out final adjustments.
The wooden spacer block provided in the kit should be a smooth, sliding fit between tyre and roller on each driven wheel. For models with smaller rollers (45mm dia), the block is 20mm thick; for larger rollers (65mm dia), it is 15mm thick.

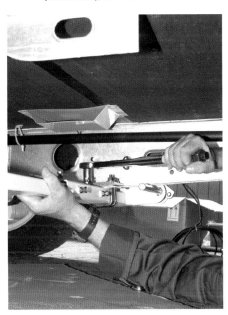

Picture 20. All bolts and nuts should now be tightened to 40 ft lb with a torque wrench, and, where locknuts are fitted to bolts, with an open-ended spanner.

Picture 21. Fit the stop-block on each side, on the opposite side to the drive wheel. This is to prevent the unit from slipping on the chassis.
Fit the block so that the bolt is tightened towards the Powrtouch unit. (On one side the bolt will stick up; on the other side it will stick down.) This will keep it in tight contact with the unit as the bolt is tightened.
Check the clearance shown in picture 20 and readjust as necessary after the first two or three times of using the unit.

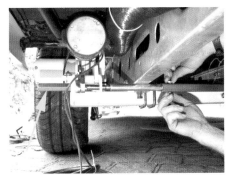

Picture 22. A cross-bar (called a PowrBar) can be fitted to the operating hexagon (arrowed). The hexagon on each side is turned with the long-lever wheelbrace supplied until the roller springs against the tyre. With the PowrBar fitted, both rollers are actuated at once, so that you can use the Powrtouch even if you only have access to one side of the caravan. This does make the hexagon significantly harder to turn, so I used an even longer wheelbrace than the one supplied, making the task much easier.

Picture 23. Phil Clarke from Powrwheel satisfied himself that our hefty Bürstner caravan would climb the very steep slope inside our gate – and it did with consummate ease. I have previously burned out a clutch reversing a caravan up this slope, and there's no room to manoeuvre a car and this length of caravan around the corner. Yet the Powrtouch did it easily. Highly impressive and highly recommended.

Picture 24. As well as upgrading the battery, I also changed the jockey wheel for one with a pneumatic tyre. This helps considerably to prevent the jockey wheel from digging in to gravel or soft grass when using the Powrtouch. It's a simple matter of removing a split pin, sliding out the axle, then fitting the new AL-KO wheel and pneumatic tyre in place of the old. Make sure you buy a compatible wheel – they're not all of the same dimensions.

INSTALLING A SPARE WHEEL CARRIER

Surprisingly, relatively few caravans are sold with a spare wheel as standard. Those that are store them in one of two places: in the centre of the front exterior gas bottle locker, or slung underneath on a purpose built cradle.

The problem with the first location is that it limits storage space and can help exceed the noseweight limit. Therefore, a useful alternative, and a common DIY fixture, is the fitting of an underslung carrier.

Picture 1. By far the most common spare wheel carrier is the type manufactured by the caravan chassis running gear specialists, AL-KO. It's designed to work in conjunction with the holes punched into the chassis behind the AL-KO axle. Under no circumstances, however, should extras holes be cut or drilled in a caravan's chassis, as this adversely affects the integral strength of the chassis.

Picture 2. The AL-KO spare wheel carrier is designed with telescopic arms, making putting the carrier in place a simple matter of extending the arms until they fit into the holes, and locking them in place with the bolts provided.

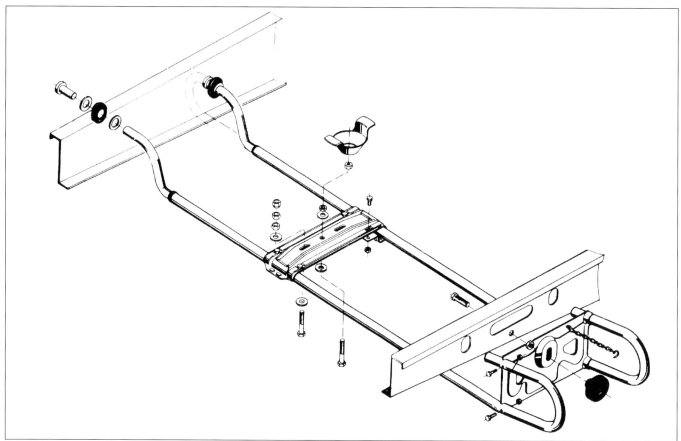

FITTING AND USING AN AL-KO SIDE LIFT JACK

AL-KO's instructions for the side-lift jack are clear and comprehensive, so there's no need to repeat them here in detail. However, it's worth noting that there are several alternative configurations, and most chassis types and shapes – including those for twin-axles – are catered for, provided the caravan has a maximum laden weight of no more than 1600kg.

Picture 1. The AL-KO side-lift jack is designed specifically for AL-KO chassis, but it can also be fitted to other types. It must always be fitted behind the axle line and – as with all jacks – must only be used when the caravan is hitched to the tow vehicle and the wheel remaining on the ground is securely chocked in both directions. It comes complete with its own robust carrying case.

Picture 4. The AL-KO side-lift jack steals a march on ordinary scissor and bottle jacks because of the way in which it slots into the bracket, as demonstrated here. (In this photo, the wheel chock is used only to support the jack.) This makes it much safer, being far less likely to slip when raised. The jack also has a smooth, easy action, though you would need to carry a pad to spread the load when jacking on soft ground.

Picture 2. Jacking brackets are fitted to the chassis, tight up against the floor, using the bolts and spacers provided.

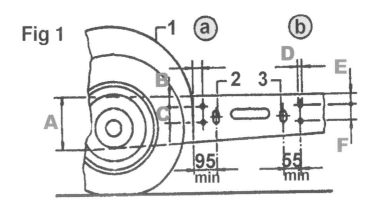

Picture 3. Position (a) shows the location position on AL-KO chassis without a spare wheel carrier (mounting hole 2), while position (b) is an alternative. If you have to drill fresh holes in the chassis, they should only be in accordance with AL-KO's instructions (if an AL-KO chassis) and holes should be treated with zinc-rich (or 'cold galvanising') paint.

INSTALLING A MANUALLY OPERATED CARAVAN STEP

Picture 3. Dave used masking tape on the underside of the floor so black ink would show, offered up the step, and marked the three mounting positions on each side.

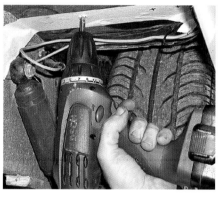

Picture 4. After checking that top-sides were clear, Dave drilled pilot holes through the floor. You need to lift the floor covering first, if you don't want the bolt heads to show.

CAK of Kenilworth manufactures an excellent range of fold-down steps, which are usually fitted to motorhomes. It even has models which fold-out electronically, so you don't have to get your hands dirty.

Using one of these certainly beats carrying around a portable step, and they are ideal if you're fed up with a loose step potentially crashing around inside your caravan, or you're worried about a step potentially tipping over in use. However, you do have to ensure your caravan's floor is strengthened to accommodate the weight that will be transferred to it when someone uses the step, and you must ensure the job is properly carried out otherwise it could damage your caravan floor, or even be unsafe.

If you want to fit one to your caravan, and your caravan is new and still in warranty, you should get the job done professionally at your local caravan dealer or workshop.

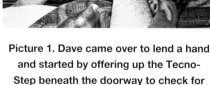

Picture 1. Dave came over to lend a hand and started by offering up the Tecno-Step beneath the doorway to check for obstructions. The caravan had been safely raised on axle stands.

Picture 2. We found that there was some wiring to be rerouted, some sealant to be carefully cut away, and the pipe from heater to warm air circulation system needed to be redirected.

Picture 5. Next, Dave pushed just one domed-headed coach bolt per side through the floor, and lifted the step into position, holding it with one nut per side.

Picture 6. Once temporarily fitted, the step was checked for position. Once Dave was satisfied, the remaining holes were drilled with the step still in situ to ensure they lined up.

Picture 7. He then bolted the step through the floor with three coach bolts per side. Dave found that, while the outer bolts could be tightened, the inner ones tried to compress the floor.

Picture 8. The drastic answer was ... I made a steel subframe. It bolted to the chassis (rear) outer floor timbers (front) and included four captive bolts (arrowed) to bolt the step to.

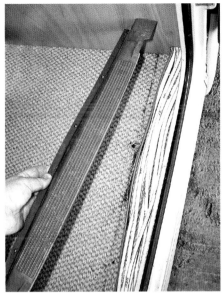

Picture 9. The outer floor timbers were solid and were accessed by removing the capping just inside the door. I used large, flat plates beneath the outer bolt heads to spread the load.

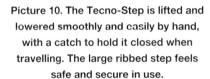

Picture 10. The Tecno-Step is lifted and lowered smoothly and easily by hand, with a catch to hold it closed when travelling. The large ribbed step feels safe and secure in use.

The Tecno-Step is a very well-made unit, made from galvanised steel. This means it will resist corrosion for a very long time. It comes with a micro-switch fitted, so that motorhome owners can wire-in a warning buzzer to ensure the step is closed before driving off. We unscrewed the switch;

it's not necessary when fitted to a caravan.

You would, no doubt, get dirty hands when using it after a wet journey, so next we'll look at turning a manual Tecno-Step into an all-electric one using the conversion kit available from CAK.

INSTALLING AN ELECTRICALLY OPERATED CARAVAN STEP

Picture 3. This large cog wheel has a squared hole, enabling it to be fitted to the shaft in the inside of the step. Tolerances were very tight but everything ran smoothly.

This is how one version of the Tecno-Step folding step from CAK can be converted to 12V operation.

If you fitted the version of the Tecno-Step shown on page 154, you could opt for manual operation but retain the option to upgrade to switch-operated electric power later. It saves you from getting your hands dirty!

Picture 1. The instructions were in Italian, but we realised that we needed to remove this pivot pin. The step was removed for easier access and the caravan safely supported on axle stands.

Picture 2. The replacement pivot pin has a square shaft (red arrow) and a bolt for screwing its lever into the threaded hole (blue arrow) in the arm on the step.

Picture 4. A cheese-head through bolt passes through the cog wheel and pivot, and the locknut supplied with the kit is tightened just enough to remove play but without 'pinching.'

Picture 5. The drive cog on the motor was liberally smeared with grease. The wires pass through the metal frame so we used a grommet to remove the risk of a short.

Picture 6. Two more long bolts and a couple of spacers are for fixing both the motor and its protection cover in place. They screw through threaded holes in the motor body.

Picture 7. We drilled a hole for an extra bolt to hold the cover more evenly at the front. We also added extra spacers to keep the cover away from the mechanism.

Picture 8. The manual step has this catch to hold it shut, but the motorised step uses the motor to hold it shut, so we removed the catch; if the catch jammed, the motor would burn out.

The conversion kit shown here, for use with CAK's Tecno-Step, means you can buy the manual step first, then – should you wish – convert it later as funds allow.

Do remember that all wiring must be carried out by a qualified electrician. Ask him to resite the fuse away from the step where it's fitted,

Picture 9. The step had already been refitted so we installed the cover plate for the last time. It still 'caught,' so we had to add even more spacers.

Picture 10. The switch was fitted after I cut a hole in the wardrobe panel with a craft knife. I measured not twice, but thrice, before cutting once – very carefully indeed!

and adjacent to the battery so that it protects the whole circuit.

CARAVAN STEPS

If you'd rather use one of the more traditional manual steps, there is a wide selection of makes and types available. Here we review six commonly available steps. Contact details can be found in 'Specialists & suppliers,' starting on page 217.

Dukdalf Quick Step 4

Frustratingly, the Dukdalf instructions are minimal, and the pivoting feet drop off too readily. However, it offers the best build quality of those tested here, and should last for a very long time. The ribbed aluminium step grips are excellent and overall stability is superb.

The only potential problem is that the centre legs could dig in to extremely soft ground – especially if you lose those feet. The lower step pivots and folds away nicely, reducing the space required when travelling.
Verdict: best build quality
Supplier: Quest Leisure Products
Height (mm) Step 1: 163
Height (mm) Step 2: 323
Overall width (mm): 635
Overall front-back (mm): 685
Weight (kg): 3.4

Milenco Original Lightweight Aluminium Double

Three of the four sides of the base of these steps rest on the ground, so only the rear corners could possibly sink in, and then only on very soft ground. Stability seems very good, there's no assembly required, and the structure appears sound.

The chequer plate aluminium steps could become slippery when wet and muddy, however, and our sample had a sharp corner (which, we we're told, is untypical). A range of different sizes are available, at different prices.
Verdict: light and simple
Supplier: Dinmore Caravans
Height (mm) Step 1: 172
Height (mm) Step 2: 348
Overall width (mm): 510
Overall front-back (mm): 590
Weight (kg): 2.6

TREM Reinforced Polypropylene

This step almost defines the word 'ubiquitous,' and almost every caravan accessory shop seems to sell them. The lightest step tested here, it has holes in the feet to allow it to be pegged down for extra stability. The step surface is well ribbed, and holed for drainage.

As with all steps, it could sink into soft ground, but the step resists tipping relatively well. It's available in four colours and gets top marks for value, even if it does lack cachet.
Verdict: could you need more?
Supplier: Almost any caravan accessories supplier
Height (mm) Step 1: 230
Height (mm) Step 2: N/A
Overall width (mm): 498
Overall front-back (mm): 346
Weight (kg): 1

Pyramid Products Double Packstep

This step may be suitable if you're on a tight budget for a double step. Some forward planning is needed, as there are no assembly instructions. The open tread design gives good grip and great drainage.

Build quality on our sample wasn't particularly good, even thought the steel construction appears strong. A few of the bolt holes didn't align, requiring modification before two of the bolts could be inserted. It's the longest, second-heaviest, and doesn't fold up, but then it is the cheapest.
Verdict: cheapest twin-step
Supplier: Discover
Height (mm) Step 1: 170
Height (mm) Step 2: 334

Overall width (mm): 410
Overall front-back (mm): 740
Weight (kg): 4.2

Dukdalf Mambo plus Safety Kit

A big set of steps, with a high price but high build quality, too. They're too large to fit through a caravan door when erected, so they're constructed to be partly dismantled and folded when travelling.

Assembly was okay, despite a lack of instructions, but surprisingly, the handle was difficult to fit, and there were a few missing parts. The 'Safety' handle (one of which can be fitted each side) is a welcome help for the elderly or infirm.
Verdict: not for everyone
Supplier: Quest Leisure Products
Height (mm) Step 1: 160
Height (mm) Step 2: 330
Overall width (mm): 690
Overall front-back (mm): 630
Weight (kg): 6.2

CAK Tecno-Step

As the only captive step here, you can't forget to take it with you, and it can't possibly tip over in use. However, it could get quite dirty when travelling, making your hands dirty when folding it.

You need 12V power for the electric model, and fitting usually requires a subframe to be added beneath the floor of the caravan to take the extra stresses. It is very convenient though, as many motor caravanners will attest.
Verdict: safe, and the simplest to use
Supplier: CAK Tanks
Height (mm) Step 1: Dependent on caravan fitting
Height (mm) Step 2: N/A
Overall width (mm): 560
Overall front-back (mm): Dependent on caravan fitting
Weight (kg): N/A

FITTING A BUILT-IN NOSEWEIGHT GAUGE

A jockey wheel that has a weight gauge built-in, so that you can check the noseweight of your caravan before hooking-up, without needing a separate gauge, is a great idea. AL-KO produces one, and fitting it to your caravan is a job at the simplest end of the DIY spectrum. This AL-KO jockey wheel ensures you've loaded up safely, and the removable winding handle also helps to clear the opening rear door on some 4x4s.

Picture 1. After applying brakes and chocking wheels, AL-KO's Kelvin Evans raises the front of the caravan with a trolley jack (although any type of jack will do) placed beneath a chassis rail.

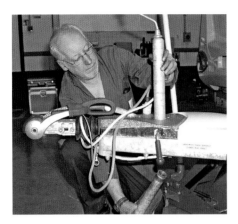

Picture 2. There needs to be enough height to remove the two halves of the old jockey wheel, after fully unscrewing the handle. They will come apart so be careful not to damage the plastic trim.

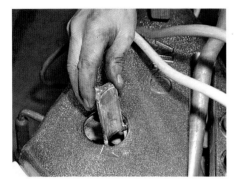

Picture 3. Inside the jockey wheel housing is a loose block which tightens against the jockey wheel shaft. Don't drop it or lose it: remove and, if necessary, clean and grease it.

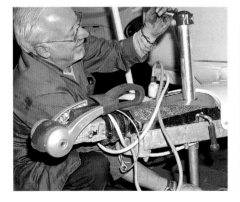

Picture 4. After refitting the clamping block, Kelvin inserts the lower part of the jockey wheel through the base of the housing, and the upper part through the top, before screwing together.

Picture 5. A feature of this device, and perhaps a useful theft deterrent, is the ability to easily remove the jockey wheel itself. Grease the detachable axle before refitting it.

Picture 6. The axle is held in place with an easy-to-use over-centre clip. Note that the wheel is extra wide so that it resists sinking into soft ground.

Picture 7. You may have noticed that the reading on the wheel gauge won't be the same as the weight at the coupling. You need to measure from road wheel centre ...

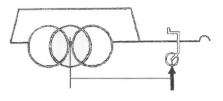

Picture 8. ... (or mid-point of twin-axles, if fitted) to the centre of the jockey wheel (we'll call it W), and from the road wheel centre to the middle of the coupling (C).

Picture 9. When loading the caravan, you read the figure on the gauge. This isn't the weight in kg, but a figure that can help you to calculate the weight later.

Picture 10. The winding handle is easily removed by pulling out the plunger, seen on the right, and sliding off the handle.

The gauge can't read the weight at the coupling, so before use, you must calculate the maximum acceptable noseweight scale reading (R), thus:

1. Establish the maximum acceptable loading (L) on your towball or caravan coupling. If several figures are quoted, the lowest figure is the safe one.

2. Calculate L (loading) multiplied by C (coupling distance) divided by W (jockey wheel distance) – see Pic. 8.

The resulting figure is the maximum you should see on the AL-KO Jockey Wheel Noseweight Gauge when you are ready to tow.

SAFETY FIRST!

• *Get as close to the maximum as possible but don't exceed it.*

CARAVAN LEVELLING DEVICES

Caravan levelling devices ensure your caravan sits firmly and evenly. Here we rate and review a selection of common devices.

Milenco Froli High Quality Adjustable Level

This German-made leveller is reasonably compact, but it's the heaviest and priciest of the ramps. Excellent quality, despite plated mild steel pivots, and the highest of all the ramps, it's effectively a one-piece unit. Each stage lies horizontally, with a curved tyre-resting place, so there's no need for an integral chock. Maximum height requires a stronger tow-car 'pull,' which could be tricky on wet grass.

Verdict: my personal choice
Manufacturer: Milenco
Approx Stored Length/Width/Height: 23.5in (595mm)/6.7in (170mm)/6.1in (155mm)
Weight per single leveller (kg): 3.6
Lift: 10mm increments from 50mm to 100mm

Milenco (Original) Levelling Ramp

These are supplied as pairs, so you'll be getting top value, especially if you have a twin-axle caravan or a motorhome. They are: wider than any other ramp we tested; provide the best stability; require more storage space. Each of the three 'steps' has a bump at its rear end to act as a small chock, but, as with the Froli, the chocking effect won't be all that great. They're big and quite heavy, but levellers don't get simpler than this.

Verdict: simplest, great value
Manufacturer: Milenco
Approx Stored Length/Width/Height: 21in (530mm)/8.75in (225mm)/4.75in (120mm)
Weight per single leveller (kg): 2.2
Lift: 40, 65 and 90mm

Milenco 4 Part Large Caravan Level Set

These have a choice of three fixed heights, and the platforms are level, minimising the chance of the caravan rolling off (although a clip-on lock is also supplied). The unit comes as four separate parts, increasing the chances of losing a part, but the attachable 'ladder' prevents a wheel from pushing the level as the caravan is pulled onto it, or a motorhome driven against it.

Verdict: plus-points for motorcaravans
Manufacturer: Milenco
Approx Stored Length/Width/Height: 19.75in (500mm)/7in (180mm)/3.75in (95mm)
Weight per single leveller (kg): 2.2
Lift: 40, 55 and 95mm

Pyramid Chockmaster

The flat base is excellent at preventing the ramp from sinking into soft ground, and none of the others had this feature. As with all sloping ramps, this will slowly move downhill unless you chock the wheels, even with the brake on. However, the chock can be hard to remove, especially if there's been rain. The clip-on 'ladder' assists driving on, and several Chockmasters can be clipped together if required.

Verdict: cheapest to buy
Manufacturer: Pyramid Products
Approx Stored Length/Width/Height: 25in (635mm)/8in (290mm)/5in (130mm)
Weight per single leveller (kg): 1.8
Lift: Up to 95mm (approx)

Bulldog V15

The Bulldog's strong construction suggests it would be unlikely to jam from twisting. This, along with the Lockloy below, should be the complete answer to levelling: there's no need to drive on, they're adjustable in-situ (ramps often need trial and error), they rise much higher, and have infinite adjustments. However, they're very hard work to use and, unfortunately, they both dissapoint.

Verdict: very hard work
Manufacturer: Bulldog Security Products
Approx Stored Length/Width/Height: 22.75in (580mm)/21.3in (540mm)/5.5in (140mm)
Weight (per single leveller) (kg): 9.0
Lift: Up to 150mm

Lockloy Aluminium Leveller

The aluminium Lockloy is lighter than the Bulldog, but takes longer to disassemble for travelling.

As with the Bulldog, even on a hard standing and using a ratchet spanner to fractionally raise our 19 foot caravan, it was a very hard work. After much effort, I had only lifted about 5mm; 150mm would have been too much effort. I later tried a 13 foot caravan and, though it was noticeably easier, it was still very hard going.

Verdict: demanding to use
Manufacturer: Milenco
Approx Stored Length/Width/Height: 23.6in (600mm)/20in (505mm)/3.25in (85mm)
Weight per single leveller (kg): 5.6
Lift: Up to 200mm

FIT DETACHABLE CARAVAN-TO-CAR PLUGS

Unsurprisingly, caravan electrics are notorious for succumbing to damp, particularly after sitting through the winter months. Rather than leave vulnerable and unprotected 12V plugs on your caravan, why not swap them for detachable ones from Maypole?

Picture 1. First, you must work out where the sockets will be sited. Too far back and the plugs could be pulled out under tension. We chose 1.5m cables.

Picture 2. When you're sure where the sockets are going to be fitted, you can cut the existing grey and black cables to length, and strip the ends ready for fitting to sockets.

Picture 3. These Maypole sockets, like most, have detachable inner sections, so the cables can be connected to the 'female' connector blocks. The sockets are reassembled later.

Picture 4. Here's a useful tip: I always use Würth car and leisure battery terminal protection spray to protect the contacts in the backs of each of the sockets from corrosion.

Picture 5. I adapted a car twin-socket mounting plate so that it could be bolted to the caravan. Use a galvanised mounting plate, not the painted type: they ALWAYS rust rapidly.

Picture 6. Having made the plate to fit, the sockets were fitted using stainless steel screws and self-locking nuts from Screwfix. They're cheap and won't rust, unlike the common mild steel versions...

Picture 7. At some point, the plastic A-frame trim cover and, in this case, the jockey wheel assembly may have to be removed to give access to a suitable mounting bolt.

Picture 8. I decided to mount the sockets on a hitch mounting bolt, which is better than drilling a fresh hole in the chassis (which chassis manufacturers say you should never do).

Picture 9. After fitting the socket plate, ensure that the bolt is tightened to the torque specified by the chassis and/or hitch manufacturers, and use new bolts and nuts if required.

Picture 10. Now you can see how the 12N and 12S sockets can be removed when the caravan is parked. Choose sockets with rubber seals in the lids if possible.

Traditional 12V plugs are open to the elements, but sockets have spring-loaded lids. However, think where you're going to locate your new caravan-mounted sockets: if you lie them horizontally, there's still a risk of water getting in; if they face directly forward, bad weather can blast water in when you're towing.

Another big plus comes when you fit Maypole's 'curly' leads. The built-in spring ensues that the cables won't dangle on the ground and rub through, or get caught in the brake mechanism when driving.

FIT A 12V SOCKET

Many electrical items are designed to run off a car's 12V cigar lighter socket: mobile phone or computer equipment chargers, tyre pump compressors, solar chargers (to charge your caravan battery), portable TVs, to name just a few. But while caravans often have a 12V, 2-pin TV socket, they rarely have the cigar lighter-type. Here we see how you can easily install an attractive socket from CAK Ltd – but do get a qualified electrician to make the electrical connections.

Picture 3. As the hole cutter broke through the inside of the cabinet, you could see why it was so important to measure, mark out and calculate where to drill before starting.

Picture 1. The components selected for this installation are: the 12V socket (a); front outer cover (b); inner plinth (c); flip-up lid (d). There are many other options available if you want more accessories.

Picture 2. We used a Würth hole cutter in the electric drill, to make a hole in the cabinet large enough to clear the protrusions on the back of the socket.

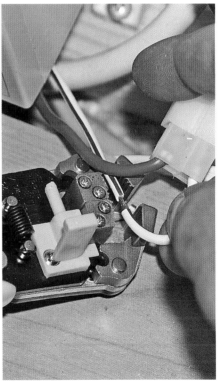

Picture 4. A qualified electrician will need to make the 12V power connections. This Würth cable stripper removes insulation from the length of the earth cable, ready for a soldered connection.

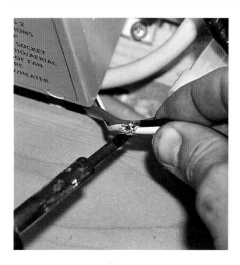

Picture 5. The negative connection to the 12V socket was made by soldering the stripped end of a sufficiently heavy cable as an improvised T-piece. The joint was then insulation-wrapped.

Picture 7. Here's the shape of the back of the socket. The spade connectors have been protected from electrical contact with shrink-fit insulation.

Picture 9. Next, the inner plinth (see picture 1, item (c)) was placed in position on the socket and screwed down with similar-sized screws. The heads must recess into the plinth mouldings.

Picture 6. The socket-ends of the cables are spade connectors, supplied with the CAK kit. They were attached to the stripped cable ends with a crimping tool.

Picture 8. The socket was next inserted into the hole in the panel and held in position with a pair of short self-tapping screws, after first drilling small pilot holes to prevent splitting.

Picture 10. Both of these components simply clip into place. The front outer cover (b) fits into the slots on the inner component, and the flip-up lid (d) pushes onto plastic pegs.

If you want to fit one of these CAK 12V sockets yourself, you could fit the socket to the cabinet but you must leave the wiring to a qualified electrician. It may 'only' be a 12V connection, and may not kill you if incorrectly wired, but it could easily lead to a fire if the wiring overheats.

If you do fit the socket yourself, make absolutely certain that there is nothing on the other side of the panel to which you are attaching it. Look first; measure and mark-out second; drill last – and only then after checking one final time.

GAS CYLINDER AUTO CHANGEOVER VALVE

An automatic changeover valve stops the gas from going off when a cylinder runs out, but it won't help if both cylinders run out because you hadn't noticed the changeover. The Gaslow Electra 2000 lets you know when an LPG auto-changeover has switched cylinders, and it can test the system for leaks, too.

Fitting one has just three steps: fit Gaslow gauges to the changeover valve; fit the Electra receiver; run wiring between the two.

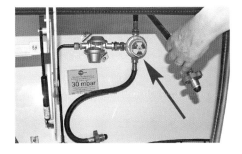

Picture 1. Our caravan already had a changeover valve, but it was too close to the top of the gas locker.

Picture 2. There wouldn't have been room to add the Gaslow cylinder contents gauges, so the pipework was reworked: a job for a Gas Safe-qualified fitter – NOT a DIY job.

Picture 3. While the changeover valve was off, I switched to the kitchen table for better access. Using a pair of spanners, the flexible hose was loosened then fully removed.

Picture 4. The gauge for the right-hand cylinder (the gauges are handed) was then screwed reasonably tightly to the changeover valve; enough to close the seal without damaging it.

Picture 5. Note, on the other side, the way in which the squared block on the gauge is used to grip the gauge, preventing it from turning as the nut is tightened.

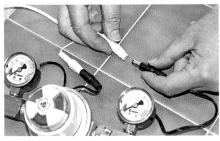

Picture 6. Each gauge has a needle reading and also an electronic output for connecting to the sensor. These are linked together using the 2-into-1 wiring supplied as part of the kit.

Picture 7. I clipped the wiring beneath the caravan floor, coming up through the bed box, and drilled an entry hole behind the fridge – after double-checking what was on the other side.

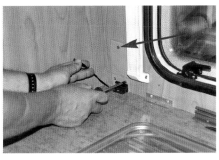

Picture 8. I removed the clip-on sink unit trim and screwed a mounting plate where the screws were hidden. Here's the cable (another hole was drilled) and the sensor fixing screw (arrowed).

Picture 9. In the gas locker, I reconnected the changeover and level gauges (2) – you can see the gas levels indicated – reconnected the wiring (1), and refitted the Gaslow Easy-Fit hoses (3).

Picture 10. The trim is now back in place and the sensor connected. The centre 'traffic lights' (inset) indicate change-over condition, and the right-hand button enables you to check for leaks.

Here's how the Gaslow Electra 2000 sensor works:

Gas working normally: centre 'traffic light' flashes green.

Cylinders in the process of auto-changing: 'traffic light' flashes yellow.

Cylinders fully changed over: 'traffic light' flashes red.

Left button: press to reset when you've fitted a fresh cylinder.

Right button: turn on gas at cylinder to pressurise system, then turn off again. Press this button and the system cleverly carries out a pressure-loss test: if pressure drops faster than it should, the system warns you there's a leak.

You shouldn't use sealant on gas connections: clean running threads and new seals are essential, but sealant could temporarily conceal a problem.

GENERATORS

As caravans become more complex and better equipped, so they have also grown increasingly dependent on a 240-volt electricity supply. However, although most commercial sites offer this as a standard facility, there are circumstances where it is not available. This is often the case on more remote sites, or those who have permission to rally on private land. A generator is a common solution, supplying a remote power source that should be adequate to deal with most mains powered caravan equipment. Commonly available from most large caravan accessory outlets, and usually petrol or gas powered, they are easy to operate and offer a greater degree of flexibility when choosing your holiday location.

When deciding on a generator, an important consideration is the power output that it delivers. This is measured in Watts and is generally shown by the designation of the generator; a smaller generator, for example, might deliver up to 650 Watts. However, it's crucial to note that this figure usually refers to the peak power output, which can only be delivered for limited amounts of time. Actual power output delivered by the generator for the majority of the time may well be around 10% lower than this figure. This 'working figure' is often shown in the owner's handbook that comes with the generator.

Therefore, when choosing which generator is best suited to your needs, it's important that you decide which appliances will commonly be drawing power from it. Add up the combined power requirements and ensure that the generator has a greater working power than this total. Once this is done, there are two further important points to consider.

First, the Hertz (Hz) rating of the generator. Most British domestic 240V products are designed to run at 50Hz. Some generators can be switched to allow the output to increase to 60Hz. This gives a higher, but less steady output, which could improve the performance of certain appliances, like hair dryers or lamps. But for more sensitive items, such as TVs or tape recorders, 50Hz may be essential. Even more sensitive items, such as computers and games machines, aren't really suited to being powered by generators, because of the fluctuating nature of their power output.

The second point to consider, is the start-up capacity required by some appliances. A microwave cooker is a good example of this. While it may require a power supply of 1000W to work correctly, to start up it may need an initial 'burst' of up to 3000W – a figure far outside the capacity of most generators suitable for caravans. All generators designed for caravanners will have some type of overload protection, cutting the power if the demand exceeds peak output.

There is one more thing to bear in mind, particularly if you're pitching near others – noise. Look at the noise or decibel rating of all the generators you are considering, and remember that decibel (dB) ratings rise exponentially: a small increase in dB means a huge increase in sound. The Caravan Club states that, on Club sites, generators shouldn't be used between 6pm and 9am, and at other times, with consideration to you neighbours. If in doubt, get expert advice.

SAFETY FIRST!
• Whenever using or transporting a petrol operated generator, take extreme care with the fuel. Always store it in the correct type of container, and keep it away from naked flames and children. Similarly, take care with petrol fumes, and remember that an empty container that's been used for storing petrol is even more flammable and explosive than one with petrol inside it.
• Whenever handling a petrol container, wear protective gloves and ensure you keep the petrol out of contact with your skin and eyes. If petrol does come into contact with your eyes, rinse them with copious amounts of running water and seek immediate medical attention.

Part 5
Security

REGISTERING YOUR CARAVAN WITH CRiS

Caravans can be registered, much like registering a car with the DVLA at Swansea. The scheme for caravans, known as the Caravan Registration and Identification Scheme (CRiS), was established in 1992 by the National Caravan Council (NCC), but unlike the government's vehicle registration scheme, it was set-up in conjunction with HPI Ltd, and is therefore a commercial organisation.

When my wife Shan and I bought our first new caravan, a Bürstner, in 2007, it hadn't occurred to us that it wouldn't be CRiS registered. But we soon realised that the scheme was set up by the (British) National Caravan Council originally to register new, British-built caravans. All caravans manufactured since 1992 by NCC members (ie British manufacturers) are recorded on the CRiS database by their unique 17 digit Vehicle Identification Number (VIN). This VIN, and the caravan description, are recorded on a form called the Touring Caravan Registration Document, which is issued by CRiS to the caravan's registered keeper.

In 1998, an important new development was introduced, and all new caravans manufactured by NCC members since then have been electronically tagged during manufacture, for added security. A tag is secreted about the caravan's bodywork, enabling a scanner (as used by the police, for example) to be used to identify the registered ownership of the caravan.

CRiS is also able to accept registration for pre-1992 caravans by allocating a new VIN – and you can also register an imported caravan.

CRiS for new caravans

If you're buying a new, UK-built caravan, the dealer must register your details with CRiS. CRiS then records these details and issues you with the first Touring Caravan Registration Document.

The document is similar, in some respects, to the V5 document issued by the DVLA for cars and motorcycles. It confirms the name of the registered keeper, the VIN, and a description of the caravan type and colour. When a caravan is sold, the seller should tear-off the lower part of the document and send it to CRiS, giving the new owner the remaining part of the document. The new owner should then fill in the Notification of Changes section, and send it to CRiS with a re-registration fee. However, this is one area where a CRiS document differs dramatically from a V5 vehicle document. Because the scheme is industry-administered, there is no compulsion on either party to follow the procedure. If you are the buyer of a used caravan, it's best to ensure you are registered as the new keeper with CRiS.

CRiS for older and imported caravans

If you have an imported caravan, or a UK caravan built before CRiS existed, you have to ask HPI to send you a document called 'Declaration For Registration of a Pre 1992 Caravan.' It might seem odd if you own a newer imported caravan, but this is the form that you have to fill in. Once completed, you should send them the top copy, and a cheque for the appropriate fee (these can be found online, and there are special rates for caravan club members). The form requires that you supply proof of identity, as well as the caravan's details.

The rest of the procedure is shown in the following photo-sequence, where Shan and I can be seen applying the CRiS treatment to our caravan.

Picture 1. Glenn Parker, the Manager at Chelston Caravans, went to a lot of trouble to point out the benefits of CRiS registration, and the fact that this can't be done by the dealer but has to be carried out by the owner, in the case of an imported caravan. Once you ignore the fact that, at the time of writing, there is no mention of imported caravans, the leaflet shown here tells you how to go about applying for CRiS registration.

Picture 2. Once again, our membership of the Caravan Club saved us money, cutting £5 off the cost of the CRiS Anti-Theft Caravan Marking Kit. The kit consists of the following: a. Degreasing wipes; b. Fitting instructions; c. Pack of 11 stencils; d. Electronic tag with stencil attached; e. Two spreaders; f. Tube of superglue; g. Tube of marking compound; h. CRiS sticker

The fitting instructions tell you to make sure that the VIN number on the stencils is correct, by ensuring that it incorporates the chassis number on the caravan. I checked and found that it wasn't correct, so I telephoned CRiS. I was informed that the following digits are altered by CRiS:

5th digit: 'S' or 'T' for single or twin axle.

8th and 9th digits: Manufacturers code such as 'BN' for Bürstner.

10th digit: The last digit of the year of manufacture, or 'Q' in the case of an import.

Picture 3. It's important to remove any traces of grease, wax, or any other contaminants from the area of the window to be marked. CRiS recommend that the windows are marked on the outside surface, at the lower right-hand corner. It provides a small number of wipes for cleaning the windows – but, in my view, nowhere near enough.

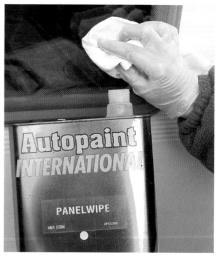

Picture 4. I'm always using degreaser in my workshop, so I have a can of panel wipe to hand. This was used to thoroughly degrease each window to be marked.

Picture 5. The marking compound etches the plastic, so there is a risk of damaging the caravan's paintwork or plastic trim if you accidentally spill any. For that reason, the bodywork beneath each window was carefully masked off. Opening the window a little would also help move the window away from the caravan's bodywork.

Picture 6. Take one of the stencils and peel it from its backing paper.

Picture 7. Making sure that it's the right way up, place the self-adhesive stencil onto the window. It's a good idea to do so lightly at first, so that you can remove it and adjust its position if necessary. Note that there is a strip of backing paper left attached to the top of the stencil, so that not all of the stencil is stuck down to the window, making it easier to remove later.

Picture 8. When you're satisfied that the stencil is in the correct position, smooth it down firmly, ensuring there are no wrinkles and – especially – that the areas around the dots are properly stuck down.

TIP!

• Use the non-waxed side of the backing paper that you removed from the stencil to give a slippery surface for rubbing down smoothly on the surface of the stencil.

Picture 9. The marking compound is in a sealed tube, the cap of which has a spike in the top which you use to break the seal.

Picture 10. If your caravan has plastic windows, you will have been provided with Plastic Marking Compound. This must be squeezed into a glass or ceramic dish.

IMPORTANT NOTE:
• If your windows are made of glass, a different type of marking compound will have been supplied, and this must be squeezed only into a plastic or metal dish.

Picture 11. Using one of the spreaders supplied, take the dish of compound to the stencil and scrape a little of it over the stencil's lettering. Make sure that each of the holes has some of the blue material in it. It's also important not to get compound on the window around the edges of the stencil. There's no risk of doing so if you ensure you don't apply too much compound at a time, but if you're concerned, you could apply masking tape to the window, especially beneath the area of the stencil.

Picture 12. The recommendation is to leave the marking compound and stencil in place for 30 seconds, although timing to the second isn't crucial. It was an extremely cold day when we did this, so we left ours for a little longer. However, CRiS makes the point that leaving the compound in place for longer than the recommended time will not improve the marking and may cause damage.

Picture 13. Making sure that you don't get any of the compound on parts of the window plastic you don't want marked, dab all of the surplus from the front face of the stencil, and then peel the stencil off the window.

Picture 14. The recommendation now is to use the wipes provided to remove the compound from the window. However, if there aren't enough wipes to clean all of the windows, there certainly aren't enough to do this as well, so I used more panel wipe.

IMPORTANT NOTE:

• If you use any solvent other than that supplied with the kit, take great care that it will not cause damage to plastic windows. Cellulose thinners, for instance, will almost certainly melt the surface of the plastic. White spirit *should* be okay, but test it on a relatively hidden corner of the plastic before wiping it onto the visible part.

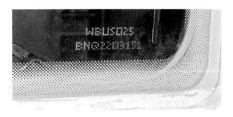

Picture 15. The process should leave you with an area etched into the window, accentuated by the blue dye in the marking compound.

Picture 16. There were more stencils in the kit than windows, so we also applied them to the two skylights in our Bürstner. One of the reasons for applying these kits is to make it prohibitively expensive for a potential thief to steal your caravan: he would have to replace all of the windows in order to disguise its original provenance. Having to replace the skylights too is an additional disincentive.

Picture 17. If you purchase a tube of marking compound for glass windows, you could also mark mirrors inside the caravan, if you don't mind seeing a VIN number every time you brush your teeth.

Picture 18. Do remember that the compound for use on glass has to be squeezed onto a plastic or metal surface: it will etch into the surface of a glass or glazed ceramic dish.

Picture 19. As we mentioned earlier, one of the ways in which the CRiS system works, is as a deterrent, letting the potential thief know that it is fitted. A self-adhesive label supplied with the kit is designed to go on the inside of a caravan window.

Picture 20. If you want it to adhere properly, clean the surface of the window with panel wipe or something similar (don't use any type of cleaner that contains silicone), and lightly place the sticker in position.

Picture 21. Positioning it lightly allows you to check that the cut-out panel in the sticker aligns correctly with the etched markings on the outside of the window. However, the space between the inner and outer layers of the double-glazed windows will throw the two out of apparent alignment.

Picture 22. The ideal situation will be that the markings are lined up with the slot in the warning sticker when viewed from standing height outside the caravan. This means that the sticker needs to be placed a little lower than the line of the etched markings, rather than horizontally in line with them.

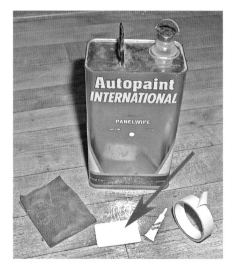

Picture 23. In order to fit the electronic tag, you will need more degreaser, some abrasive paper, the tag itself (arrowed), the superglue, and the other spreader supplied in the kit.

Picture 24. There is a separate set of instructions on the back of the leaflet showing you how to fit the electronic tag. The important point is that the police need to be able to read the tag from outside the caravan. This limits the possible fitting positions, as the tag cannot be read through metal. The tag can, however, be read through all other non-metallic materials.

Approx. front-end locations

Approx. rear-end locations

Picture 25. Now you need to decide where you're going to fit the tag. These are the locations recommended by CRiS, and therefore the ones that the police are most likely to scan, if and when they have to check you caravan.

At one point, I considered placing the tag inside the compartment into which the chemical toilet holding tank is slid. However, the holding tank is fitted inside a metal frame, ruling out that location. Another position

I considered was inside one of the cupboards at the front end of the caravan, behind the bulkhead. Then I realised that the bulkhead was fabricated in aluminium – another no-go. In the end, you will be left with areas that you can reach behind the plastic panelling at the front or rear of your caravan.

Picture 26. I used fine abrasive paper to roughen the surface of the tag, and the area to which it was to be fitted inside the caravan end panel. Then, more panel wipe was used to remove every trace of dust or grease, bearing in mind that there may well be release agent on the surface of the plastic left from its manufacture, and this too needs to be removed. Bear in mind, also, that the surface to which the tag is to be fitted must be flat, so that as much of the tag as possible is in contact with the panel. Use masking tape to hold the tag in position while the superglue sets.

IMPORTANT NOTE:
• Wear plastic gloves to avoid any risk of supergluing your fingers together, and keep the glue well away from face and lips.

Picture 27. When you've finished, fill in the postcard supplied with the kit, sign it, and post it back to CRiS. The card tells CRiS the location of the electronic tag and enables completion of your registration.

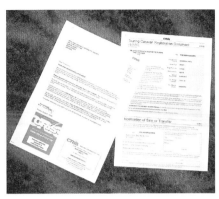

Picture 28. You will then receive a CRiS Touring Caravan Registration Document and a Caravan Information Card. You can keep the card in your wallet, taking it with you on your holiday: it carries the caravan's VIN, so you can notify the police if the caravan is stolen. A blue sticker, which CRiS recommends you place inside a cupboard door in your caravan, to help remind you and any future owners to keep your registration up-to-date, is also included. If you move house, informing CRiS is free, and ensures that the correct information is always on file.

CRiS EXTRA
For a small extra cost, you can purchase a 'CRiS Extra Pack' security kit. This consists of another (and completely different type of) electronic tag, a number of tamper-resistant labels, a permanent marker, and about 1000 micro-dots, designed to show up under ultra-violet light.

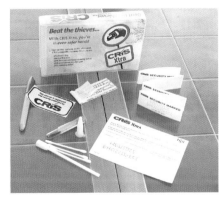

Picture 29. With this kit's contents applied, it would be virtually impossible for a thief to disguise the true identity of your caravan.

Picture 30. This identity tag is housed in a glass cylinder, and is capable of being read by a police scanner at a distance of about four inches – so common sense suggests that the tag should be fitted at a convenient height for someone using a scanner (a location tight against the ceiling or floor would be most likely to be missed). You need to drill a 4mm hole, about 35mm deep, in a suitable wooden panel. The tag is inserted, and then sealed in with suitable filler, such as the epoxy resin that we used here. Place the tag in a cupboard edge that will not be easily visible to the thief, such as a hinged edge.

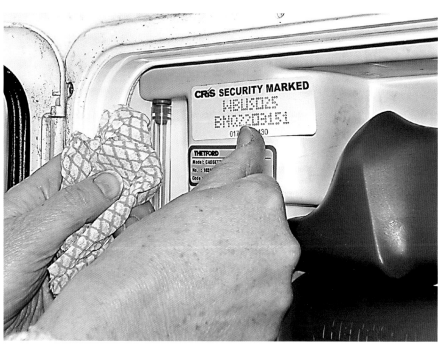

Picture 32. Tamper-resistant labels are best applied to inner areas, such as the toilet cassette compartment, inside the gas locker, and inside the top of the shower compartment – anything that will be very expensive to replace. After a 24-hour curing period, the labels will be extremely difficult to remove, and can't be removed in one piece.

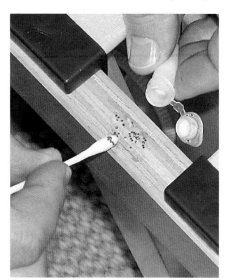

Picture 31. Micro-dots are clearly visible as black specks, especially when placed on a light surface, and glow purple when ultra-violet light is shone upon them. They can also be read with a scanner, and will show the CRiS VIN number of your caravan. You apply them to fixed areas of the caravan using the adhesive and bud supplied with the kit.

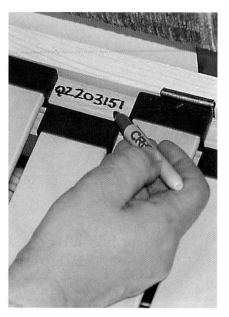

Picture 33. Permanent marker pen ink is extremely difficult to remove. Write the last eight digits of your VIN onto suitable fixed areas of your caravan. You could also use it to write your postcode onto the rear of removable items, such as your TV or DVD player.

Picture 34. Last, but not least, add the warning sticker somewhere suitable, such as the caravan door window, to deter potential thieves. After you've finished, be sure to send your registration card to CRiS so that it knows where you have fixed the second electronic tag, and so it can issue you with the appropriate documentation.

FITTING AN ALARM

Keen Electronics Ltd describes itself as the leading UK manufacturer of touring caravan alarms, supplying to manufacturers and dealers. The 2002 Concept KEL alarm is suitable for DIY fitting – provided that you have some basic competence.

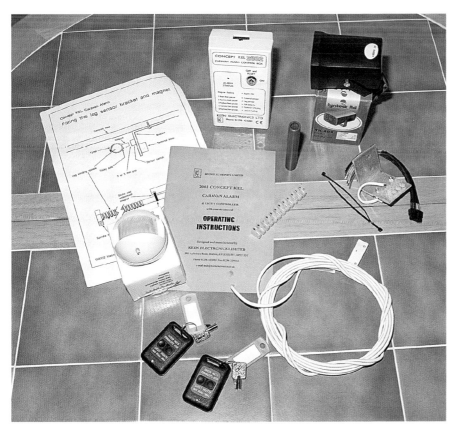

Picture 1. These are the components supplied in the 2002 Concept KEL caravan alarm kit. Reading clockwise from top-centre: Control box, with integral PP3 battery backup holder and lead with plug and terminal block; Siren; Leg sensor; Cable (only for wiring the PIR – you have to supply your own for wiring for the power supply); Remote controls and override keys; Internal PIR sensor; Operating and installation instructions, with wiring diagram.

Picture 2. Your first job is to consult the wiring diagram and decide where everything needs to go. This takes some careful thought: you want to route cables through the insides of lockers wherever possible, but also want to fit them so that they're not dangling obtrusively in the lockers. We used a number of Würth self-adhesive pads, intended for fixing wiring in precisely this sort of location.

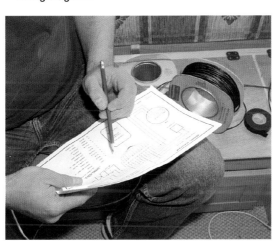

Picture 3. Siting the PIR sensor proved tricky: it needs to be fitted at (or just above) eye level, looking along the length of the caravan's interior. Ideally, the sensor shouldn't be sited pointing straight at a window, as it could then be affected by direct sunlight. You also need to bear in mind the location of the wardrobe and other obstructions in a larger caravan. We used a combination of double-sided tape and a single screw into the roof panel, for extra security. The material used on our Bürstner caravan is thick enough to take a solid fixing, but I didn't want to drill into the woodwork.

Note that the sensor wiring has already been fed through the corner cupboard, passed through a knock-out hole in the back of the sensor backing plate, and will need to be cut to length when the PIR sensor is fitted.

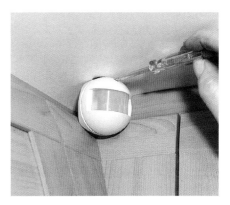

Picture 4. Following the instructions supplied with the sensor, the wire has been stripped and screwed to the relevant connections on the back of the PIR sensor head, before the head itself is screwed to the backing plate.

Picture 5. The leg sensor is an excellent feature of the KEL alarm. The way it works is explained in these drawings. The lower drawing shows a typical type of leg, but on some, the spindle may be too short to take the magnet. In this case, a length of plastic tubing supplied with the kit is knocked onto the end of the spindle, and the magnet attached to that.

The principle of the leg sensor is that the sensor switch will detect movement of the magnet past its face. If you fit the leg sensor to one of the rear legs, it would be extremely difficult for anyone to move the caravan without raising the leg and, thus, setting off the alarm.

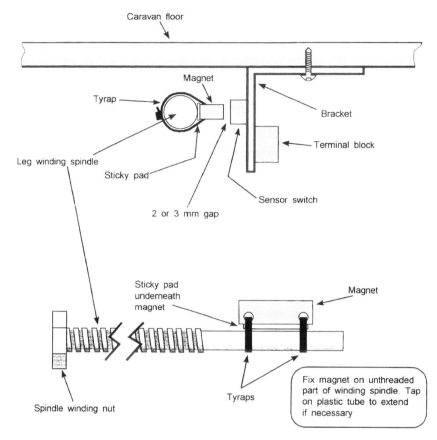

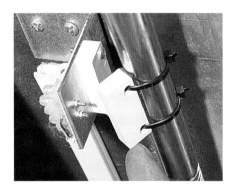

Picture 6. On the Bürstner, there is a long, unthreaded portion of the spindle, to which the magnet could be attached. Here, you can also see the sensor switch and terminal block bracket screwed to the floor.

Picture 7. At this point, I removed the bracket from the caravan and made my own modification. I removed the junction block from the back of the bracket and encased it in epoxy resin, using the bottom of a plastic container as a mould (the wires having been previously connected, obviously). This meant that there would be no chance of moisture getting into the connections and causing

a malfunction in future. Malcolm Keen, at Keen Electronics, suggested that this was overkill, and that if I really was concerned, a squirt of silicone sealant would have sufficed. Having experienced electrical malfunctions through exposed connections on cars, I'm not convinced, and I'm happier having done it this way. Incidentally, it struck me that a thief might be able to overcome the leg sensor simply by cutting the cable ties and pulling the magnet off the spindle. To prevent that from happening, I ran a bead of epoxy resin down each side of the magnet, to prevent it from being easily removed.

Picture 8. The type of switch used for the leg sensor is known as a reed switch (you can buy an accessory reed switch from Keen Electronics). These can be used to protect caravan doors, or even a caravan mover. It makes the most sense to fit such a switch to the battery box door: a thief would then find it difficult to disconnect the power supply. However, if you fit the PP3

battery to the control box, disconnecting the leisure battery will sound the siren.

The switch (a) is fitted to the door frame, and the wires connected in series with those from the leg sensor.

The magnet (b) is fitted to the door so that there is a gap of about 2mm between the two when the door is closed.

Opening the door with the alarm turned on will trigger it, just as moving the magnet against the switch on the leg sensor would.

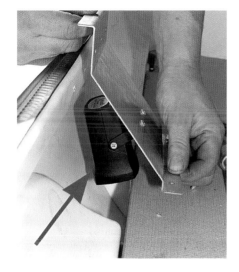

Picture 9. Next, we fitted the siren. If a thief could easily get to the siren, the alarm would quickly be rendered useless, so you'll need to fit the siren where the sound can easily pass to the outside, but also where it's protected from intense road spray or rain (although it is splash-proof), and so that it's not easily accessed. This reinforcing plate on the Bürstner seemed like a good place to fit the alarm as, even if a thief could find it, some dismantling would be required in order to reach it. As Malcolm Keen says, "Make sure that the sound can get out – it's no use if all the sound is heard in the bed box only!"

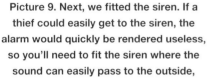

Picture 10. The control box is best fitted inside a cupboard or a bed box. A white mounting plate is fitted to the panel to which the box will be installed, and the control box is then fitted onto the mounting plate, and slid down until it clicks into the locked position. We used a length of white plastic trunking, available from any DIY store, to conceal the wiring, so that it doesn't look unsightly and, even more importantly, doesn't become disturbed when you pack the bed box or cupboard.

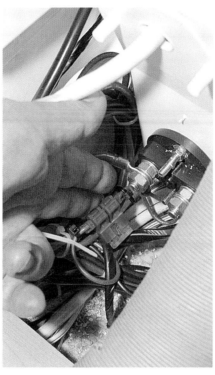

Picture 11. The final job is to connect the supply lead to the 12V supply, usually found in the bed box at the rear of the battery box. Note that a fuse needs to be fitted in the main supply, as close to the battery as possible. In some cases, the supply will be taken direct from the battery, requiring the drilling of a hole through the inner face of the battery box, so the wiring can be passed through. The edges of the box should be protected by fitting a wiring grommet into the hole before passing the cables through it.

The final stage is to check each of the alarm's features to make sure that they work:

• Try the panic feature by arming the alarm (indicated by two cheeps on siren), then holding both of the fob buttons down for a few seconds.

• Arm the system, and check that the PIR sensor sets off the alarm without a delay when you step into the caravan.

• With the system armed again, wind the alarmed corner steady leg: this should trigger the alarm instantly.

• If correctly installed, coupling or uncoupling the 12N plug (the black

Picture 12. You also have the option of connecting the KEL alarm to an exterior light on your caravan. The remote fob can then be used to operate either the alarm, or the external light. The small downside is that you have to leave the light switched on inside the caravan, and then use the remote fob to turn it on and off, but that's a small price to pay for being able to light your way back to your caravan in the dark. Also attached to the remote, is the key used for enabling or disabling the control box, shown earlier.

one) will trigger the alarm. In addition, with the 12N plug inserted, operation of the foot brake on the tow vehicle will re-trigger the alarm. Note that Keen Electronics recommend that the 'van must be coupled to the tow vehicle to provide an assured earth connection between the two. Alternatively, the 12S plug (which includes the earth connection) can be inserted.

• With a PP3 battery fitted to the control box, try disconnecting the 12-volt leisure battery: this should trigger the alarm, now operated by the internal battery in the control box (arm the alarm first).

INSTALL A TRACKING DEVICE

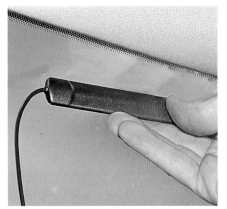

Picture 2. The mobile phone GPRS unit is installed inside the caravan, giving a second line of defence to the satellite unit, that other systems use in isolation.

Picture 3. A SIM card fits in the main control unit, and communicates the caravan's whereabouts via a mobile phone network – hence the need for subscription charges.

Caravan insurance is very expensive, simply because they're so easy to steal. The ultimate recovery protection has to be a Cobra tracking unit that instantly locates a stolen caravan using satellite and mobile phone technology.

The Cobra is Thatcham-recognised and has been developed specifically for caravan use. There is a subscription charge, but it provides satellite tracking plus a mobile phone tracker, covering all of Europe, and you can check the position of your caravan from anywhere that provides internet access. Additionally, having this system fitted can significantly reduce insurance costs.

Here, we follow security specialists Auto Tec as they fit a Cobra tracking device.

Picture 1. This is the heart of the unit, the CobraTrak 'black box.' Of course, the potential thief doesn't know the CobraTrak is installed, so it will be working without his knowledge.

Picture 4. Anyone familiar with the fitting of a GPS satellite navigation system will recognise the satellite tracker, which must be fitted to the caravan in a position where it can 'see' satellites.

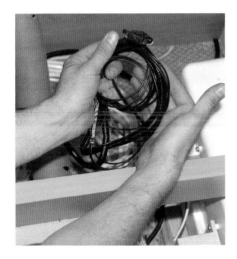

Picture 5. Some dismantling is required, in order to locate and hide the control unit. Additionally, wires need to be run for the satellite and mobile phone sensors and power.

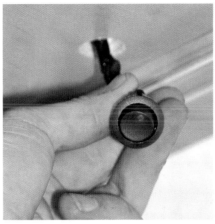

Picture 8. Jason passed the switch wiring through the panel. Auto Tec only make soldered electrical connections, which take a little longer, but aren't prone to breaking down over time like other collections.

Picture 9. The control unit, satellite, and mobile phone network sensors are connected into the wiring harness. When the switch is illuminated, the caravan is in 'travel' mode; when off, it's being watched by Cobra.

Picture 6. When fitted to a car, the ignition switch triggers a signal to the Cobra control room, showing that the vehicle is being moved. In a caravan this has to be done manually.

Picture 10. With the Attivo service, you can track your caravan's location online, as Auto Tec's owner, Julian Willis, demonstrates. The caravan's VIN and the unit's code number have been registered with Cobra.

Picture 7. After drilling its fitting position (the location can be selected by the owner, provided it's practical), engineer Jason soldered the switch terminals onto the back of the switch.

Auto Tec recommend the Cobra because it has a dedicated control room, and the system covers all of Europe.

Here's how it works. When a theft is reported, or when Cobra is alerted by the movement sensor installed in the caravan, the Cobra 24/7 Control Room contacts the caravan's owner. If the owner confirms the theft, they track and monitor the caravan on its control screens, liaising with the police to help recover the caravan. The caravan is recovered to the owner as part of the package.

WHEELCLAMPS

Caravan wheelclamps come in a wide variety of designs and colours, but all do roughly the same job. Whichever one you choose, you should make sure that it fits right around the wheel and, once fitted, can't be slid off, even with the tyre deflated. Be sure to check, too, that the lock can't simply be removed by hammering a hole punch into it. It might sound unlikely, but stories of thieves removing wheelclamps in under 30 seconds are too common to ignore.

AL-KO WHEEL LOCK SYSTEM

Caravans are easier to steal than modern cars, which is why insurance is so expensive. At AL-KO's UK headquarters, I saw first-hand what's involved in fitting its revolutionary wheel lock.

Most caravans with an AL-KO chassis from 2001 can use an AL-KO Secure wheel securing device, the most effective caravan theft deterrent currently available. For 2006-on caravans, you simply buy and use, but earlier models require the use of dealer-fit parts.

Picture 3. AL-KO's Kelvin Evans starts to fit a Premium Kit, first removing the brake drum, then disconnecting the brake cable and taking off the brake backplate complete with brake shoes.

Picture 1. Caravans from 2006/07 (those whose lock receiver was fitted at the time of manufacture) require the **COMPACT KIT.** You line up the hole in the wheel with the receiver, then fit the lozenge.

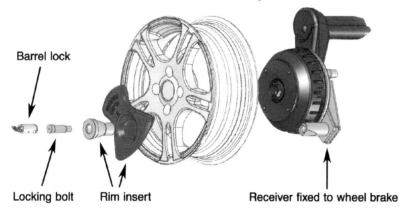

Barrel lock

Locking bolt   Rim insert

Receiver fixed to wheel brake

Picture 2. The **PLUS KIT** (inset) is for 2006/07 caravans with pre-punched fixing holes in the brake backplate. The **PREMIUM KIT** (right) is for 2001-05 model year caravans, which don't have backplate holes.

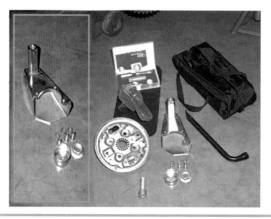

Picture 4. The stub axle (see alignment marks) sets the toe-in and camber settings, and must be fitted by trained personnel. That's one reason why AL-KO doesn't sell fitting kits to the public.

Picture 5. A second reason is that the large bolt holding the stub axle and backplate to the trailing arm requires a massive 370Nm torque, requiring a huge torque wrench and exacting safety standards.

Picture 6. A third reason why AL-KO doesn't regard this job as DIY-able, is that the brake components need to be removed from the old backplate and fitted to the new one.

Picture 7. Three bolts – one of them held in Kelvin's left-hand – allow the immensely strong lock receiver, shown being offered up here, to be fitted to the new backplate.

Picture 8. The three M12x16 Torx bolts are self-locking, use-once components. Once the lock is fitted, to remove the receiver without the key involves working from beneath with oxyacetylene, but see right.

Picture 9. On the latest versions, the receivers are even oxyacetylene resistant, and incredibly difficult to remove. The 'one-shot' brake drum nut requires a whopping 290Nm – way beyond any DIY torque wrench.

Picture 10. Kits cover 20 different wheel designs, and the latest versions include a plastic cover for the lozenge, to protect wheel surfaces. Twin-axle caravans require two kits to be fitted, otherwise it would be possible to let down a tyre, or raise one end of the caravan.

The owner must register, and this registration goes to the lock manufacturer, not to AL-KO: AL-KO do not keep the key details. If you don't register, it won't be possible to obtain a replacement key, and it may be necessary to cut the entire axle off if the key is lost with the lock fitted. Receivers are now fitted with a special material so that they cannot be cut through with oxyacetylene.

HITCHLOCKS

Hitchlocks, as the name suggests, lock over the hitch of the caravan, making them inaccessible to a potential thief's tow car bracket. They should be fitted as an additional security measure, along with a wheelclamp, as alone they can be quite ineffective, as thieves have been known to simply put a rope around the hitch, lock and all, and use it to tow the caravan.

If you do fit a hitchlock, make sure that it covers the bolts that attach the hitch to the caravan's A-frame. Otherwise a thief can simply unbolt and remove the locked hitch, fit an unsecured one in its place, and make off with the 'van.

Many caravans are stolen when left unattended for a short while in a layby, or at a motorway service-station. In order to protect caravans in such circumstances, some hitchlocks are designed to lock the caravan onto the car when the outfit is stationary, making it difficult for the caravan to be removed. However, under no circumstances should such a hitchlock be attached to the outfit when it is on the move.

Some insurance companies have been known to insist on the use of a hitchlock, in which case you have no alternative but to comply. Check your insurance policy.

Picture 1. The AL-KO hitchlock is designed solely for AL-KO hitches, and can easily be used in conjunction with the relevant stabiliser. You place it on the hitch, locate the peg on the hitchlock with the groove in the hitch, then slide the hitchlock forward. You can only do so with the lock in the unlocked position, shown here.

Picture 2. You can't push the locking pin home unless the key is in the barrel, and there's a little jiggling involved to align the locking pin with the recess in the hitch. However, it's a beautifully made piece of kit, and there are several models available, each relating to the different AL-KO hitch types.

Picture 3. The Safety Ball is an essential, if very inexpensive addition. You use it before fitting the hitchlock, by opening the hitch clamp and inserting it into the hitch.

Picture 4. With the hitch closed and the hitchlock in place, the Safety Ball prevents a thief from tying the recess in the hitch to a towball (which is possible even with the lock handle down), and advertises its presence with the red handle, which hangs clearly below the hitch.

Picture 5. Finally, this padded Deluxe Hitch Cover (for AKS2004/3004, or a separate version for AKS 1300) fits snugly over the AL-KO hitch ensemble. An eyelet enables the fitting of a padlock to the cover, and Velcro strips allow quick fitting and removal.

SECURITY POSTS

Security posts effectively block a caravan's removal from its storage position by locking into the ground in front of the caravan. Some are also designed to act in conjunction with a hitchlock, allowing the caravan to be locked onto the top of the security post. However, they are only as strong as the locks that hold them in place, so if you are relying on a security post to protect your caravan, make sure that it's built of high-grade steel and has a high-security lock.

CORNER STEADY LOCKS

Locking one or more of the caravan's corner steadies obviously makes it difficult to move a caravan. However, caution should be taken when relying solely on this form of security: it can be countered by a thief simply sawing off the corner steadies.

TYRE RUN-FLAT SAFETY

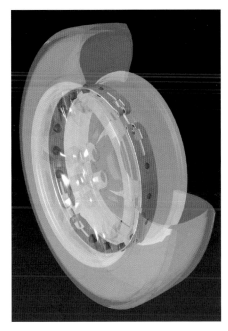

Every caravan wheel has a well inside its rim, which allows the tyre bead to drop into the wheel so it can be fitted. Pressure in the tyre keeps the bead secure, but if the tyre loses pressure due to a puncture, the bead will come away from the wheel rim, dropping into the tyre well. The tyre will come loose, flail around on the wheel, and cause significant damage – or even flip your caravan over.

Tyron MultiBand is a steel band that is fitted inside the tyre, temporarily blanking off the well in the wheel. If the tyre deflates, it will now stay in place on the wheel giving a run-flat capacity of at least 4km (2.5 miles) at high speed, and possibly an even longer distance at lower speeds. Hopefully, this will be enough to enable you to spot the problem and do something about it before catastrophe strikes.

Bearing in mind that more people are killed on the hard shoulders of motorways than while driving on the carriageways, you may also have the opportunity to drive at low speed off the motorway, to find a place where the wheel and tyre can be safely changed.

Picture 1. The first step when fitting a Tyron MultiBand, is to let out all the air from the tyre by removing the valve, and then break the seal between bead and tyre on the side of the valve. It's important that the seal on the other side of wheel and tyre is left intact.

Picture 2. Tyron's clever device for holding the tyre down on the wheel makes the process easier.

Picture 3. There are very many different shapes of wheel, and Tyron produce this set of special plastic gauges, used to judge the correct band for a wheel. This is crucially important and the fitting instructions supply tyre fitters with all the information they need.

Picture 4. The blue stops ('feet,' as Tyron calls them) on the bands sit on the floor of the well, and the bands are held in place with the two special fixing screws shown here.

Picture 5. The two bands are inserted into the space between wheel and tyre, and one of the joints is arranged so that it is spaced equally either side of the valve, but without touching it.

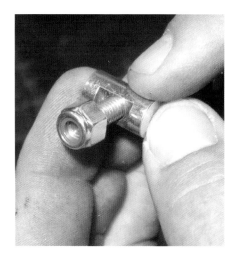

Picture 8. Iain now tightens both of the fixings, making sure that he does so evenly, that there is a gap of no less than 5mm between the ends of the fixings, and that they remain evenly spaced either side of the valve. Final tightening must be carried out with a torque wrench.

Picture 6. The fixings have to be arranged in such a way that the locknuts are prevented from turning by the slots in the appropriate fixing ends.

Picture 9. Before inflating the tyre, Iain uses tyre lubricant on the band itself, as the bead of the tyre will have to slide over it.

Picture 7. It's important that the Tyron band is not pressed against both sides of the well, as this could cause stresses on the wheel, leading to damage. Iain Vincent, from Tyron, who is carrying out this work, ensures that the band is touching only lightly on the valve-side of the well, but that there is clearance all the way around on the other side. Bands come in a wide range of sizes and are capable of being fitted to almost every type of wheel.

Picture 10. He refits the valves, and makes sure that there is a sticker adjacent to each one showing that Tyron bands have been fitted. This is so that, if a tyre needs changing, your fitter can see that Tyron is fitted, and must be removed before he can remove the tyre.

Picture 11. This Avondale is being towed by a Volvo estate, on a wet test track with a completely deflated right-hand tyre, but the Tyron MultiBand keeps the tyre on the rim and allows the caravan to be towed safely to a place of refuge.

TYRE PRESSURE MONITORING AND MAINTENANCE

Arguably, caravan wheels and tyres are even more safety-critical than those on cars: the driver can't sense when there's a problem with them, and failures tend to be catastrophic, with blow-outs and wheel loss all too common. Yet, little maintenance is required.

Here we look at tyre pressures and torque wrenches – and there's more to them both than meets the eye.

Picture 1. This brass-bodied ITC gauge gives consistent results, but be prepared to waste air until you get the hang of pressing the gauge quickly and squarely onto the tyre valve stem.

Picture 3. Bosch used to make this excellent rechargeable air pump, wonderful for topping up tyres away from a 12V socket. You can sometimes find them on eBay UK.

Picture 2. Putting air in is very hard work with a foot pump. This is the compressor that comes with the excellent Dunlop Fill & Go tyre puncture rescue kit: it's much quicker.

Picture 4. Ultraseal's Tyre Pressure Monitors are cheap at under £3 per wheel, and you're more likely to glance at the cap than to use a gauge.

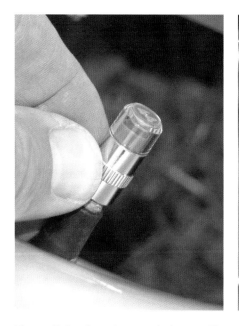

Picture 5. Purchased to match the specific pressure required, the Ultraseal Monitors turn orange, then red, when the pressure drops. Not as accurate as a gauge, but a great visual safety check.

Picture 6. Some say nitrogen in tyres isn't worth bothering with. Yet F1 teams and aircraft engineers both use it. The cost is low, but potential benefits make it worth a try.

Picture 7. The air is removed, nitrogen is pumped in, and the tyres stay inflated for longer. It works quite well, and the reduction in oxygen also discourages corrosion from forming inside the wheel.

Picture 8. Don't lubricate wheel bolt threads: you won't be able to 'torque' them accurately. But copper grease on the bolt seat, where it bears on an alloy wheel, will prevent corrosion.

Picture 9. There's a real danger of caravan wheel bolts coming loose and wheels flying off. Slacken all bolts in turn to ensure they're not too tight, then retighten with a torque wrench.

Picture 10. Set the gauge to the figure required, and when the bolt is correctly tightened, the wrench 'clicks,' and you must stop turning. Be careful: there's nothing to stop you harmfully over-tightening after the click.

Wheels and tyres, unless properly maintained, *will* become dangerous. Tyre blowouts, possibly causing a roll-over, are almost always caused by badly maintained, under inflated tyres. Wheels coming off are almost always caused by loose or over-tightened wheel bolts.

Many owners think that a 'good tightening' of wheel bolts is all that's required, but over-tightened bolts can be even more dangerous than loose ones. Over-tightened bolts shear suddenly, coming off very quickly, and the loss of a wheel will be almost instantaneous. Always fit and check with a torque wrench.

Stabilisers are sprung devices fitted to a caravan's hitch or A-frame, and are designed to dampen the swaying motion encountered by caravans in strong winds, or when being overtaken by a high-sided vehicle. Before fitting, it's essential to make sure that the caravan is loaded correctly, in good mechanical order, matched with a suitable towing vehicle, and that both the caravan and tow car's tyres are inflated correctly.

In addition, stabilisers should never be relied upon to improve the

BASIC STABILISER TYPES

towing characteristics of an inherently unstable outfit.

The most common type of stabiliser is the leaf-type, fitted from the tow car's towing bracket to the side of the caravan's A-frame. It's imperative that this type's adjustable bolt is correctly set, otherwise the stabiliser will not work correctly.

To adjust and alter the setting, it's essential that you refer to the manufacturers instructions, as each type will have a slightly different method of adjustment.

IMPORTANT NOTE:

• It is strongly recommended that you try towing for the first time without a stabiliser, so that you gain a feel for what's involved when the 'tail' (caravan) tries to wag the 'dog' (car). A stabiliser will make the combination far more secure-feeling during normal towing but any instability inherent in the set-up will simply be transferred to a higher and more dangerous speed.

FITTING A BLADE-TYPE STABILISER

The blade-type stabiliser is by far the least expensive method of improving the stability of your towing combination.

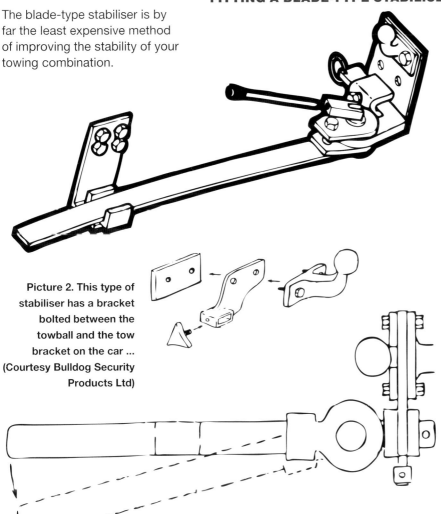

Picture 2. This type of stabiliser has a bracket bolted between the towball and the tow bracket on the car ... (Courtesy Bulldog Security Products Ltd)

Picture 1. The stabiliser consists of a friction damper bolted to the tow car, either projecting beneath the tow bracket (as in this case), or to one side of the tow bracket, and a guide bolted to the caravan. As turn a corner, the blade slides through the guide as it turns on the friction damper; as travel along a straight road, the effect of the friction damper is enough to hold the caravan more securely than it otherwise would be.
(Courtesy Tow Sure Products Ltd)

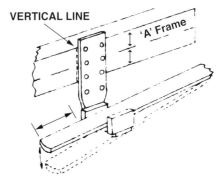

Picture 4. When fitting a stabiliser of this type, it's important that the guide is precisely located on the caravan chassis. If a fairing is fitted, you will have to remove it, and cut it so that it fits around the guide bracket. It's also most important to follow the fitting instructions precisely so that the guide is correctly positioned on the caravan's A-frame.
(Courtesy Bulldog Security Products Ltd)

Picture 3. ... and the stabiliser bar slots into the bracket, and is held with a thumbscrew while travelling. (Courtesy Bulldog Security Products Ltd)

Picture 6. A swan-neck type tow bracket is almost always acceptable for using an AL-KO hitch.

Picture 8. Presenting the tow vehicle to the caravan is done in the conventional way. Shan reversed slowly back while I directed.

TOP TIP!

• *Before going any further, remember the cardinal rule: remove all traces of grease and paint from your towball before connecting to a friction stabiliser. Grease in particular will make the friction pads useless. Plating and paint on the ball will encourage the ball to creak and groan in use. After you've removed the grease, use an abrasive kitchen pad to clean off any coating on the ball.*

Picture 9. As the tow vehicle approached the caravan hitch, I wound the jockey wheel up, until it just cleared the top of the towball. Note that the stabiliser arm is in the up position, and the coupling lever is about to be lifted, before winding the caravan hitch onto the towball. On the AL-KO hitch, the coupling locks temporarily in this position.

Picture 10. At this stage, it's worth exploring one of the later Discovery's most interesting features: height-adjustable rear suspension. Here, the vehicle is lowered, not only making it easier to get in and out of, but also easier to hitch a caravan to.

Picture 11. When the hitch on the caravan was directly over the ball, the caravan was lowered at the jockey wheel. As the hitch is wound over the ball, the coupling snaps down.

Picture 12. To show that the ball is in place, and as an extra safety check, ensure that the safety indicator button on the top of the hitch is showing its green segment.

Picture 13. The arrows on the front of the head must point to the area shown, to indicate that the left and right friction pads are in good order. In addition, the segment on the coupling handle (Pic 1, item 7) must also show green, otherwise the front and rear friction pads, the coupling mechanism, or the ball are worn.

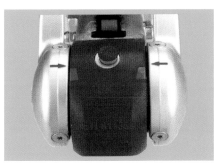

Picture 14. When the arrows point here, left-right friction pads need replacing.

Picture 15. Make sure that when you raise the jockey wheel, the wheel arms are recessed into slots in the tube; this prevents the winder from unscrewing itself as you drive along.

Picture 16. Note that if your tow vehicle comes with a 13-pin socket, you will have to fit an adapter to connect a caravan with 12N- and 12S-plugs.

Picture 17. Make sure that with the extra length, the cables don't drag on the ground. Winding the caravan's cables around the hitch might do the trick, but be careful not to foul the overrun/brake mechanism, and ensure you leave enough slack for manoeuvring tight corners.

Picture 18. If your break-away cable is of the heavy-duty type (available from AL-KO as an extra), you can clip it directly to a suitable clip on the car. Otherwise, it must be doubled-back on itself, and connected like so. If you don't, in an emergency the clip can pull open before the brakes are properly applied.

AL-KO ATC ANTI-SNAKING SYSTEM

Picture 3. Beneath your caravan, on the axle, is the brake equaliser. This transfers forces from the hitch to the brake on each wheel. The rod adjuster thread has to be shortened.

The ATC 'Electronic Snake Control' system is one of the biggest steps forward in towing safety. Here, we explain how it works, and how it can be retrofitted by AL-KO.

Many caravans from 2008 onwards will be factory-fitted with this device, but it can also be retrofitted to most caravans with an AL-KO chassis (which is most caravans), but only by AL-KO itself at Southam, near Warwick, or at Burton-on-Trent.

Picture 4. Once the centre brake actuator has been shortened, and the threads cleaned up, the other brake rod in the kit is screwed and locked onto it, extending its effective length.

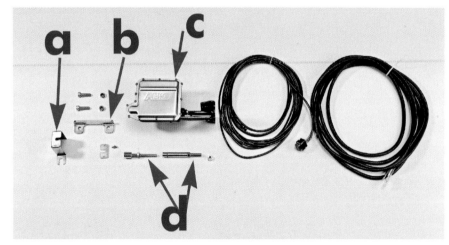

Picture 1. The kit contains:
a. Check light brackets; b. Mounting bracket; c. Control unit; d. Brake rods. Wiring must be carried out by a trained engineer – hence, no DIY kit.

Picture 2. First, a brake rod is fitted to the control unit. This contains the sensors for detecting lateral movement (snake), and the brake operator. There are six different units to cater for the range of caravans.

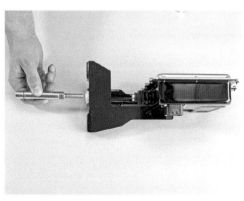

Picture 5. The control unit is offered up and slid into position. The extension rod, just fitted, can be 'pushed' by the unit, gently applying the caravan brakes if required.

Picture 6. The control unit is fixed in place via this bracket (arrowed), which is attached to the normal caravan brake bracket, welded to the caravan's axle tube. No extra drilling is required.

Picture 7. The final job, on the mechanical side, is to adjust the brake rod clearance. This is a once-only job, and no maintenance is ever required for the ATC unit.

Picture 8. A tell-tale light lets you know when the unit is powered and operating. It has to be fitted to the hitch cover which, of course, needs to be drilled.

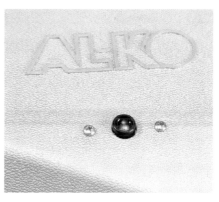

Picture 9. Depending on model, it fits either on a steel bracket bolted to the A-frame, or to a steel reinforcing bracket placed on the inside of the hitch cover.

Picture 10. It's vital that the systems' wiring looms are correctly connected to the caravan's wiring system. Then, it's simply a matter of plugging it in to the control unit.

Anyone who's ever experienced severe snaking, or has seen the results, will know that it's the caravanner's biggest fear. If you've ever seen a caravan snaking uncontrollably across the lanes of a motorway, or pictures of a flipped-over caravan, you'll know that its consequences can be horrifying.

AL-KO's ATC system uses an electronic sensor to detect snake, even before the driver notices it. It then gently applies the caravan's brakes, slowing the unit. I've seen the unit tested in extreme circumstances – and I think it's a brilliant system!

FITTING AN AL-KO POSITIVE COUPLING INDICATOR

It's often said that some of the best ideas are the simplest ones, and this is certainly true of the AL-KO Positive Coupling Indicator. This device is fitted as standard to many caravans from 1993 onwards, and replaces the standard coupling head with a modified version incorporating a button on its top. When the caravan is correctly hitched onto a towing bracket, the button raises slightly to reveal a green band.

Picture 4. Remove the coupling head bellows from over the rear flange, if fitted, and lift the coupling head from the overrun shaft. (Courtesy AL-KO Kober Ltd)

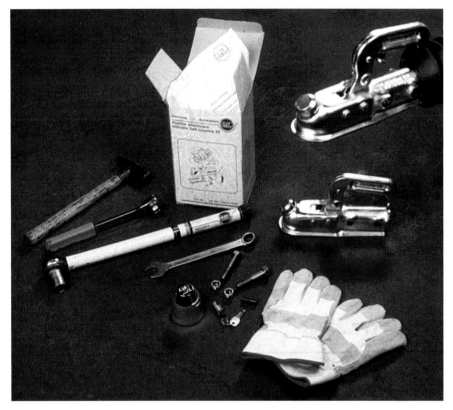

Picture 1. The Positive Coupling Indicator is an excellent way of ensuring your caravan is correctly hitched to your tow car, and can be fitted to any caravan equipped with a standard AL-KO hitch. Kits can be obtained from larger caravan dealerships. (Courtesy AL-KO Kober Ltd)

Picture 5. Position the replacement Positive Coupling Indicator onto the drawshaft, ensuring that both the fixing holes are aligned.
Fit one of the new bolts supplied with the kit into the front hole and attach the Nyloc nut. Use the other new bolt supplied to drift out the damper retaining piece, and attach the second Nyloc nut.
(Courtesy AL-KO Kober Ltd)

Picture 6. Using a torque wrench, ensure that both fixing nuts are torqued to the figure specified with the model of coupling you are fitting. (Courtesy AL-KO Kober Ltd)

Picture 2. For safety, ensure that the caravan's handbrake is engaged before starting work. Undo and remove the front coupling head bolt ...
(Courtesy AL-KO Kober Ltd)

Picture 3. ... and use the retaining piece, supplied with the kit, to drift the rear bolt out. This retaining piece ensures that the overrun damper is retained in its correct position. (Courtesy AL-KO Kober Ltd)

Picture 7. Replace the coupling head bellows over the rear flange, if fitted. (Courtesy AL-KO Kober Ltd)

TOWING MIRRORS

Hitch a caravan behind your car, and you'll soon notice that the car's wing mirrors are, generally, useless for seeing behind the caravan. Having a good view of what is going on behind the caravan is obviously vital for road safety, particularly when overtaking and reversing. Therefore, it's essential that extension towing mirrors are fitted.

The law on towing mirrors is a little vague, stating that the driver must have an 'adequate' view along the sides of the caravan, to the rear, although the word 'adequate' is not defined. Towing mirrors come in a wide variety of shapes and sizes, but there are basically only two types: door-mounted and wing-mounted.

The benefit of door-mounted types over wing-mounted types, is that they can be adjusted from the driver's seat, rather than having to rely on somebody else adjusting them to give the driver a clear rearward vision, which is the case with wing-mounted types.

Picture 2. Wing-mounted mirrors, as the name suggests, attach to the front wings of the car, by means of clips and elastic straps. Like the door-mounted variety, many are fitted with reflectors on the back, so that they are visible to on-coming motorists at night.

REAR VIEW MIRRORS

Picture 1. Door-mounted towing mirrors are either attached directly onto the car's existing mirrors, or clipped onto the car door. Of the mirror-mounted variety, some will obscure the car's existing mirror, in order to give a wider rearward view, while others will still allow at least a small amount of vision from the standard mirrors.

Almost all mirrors of this type are held in place by fixing adjustable rubber straps around the back of the car's door mirrors. It's essential that these straps are fixed as tightly as possible: you don't want the towing mirrors to become disconnected when the outfit is on the move.

Door-mounted types often slide-in at the top of the door, between the side of the window glass, and are then steadied at the bottom with a heavy-duty elastic strap.

As a responsible caravanner, you'll want to have the best rear vision available when you're towing and, in practice, all except the widest tow vehicle will need to be fitted with a pair of extension mirrors. So, which ones are best? The choice is wide, but the problems with some can be quite significant.

CLIP-ON MIRRORS

Milenco Easi View and Raydyot M800/802

Verdict: lowest price

General: These, apparently identical mirrors, are probably the most widely used model.

Plus points: Among the quickest and easiest mirrors to fit, and suitable for a wide range of cars. Leaves existing mirrors unobstructed. Cheap to buy, lightweight and easy to store. Larger sizes for bigger door mirrors also available.

Minus points: Among the worst mirrors for vibration, obscuring detail at motorway towing speeds. Can't be fitted to larger, taller door mirrors.

Head dimensions: 158mm x 117mm

Glass type: Flat or convex
Suppliers: Milenco and Raydyot.
Supplier/retailer: Towsure

Rock Steady Towing Mirrors

Verdict: superb value
General: Supplied as a pair, each with its own bag. Each mounting has its own steady strap, increasing stability.
Plus points: Vibration average, but acceptable. These mirrors are said to be universal (but see below). Different sizes of attachments (plus spare fixing pads) are supplied with the mirrors, widening the range of vehicles that these mirrors will fit.
Minus points: Distorted glass on our sample driver's mirror. If the top edge of the mirror casing is strongly curved, it may be impossible to fit the brackets, because they are held in a level plane by the mirror bar. On our VW T5, the mounting brackets just fouled the door mirror glass.
Head dimensions: 190mm x 127mm
Glass type: Flat for driver's side; convex for passenger's.
Supplier: Pyramid
Supplier/retailer: Towsure

Raydyot Ultra-View M88/M89

Verdict: very stable
General: Takes an entirely different approach, in that it clips to the front wing rather than the existing door mirror. It's a simple matter to open the bonnet, hook the lower arm under the wing, and pull the two upper arms up and over the front wing channel.
Plus points: The most stable of all the mirrors tested, with the least amount of vibration at the mirror head. Very quick to fit. Very well constructed.
Minus points: Can't be fitted to vehicles with unusual bonnets (such as clamshell designs), or those with steeply sloping front-ends. The mirror can't be adjusted from the driver's seat. Takes up a large amount of storage room.
Head dimensions: 188mm x 137mm
Glass type: Flat or convex
Supplier: Raydyot
Supplier/retailer: Riversway Leisure

Milenco Towing Mirror

Verdict: solidly made

General: The attachment system is an unattractive array of brackets and knobs. To fit the mirror, slacken all knobs, and push brackets onto mirror casing. A rubber strap is then fitted for added security.
Plus points: Vibration is average, but acceptable. Said to be universal (but see below). Reasonably compact for storage when you're on-site.
Minus points: If the top edge of the mirror casing is curved, it may be impossible to fit the brackets. The rubber pads have an annoying habit of dropping off, and are fiddly to refit. On our VW T5, the mounting brackets, which are thicker than those on the Rock Steady mirrors, prevented the door mirror glass from being adjusted.
Head dimensions: 188mm x 125mm
Glass type: Flat or convex
Supplier: Milenco
Supplier/retailer: Towsure

Vision View Universal Towing Mirror

Verdict: promising but flawed
General: This is a radically different mirror, the best looking of those here, but it's badly let down by its clips (see below). There's a ratchet built into the body of the mirror, which tightens a strap with a clip on each end. These clips are placed over the edges of the door mirror casing. Turn the ratchet to tighten the strap and pull the feet on the towing mirror tight against the door mirror casing.
Plus points: Good looking, and best for vibration, of all the door mirror-mounted models. Very quick to fit once the clips are in place. Neat and

compact when stored, especially in the optional storage bag.

Minus points: I broke a plastic clip when tightening the mirror. The ratchet is extremely difficult to release when fully tightened. I found it almost impossible to fit one of these mirrors where the door mirror casing was over 5mm thick. The optional, wider plastic clips weren't usable. I called the American suppliers (they hadn't responded to an earlier email), who suggested "shaving a bit off," but they still didn't work properly. The optional aluminium clips would have broken the mirror glass on my vehicle, had I used them. What a shame: these could have been superb mirrors.

Head dimensions: 125mm x 115mm
Supplier: Vision View Mirrors
Supplier/retailer: Riversway Leisure

Suck-It-And-See Tow Mirror

Verdict: my top choice

AUXILIARY MIRRORS

If your vehicle is wide enough to not need mirror extensions, you may still benefit from adding an auxiliary wide-angle mirror.

Hercules Big Auxiliary Mirror
General: Fixes to the door mirror casing.
Plus points: Excellent panoramic view.
Minus points: Rather plain.
Head dimensions: 63mm x 125mm
Supplier/Retailer: Riversway Leisure

Wide-Angle Mirror
General: Fixes to the door mirror casing.
Plus points: Good looking.
Minus points: Doesn't offer much extra view.
Head dimensions: 63mm x 125mm
Supplier/retailer: CAK

General: To fit the Suck-It-And-See Tow Mirror, hold the sucker against the door mirror glass, and turn the knob to activate the suction device. Said to have been tested to 120mph, and showed no sign of coming off when I tried them at motorway speed.

Plus points: Developed specifically for UK RHD vehicles. Easily the fastest and easiest to fit, and the only mirrors you can set using the vehicle's internal door-mirror adjusters. Small, light, and easily stored in the bag provided. Low vibration. Safety strap included.

Minus points: The flat mirror's view area is small, but the (UK-specific) convex models is spot-on.

Head dimensions: 130mm x 100mm
Supplier: Pyramid Products
Supplier/retailer: Towsure

Picture 1. Hercules Big Auxiliary Mirror.

Picture 2. Wide-Angle Mirror.

FITTING A REAR VIEW CAMERA

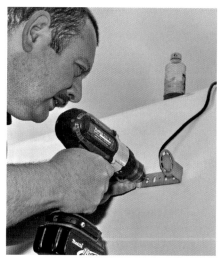

Picture 2. Here's the bracket for the Waeco rear-view camera, being fitted to the rear of the caravan. There's also a version with a protective shutter to keep the lenses clean when not in use.

Even with extended or auxiliary mirrors, you may not be able to see what's following you when towing a caravan.

Conrad Anderson worked with Waeco to produce a rear-view camera system, specially for caravanners. With this system, you'll not only be able to see what's following your caravan, you'll also be able to see when reversing the caravan onto a pitch, and there's the extra bonus of a reversing camera for your tow vehicle.

Here's how Conrad Anderson wired our caravan and tow vehicle to provide rear vision. It's not an easy DIY job, though!

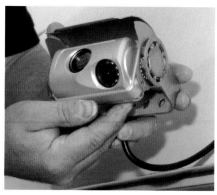

Picture 3. I chose the Waeco RV590 video system, with twin colour camera modules in a single housing. This provides close-up camera views for reversing, or long distance views for the open road.

Picture 1. The kit shown in the main picture includes an option that provides views along the sides of the caravan, too. Whichever system you select, it requires wiring to be installed along the entire length of the caravan.

Picture 4. An optional Conrad Anderson system has a single lens rear camera, and two small cameras mounted on the camera sides, to provide extra side views when manoeuvring the caravan.

Picture 5. Of course, the vehicle has to be wired, too. Here, the cabling for the reversing camera being fitted to the rear-end of our tow vehicle is being positioned.

Picture 8. The reversing camera on our T5 Volkswagen fits nicely here, after having moved the number plate down. On most cars, it's best fitted towards the top of the tailgate.

Picture 6. Inside the vehicle (or the caravan, depending on installation), the Waeco control box is tucked away. Operated by a dash-mounted switch, it allows you to select between cameras from the driver's seat.

Picture 9. The 5 inch Waeco monitor is switched to the vehicle's reversing camera. The towball is easily visible – great for hitching up accurately, and without causing damage to the tow vehicle.

Picture 7. Conrad Anderson developed a special plug and socket to connect the caravan cameras to the tow vehicle. Wireless systems, incidentally, are very prone to interference and picture loss while driving.

Picture 10. The dash-mounted switch, and remote control, were used to show this view of a car, parked 10m behind the caravan.

Rear view mirrors are essential and a legal requirement (see page 192), but I've noticed some huge advantages with a rear view camera. On A-roads, you can tell if there's anyone speeding up behind you – especially useful if waiting to make a right turn. Better still, if you need to pull out to overtake on the motorway, you can be sure you're in the clear.

Incidentally, some people believe that, because it's illegal to watch a TV when driving, the same applies to a rear view monitor. It doesn't: the law specifically allows for views of the vehicle or the road.

REPLACE SIDE-MARKER LIGHTS WITH LED UNITS

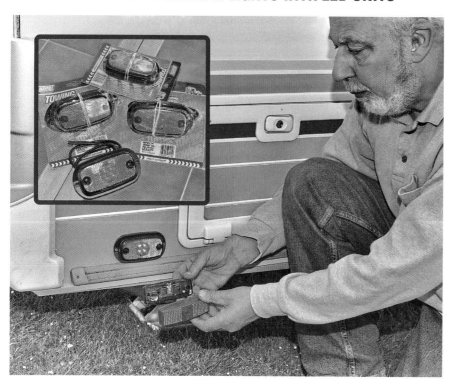

Picture 3. After removing the old light unit, there will undoubtedly be lots of sticky mastic still attached. White spirit can help, but I used Würth Silicone Remover, to also remove all other contaminants.

I removed our caravan's old side-marker lights, and replaced them with new LED lamps.

All caravan incandescent lights seem prone to leaks. LED lights are (theoretically) fully sealed, and shouldn't leak. The 'bulbs' should last indefinitely, and they consume much less electricity. The hassle of changing should be offset by never having to touch them again.

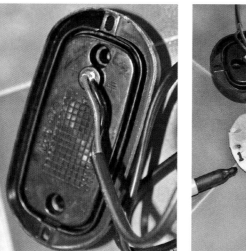

Picture 1. There are many different sizes of light unit available, so ensure the ones you buy cover the existing light fixing holes. Remove the old unit to check for bodywork cut-aways.

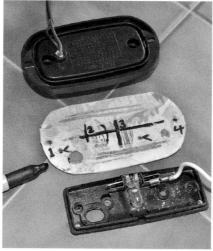

Picture 2. You also need to make a note of the existing wiring. I made a cardboard template to allow for the shape of the new light, its fixing holes, and the location of existing electrics.

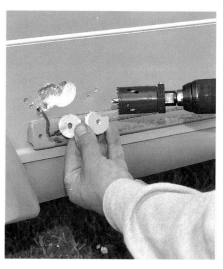

Picture 4. A cordless drill is safest when working outside, and the Makita has enough power to use with a hole cutter. These two overlapping holes allowed for moving the wiring ...

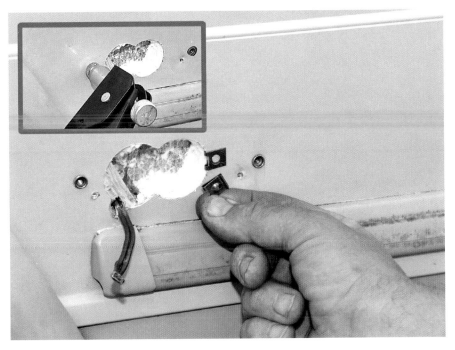

Picture 9. ... so that, when disconnected, the live cable will be a little safer. I used a strip of butyl mastic on the back of the light unit, to make sure that no water would reach the fixing holes.

Picture 5. ... and for the protrusion on the back of the light. I used Würth rivet nuts where there was no rear access available, and push-on spire clips where I had side-access.

Picture 6. Having removed surplus insulation, I removed the old electrical terminals, and stripped the wire endings with the wire stripper. It's quicker and more reliable because ...

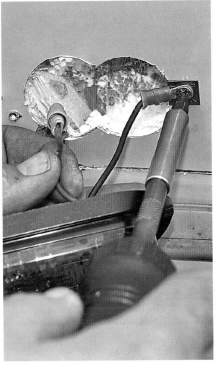

Picture 10. Stainless steel screws were screwed into the rivet nuts, with a dab of non-setting mastic (NOT silicon sealant) beneath each screw head to further guard against water ingress.

You are strongly advised to buy a branded unit supplied in the UK. Also, look at the number of LEDs fitted. Depending on the type of LED used, the fewer there are, the less the lamp will cost. However, there are more expensive single-LED types available, so check carefully.

I have also known cheap LED light units to be badly sealed, allowing internal condensation, and leading to almost certain rapid failure.

Of course, the information shown here for fitting LED lights would also apply if you were simply replacing bulb-type incandescent units with new ones of a similar type.

Picture 7. ... you don't accidentally remove any strands of electrical cable. I crimped a new female connector to the power feed cable, with a new mail connector crimped to the cable on the light.

Picture 8. A ring terminal was used to screw the earth cable to the spire clip on the caravan body. Always use a female connector on the live feed from the caravan ...

FITTING A SAFE

If you're planning on leaving valuables, spare car keys etc, in your caravan, a safe is a sound investment. Be aware, however, that a cheap safe probably isn't much of a deterrent, and that in order to be sufficiently strong, there is inevitably a weight penalty. The AL-KO safe, shown below, weighs 8.5kg, which is very reasonable given the strength of the components used.

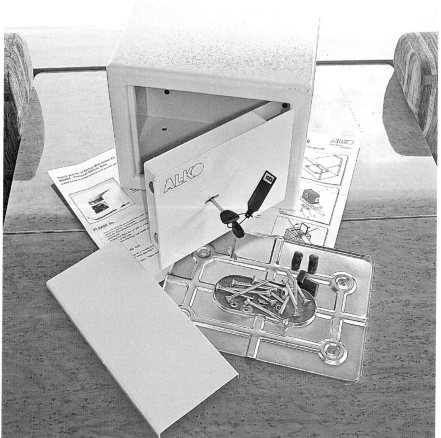

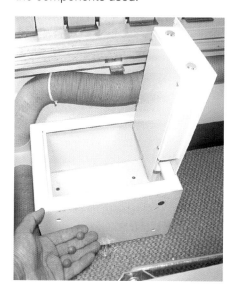

Picture 1. Usually, safes are fitted with the door facing upwards. If you're fitting it this way up, use one of the fixing screws to push the four blanking grommets out of the floor of the safe, and put them in the now-redundant holes in the side.

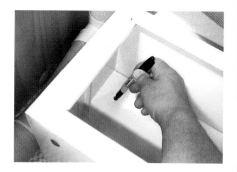

Picture 2. Place the safe in a suitable position, where there are no wires or pipes beneath and without blocking any ventilation holes. Mark the positions of two diagonally-opposite holes, and remove the safe.

Picture 3. Drill through at the two positions you have just marked.

TOP TIP

• With a thicker floor it's essential that the hole you drill is truly perpendicular to the floor.
• Use a set-square or a square-sided box to give yourself something against which to judge the angle of the drill.

Picture 4. Push screws through the two holes in the floor, facing down. Place the galvanised metal plate beneath the caravan floor, and hold it on with a couple of plain 6mm nuts – not the lock-nuts supplied, but ones you can easily fasten on the thread with your fingers.

Picture 5. Now drill up through the floor, using the other two holes in the plate as a template.

Picture 6. To prevent water from seeping between the plate and the floor, I used Würth PU Bond+Seal on the metal plate.

Picture 7. The instructions say that you shouldn't use the safe key to open the door, because it could break, and no replacement keys are available. So, to attach a knob to open the safe, first unscrew the liner from the rear of the door, and then drill a hole (arrowed) through it. Note that steel swarf could cause the locking mechanism to jam, so after drilling the hole, use a pick-up magnet, or similar, to extract every last bit of swarf.

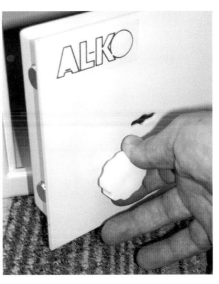

Picture 8. Then screw a suitable knob in place on the door.

Picture 9. The safe should now be placed back in position, with the holes in the safe aligned with the holes in the floor.

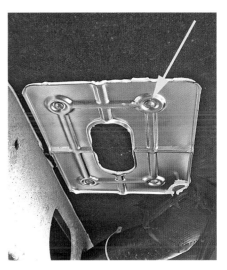

Picture 10. Beneath the caravan, the plate is held in position and the correct length screws (there are three lengths to choose from) are pushed from beneath, through the caravan floor and into the holes. An extra pair of hands is useful here, but not essential. Each of the screw(arrowed) is given a sharp tap with a hammer, seating its squared shank in the pressed square in the plate, and gripping it, preventing it from falling out. This is a nice touch from AL-KO's design engineers, and was much appreciated.

If the floor of your caravan is of the composite, insulated type, with polystyrene sandwiched between two sheets of board, be careful not to overtighten the fixing screws, or you risk crushing the floor board.

The actual location of the safe is, of course, up to you, but do test the door opening before fitting, to ensure it doesn't foul on surrounding panels, framework, or cupboards.

FIAMMA DOOR SECURITY ARM

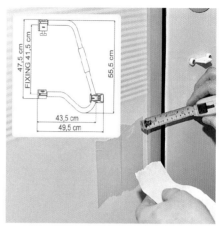

Picture 2. The most difficult part was working out where the arm could go, without clashing with any internal fittings. The instructions are not particularly helpful.

Door security arms are a useful modification: if you're a little unsteady, or are worried about slipping off the caravan steps, a Fiamma Door Security arm is ideal. Plus, it will act as a highly visible theft deterrent.

In this section, caravan engineer, Rob Sheasby, shows how to fit a door security arm to a caravan.

Picture 3. After establishing approximate positions, Rob applied masking tape to the wall of the caravan, so that accurate pencil lines could easily be drawn. After measuring the door frame surround, the arm was offered up to the precisely drawn lines.

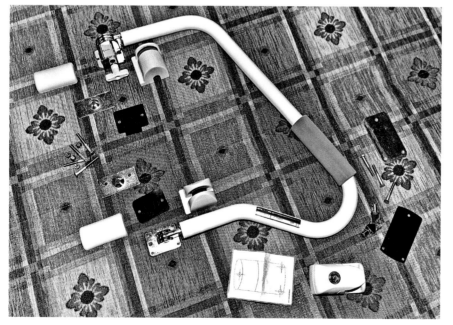

Picture 1. We fitted the larger, 46cm version of the Fiamma Security Arm, but, in retrospect, the shorter arm should have been chosen for our caravan, to put less strain on the wall.

Picture 4. Don't try using a spirit level on a caravan: it almost certainly won't be level. Rob drilled a very small pilot hole using a 6.5mm diameter bit.

Picture 5. After making a strengthening board for the inside of the caravan, the same bit was used to drill through both caravan wall and board. Edging and varnishing were done later.

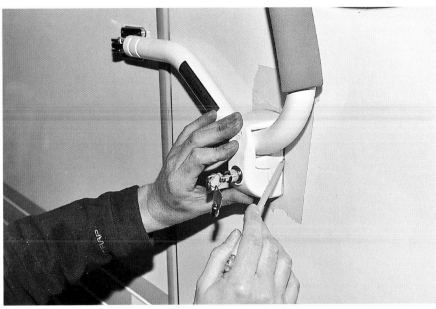

Picture 8. Once the arm was in place, Rob turned his attention to the separate lock, the position of which was marked on the door using the same masking tape approach as before.

Picture 6. Note that Rob applied non-setting caravan mastic around each hole, on the outside of the caravan, before inserting the stainless steel bolts and rubber pad.

Picture 7. While gripping the bolts to prevent them from turning, the Nyloc nuts were tightened onto the metal plate supplied with the kit (a second pair of hands will be required for this).

Picture 9. Again, a metal plate is supplied for the inside of the door. Note that you have to make sure you're in a clear space. I found some plastic nut caps to improve the appearance.

Picture 10. While the hinges aren't too ugly, Fiamma supply clip-on plastic covers. Inevitably, there will be some squeezed-out mastic to be cleaned off before you've finished.

Fiamma Locking Security Handles are made of 2mm thick, 30mm diameter anodized aluminium tube. When open, a Security Handle makes entering and leaving the caravan easier and safer. When closed, it's a useful anti-theft device, and also prevents accidental door opening when travelling.

Though the Security 46 Pro used here is very strong, the weakest link is likely to be the structure of the caravan to which it's attached. The longer the arm, the greater the leverage you can inadvertently put on the body of the caravan. Both the strength of the unit, and its security function, are dependent on having a good, solid fixing.

LOCKER LOCK REPLACEMENT

Caravans are often notorious for having hard to find special fittings installed by the manufacturer. Here's how to fit a 'standard' locker lock.

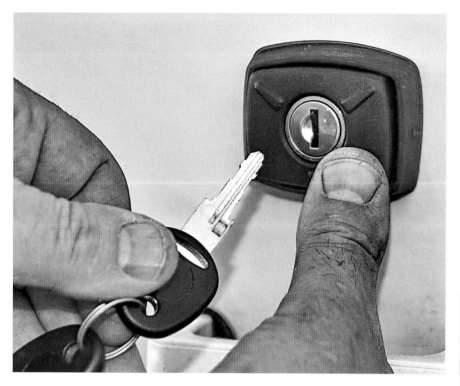

Picture 1. On this fibreglass (GRP) caravan, the locker lock broke, and we couldn't find a like-for-like replacement. It was simpler (and probably cheaper) to remove the old lock and fit a standard item, for which replacement keys could be found if necessary. We used a version from CAK.

Picture 2. The old locker lock was a strange and difficult device to use, even before we lost the last remaining key! You have to ensure that the latch on the replacement ...

Picture 3. ... is, or can be, bent, to match the distance from the back of the old lock. The hole in the locker door wasn't large enough, so the door was removed ...

Picture 4. ... and a strong piece of scrap wood tightly clamped to the back, before carefully and accurately drilling a pilot hole, right in the middle of the hole for the old lock.

Picture 5. The piece of wood was used because a hole cutter (used to make the larger hole) can't enlarge an existing hole unless there is something to support the centre of the bit.

Picture 6. I separated the lock's components, inserted the housing, and used it as a guide for drilling the holes for the fixing screws. Use a breathing mask when machining GRP.

Picture 9. ... to adjust its position on the shaft or, if necessary, bend and reshape the lever. You'd need a vice to reshape steel this thick.

Picture 7. You need large washers to spread the load when bolting through any type of plastic. These had to be trimmed to fit. Also, use locknuts or shakeproof washers.

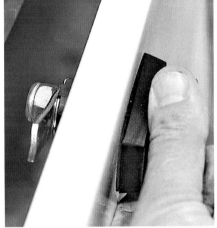

Picture 10. In the event, all I had to do was bend the lever flat. Now, when shutting the door, the lever fitted snugly against the fixed panel on the caravan.

Picture 11. Once I had established that everything was in the right position, and that the lock was working properly, I tightened the locknut, gripping the lever with an adjustable spanner.

Picture 8. The lock assembly was inserted into the housing. I hoped that the lock lever would be in the correct position, although I expected to have to use washers ...

If you've got odd or foreign (literally, in this case) locks, and you want to replace them, there are several measurements that you'll need to confirm against the replacement lock.

First, you can get away with widening a hole, but fitting a smaller lock into a larger hole can involve much remedial work, even if it is possible.

Second, you need to make sure there's enough clearance at the door and opening for the new lock mechanism and knob.

Finally, ensure the lever can be adapted to fit your installation, or you'll need the skills required to make a new one.

Part 6
Entertainment

USING A STAND-ALONE TV AERIAL

A roof-mounted, omnidirectional aerial can be useless for Freeview digital TV. If you want to pickup digital TV, wherever there's a signal, with a high-efficiency, jockey wheel-mounted aerial, here's how to install a Maxview digital aerial, mast, and signal finder – and how to use your laptop as a flat-screen TV.

Picture 1. Here's the kit as supplied by Maxview. For optimum performance, especially in low-signal areas, Maxview recommends the use of a signal booster (although our kit didn't come with one).

Picture 2. The Maxview Weatherproof Socket provides a weatherproof cable entry into your touring vehicle. Use this seal as a template, but double-check which holes you'll need before marking them.

Picture 3. It's best if the internal cable is hidden inside a locker or cupboard, and it's essential to drill *away* from internal components, seals, or structures. Check first with your dealer if necessary.

Picture 4. After fitting the self-adhesive sealing pad, internal cables are pushed through from the inside and connected to the socket, the backing paper is removed from the seal, and the socket stuck in place.

Picture 5. Cable entry points must be double-sealed using a suitable flexible sealant. Pilot holes for the mounting screws are drilled after the socket has been stuck in place, and stainless steel screws should be used.

Picture 6. The aerial is easily assembled using the bolts and wing nuts supplied, and breaks into four sections, so that it takes up little space when you're travelling.

Picture 7. The jockey wheel attachment is excellent, as it doesn't require the mounting of permanent brackets. It was amply strong enough, too, even in a fairly high winds.

Picture 8. The TV signal strength meter plugs into the aerial cable, and enables you to tune the aerial position without having to see the TV screen.

Picture 9. It's only sensible to trial-fit and test your new TV system before setting out. You'll certainly want to get to grips with the Hauppauge Win-TV's programme recorder and TV scheduler.

Picture 10. With the Hauppauge Win-TV plugged into a USB port, your laptop can be used as a TV, with remote control, electronic program guide, and recorder.

My first instinct was to be the most excited about the Hauppauge Win-TV. It enables you to watch and record programs, via Freeview Digital TV, in a window or full screen. You can also listen to stereo DVB-T radio.

However, if you can't pick up a decent signal, you can forget about digital TV.

The Maxview digital aerial is very light, but performed really well, even without a signal booster (though I recommend one for weak signal areas).

FIT AN EXTERIOR TV AERIAL SOCKET

This project enables you to plug-in to the TV point on a caravan site's power bollard, via a socket on your caravan.

Most caravans have a roof-mounted aerial, and the signal from this is often weak, but most caravan sites have TV points available. With this socket and switch, you'll be able to select whichever one you want, without loose wires inside the caravan.

Picture 1. If possible, fit the socket inside the battery box. The socket has a waterproof cap, but this placement helps further. The aerial wire can pass through the recess for the mains cable.

Picture 2. Make sure that the socket will be clear of all obstructions. It's best to drill a small pilot hole first, then, if you've made a mistake, it'll be a small one.

Picture 3. Use the correct size of hole saw, or a (tapering) stepped drill, but don't make the hole too big. Here, the aerial cable attached to the socket is passed through the hole ...

Picture 4. ... and the aerial socket (with the flap open) is pushed into position. If you're fitting it outside the battery box, the socket flap hinge should be at the top.

Picture 5. Here's why the main hole mustn't be too big: you need to drill pilot holes near to the edges of the main hole. This inexpensive Clarke angle adapter is a boon.

Picture 6. A stubby screwdriver is used in the confined space, to screw the stainless steel self-tapping screws that we used. They're available quite cheaply from Screwfix.

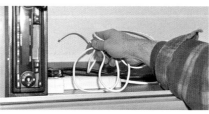

Picture 7. If the supplied aerial cable isn't long enough, you'll have to extend it. Fitting a conduit and planning a hidden route through cupboards and bed boxes can be time-consuming.

Picture 8. You'll need F-plugs to connect to the back of the switch. Use a very sharp knife on the coaxial cable, and ensure you cut away from your fingers, on a piece of wood or cardboard.

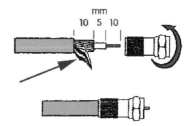

Picture 9. Prepare the cable as shown, twirling the braided section (arrowed), and wrapping it back around the insulation. Push and screw-on the F-plug connector, making sure the centre protrudes as shown.

Picture 10. I fitted the switch, semi-concealed inside a cupboard. One button selects the caravan aerial; the other, the external on-site TV supply. I added a label to indicate which is which.

This has been a really useful, low-cost modification to make. Previously, when connecting to on-site TV aerials, it was a matter of disconnecting the coaxial cable from the back of the TV, and draping another cable across the caravan, through a window, and over to the power supply bollard.

Now, all the coaxial cables are neatly fitted permanently inside the caravan, and a simple switch selects between on-site and on-caravan aerials. Connecting to the on-site TV supply, when required, is simply a matter of plugging into the socket in the battery box, and running the coaxial cable alongside the mains cable to the power supply bollard.

FITTING AN OMNIDIRECTIONAL TV AERIAL

Caravan TV aerials (and even satellite dish systems) are readily available in a number of different forms and styles. Indeed, many of today's upper range caravans are available with TV aerials as standard equipment.

There are two main types of TV aerials available for caravans: omnidirectional and monodirectional. Each type comes as either permanently fixed, or removable, although, obviously, the monodirectional aerial isn't suitable as a permanent fixture, as you would need to turn your caravan to face the right direction before tuning in the TV!

Bear in mind, too, that a TV aerial mounted permanently on a caravan's roof can cause problems with headroom, when going under low bridges, or boarding a ferry. The pinnacle at the top of the widely fitted Grade Status omnidirectional aerial is removable to counter this problem.

The difference between omnidirectional and monodirectional aerials basically comes down to technology and money. Omnidirectional aerials are, generally, permanently attached to a caravan, and respond to the strongest TV signal coming from any direction, without having to 'aim' the aerial to a specific bearing. Unfortunately, such benefits mean that they're generally more expensive than monodirectional models.

Monodirectional aerials must be specifically positioned whenever you arrive at a new destination, in order to get the best reception. This is simply a matter of trial and error: one person, outside, positions the aerial, while another person, inside the caravan, observes the quality of the TV picture, giving a signal when it's at its best. As a tip, and to cut down on the amount of time spent in such pursuits, it's worth, first, simply taking a look at the TV aerials on houses in the vicinity, and noting which way they're pointing.

Sometimes, no matter what type of aerial is fitted to your caravan, you'll still get a sub-standard picture on your TV. One solution is to have a booster fitted inline. Boosters help amplify a good signal, where, perhaps, the aerial is a long distance from the transmitter. However, it should be noted that inline boosters also increase the strength of a noisy signal, along with interference that can cause problems with the signal.

TOP TIP

• One tip for improving the reception on your caravan's TV is to make the length of the aerial cable as short as possible. Leaving lengths of aerial cable coiled up often detrimentally affects the quality of TV reception.

Fitting a Status TV Aerial

One of the most popular TV aerials available for caravans, is the Status omnidirectional combined TV and FM radio aerial, from Grade, that comes with its own booster/power pack. The Status comes in kit form and is available from caravan accessory shops, and includes most of the items you'll require to fit it. In addition to the kit, however, you'll need an electric drill, drill bit, cable clips, and non-drying sealant.

SAFETY FIRST!

• Whenever working on the roof of a caravan, be particularly careful not to stand or sit upon it – this could easily dent and damage the roof. If you use a ladder, ensure that it's properly supported, and if possible, have somebody with you to steady it, in case a problem occurs.

Picture 1. First, decide where aerial is to be positioned. Over the caravan's wardrobe is one recommended place, allowing you to drill a guide-hole from the inside, and making sure that you're not drilling into any pipes, walls or wires. Then, from the outside, drill through the roof, ensuring that you leave no sharp edges that could cut into the cable.

Picture 2. Carefully feed the aerial cable through the hole you've drilled, and position the base of the aerial over the hole. The base can be adjusted so that the aerial is level – ideal if the surface you're fixing it to is sloping. Then apply plenty of silicone sealant to the bottom of the aerial base, to prevent water penetration.

Picture 3. Screw the aerial base into position, allowing any excess sealant to squeeze out onto the caravan's roof. This should be cleaned up with some white spirit and a clean piece of cloth.

Picture 4. Feed the aerial's coaxial cable through, making sure that it isn't catching on any sharp edges, or becoming coiled in the aerial base. Place the central area of the aerial into place, in the base, and lock it into position with the allen key provided.

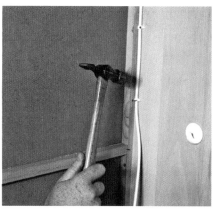

Picture 5. Inside the caravan, find a suitable route for the aerial wiring, through the wardrobe, to wherever you've decided to place the aerial socket. To keep it tidy, try to keep the cable in the corners of furniture, and use cable clips to keep it in place.

Picture 6. Next, decide where you're going to position the aerial's booster unit/power pack. This can either be placed next to where you will put your TV, or, if you prefer, it can be hidden away in a roof or bed locker, with some extra cable threaded to a remote aerial point. Secure the booster/power pack using the two screws supplied.

Switch on the power pack, turn on the TV, and tune in. Check that the gain control is set to normal 'NML;' this

Picture 7. Wire the booster/power pack to a 12-volt power supply. Ideally, this should be a direct connection to the battery, or a suitable terminal strip. Don't connect it to any other 12-volt power cables, as they may carry electrical interference from an invertor or a transformer.

Picture 8. Plug the coaxial cable into the 'ANT.IN' socket of the booster/power pack. Then run another length of coaxial cable from the caravan TV to either 'TV1.FM' or 'TV2.FM,' on the booster/power pack.

may need to be adjusted, depending on the strength of the local television transmission.

INSTALLING AN INTERNALLY ADJUSTABLE DIRECTIONAL TV AERIAL

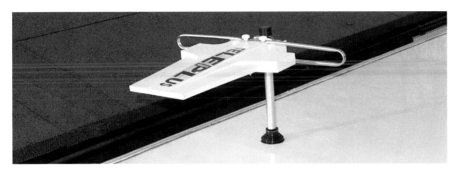

Picture 3. You need to seal the top flange – it swivels for sloping roofs. There's a rubber cover (right), and a spring seal (left). Smear Vaseline into the housing to lubricate the mast.

TV reception from the aerial on your caravan's roof is usually not very good. Round, omnidirectional aerials aren't as good as directional aerials. CAK's digital-friendly Teleplus aerial appears to provide the best reception of all.

The adjustable mast, that can be purchased from CAK as a separate item, turns the powerful Teleplus aerial into one that's very easy to set up, even in wet weather – and you don't even need to go outside.

You'll need to cut a hole in the roof, fit the support bracket inside the caravan, and fit a new aerial cable.

Picture 4. Inside, the mast tube is held with a rubber washer and screw-on flange. The hole for this tube MUST be drilled upright, so check with a spirit level when drilling.

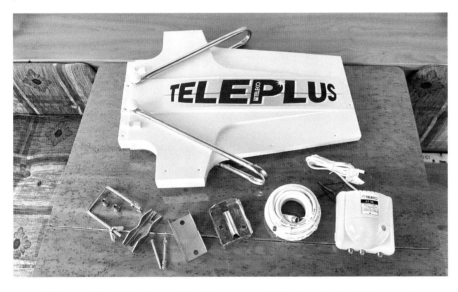

Picture 1. The Teleplus aerial as it comes out of the box. Included is a good quality, adjustable signal booster that can run from either 12V or 230V. The clamps are galvanised.

Picture 2. You might need to remove the old aerial before drilling (we did), depending on where you want to site the mast. The mast kit (available separately) is shown inset.

Picture 5. Space restrictions inside our caravan meant the mast had to be cut down, reducing the available aerial height. The aerial was fitted first, before measuring and cutting the aluminium tube.

Picture 6. Because the aerial cable has to be inserted into the weatherproof cap, it's easier to feed the aerial wire into the mast before inserting it into the mast tube.

Picture 9. The aerial wire is best held to the mast with a cable tie. The cable must loop down, then up again to the aerial, so that water runs off.

Picture 7. If the mast is used full-height, the clamp is best mounted on a wall. In our case, it was okay to mount the clamp, on a bracket, against the roof.

Picture 10. Before fitting the top cap, we used Würth Bond+Seal to make a fully waterproof seal, and to ensure that the cap couldn't be blown off.

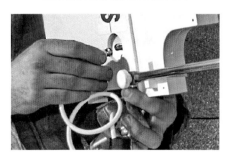

Picture 8. Before fitting the Teleplus aerial to the mast, remember to screw-on the aerial cable. Seal it with more Vaseline, to stop corrosion – otherwise **TV picture quality will slowly deteriorate.**

We live in a very poor TV reception area, yet for the first time in a caravan, we were able to pick up all the analogue channels, and many (but not all) of the digital ones, via our digibox. The Teleplus aerial picked up very good analogue signals on its own (which is more than our house aerial will do), and the booster reached the digital signals.

It's easy to 'find' the transmitter from inside the caravan, too. Unlike satellite receivers, the Teleplus picks up a TV signal over a wide sweep, so it's not at all difficult to tune-in.

FITTING A MANUALLY ADJUSTABLE SATELLITE DISH

Picture 4. The Semitronic mechanism was passed to Graham, while Andy inserted the tubular mast from beneath. The cables were fed through the centre of the mast.

Picture 5. With the two clamp support legs secured over the stainless steel disc, and the mast pushed up into the clamp, the two Allen key bolts where tightened.

Satellite TV provides the best quality picture, and almost guarantees reception of British programmes anywhere in the UK – anywhere in Europe, in fact. Hundreds of free channels are available; you just need to avoid nearby trees or building obstructions when on site.

Conrad Anderson, one of the country's leading suppliers and fitters of caravan electrical and electronic equipment, demonstrate what's involved in fitting a satellite dish to your caravan.

Picture 1. This is the well-made Maxview Omnisat Semitronic kit. At much less than the cost of cheapest fully-automatic systems, it's a great compromise between convenience and price.

Picture 2. Graham, from Conrad Anderson, first drilled a pilot hole, upwards from inside the wardrobe, and then cut a larger hole from above. He then fitted the mast pivot assembly to the top of the roof.

Picture 3. The stainless steel and plastic components were fitted with plenty of sealant to prevent leaks. Tapering rubber seals allow fitting on some sloping caravan roofs.

Picture 6. The last job, topside, was for Graham to attach the dish to the Semitronic motorised unit, using the stainless steel bolts and lock washers provided with the kit.

Picture 7. Inside the caravan, the mast was bracketed to the inside wall of the wardrobe. The threaded mechanism allows the unit to be locked for travelling, and when tuned to the satellite.

Picture 8. Graham fixed the control box in place. Luckily, he found a fused 12V feed from inside the wardrobe base (otherwise, he would have run a new one from the battery).

Picture 9. Next, power and antenna cables were connected to the control unit. One button raises the dish to the exact required elevation; another folds it away again.

Picture 10. Turning the dish to 'find' the satellite comes next. This Avtex TV/DVD player is widely praised for presenting high quality satellite images to their full effect. Cheaper sets display pixelation.

You don't need to pay much for a little satellite dish in a box, but ones that 'finds' satellites automatically are very expensive. The Maxview Omnisat Semitronic seems, to me, to offer the best compromise.

Setting the elevation requires pressing a button until the angle shown on a chart appears on the control box. Turning the dish takes much longer, up to 30 minutes at first, though experience 'tuners' can do it in two minutes.

Self-fitting is fine provided you're fully proficient, and you don't drill though anything important in the roof.

SELF-SEEKING SATELLITE TV SYSTEM

How can you connect instantly to all the digital TV channels, anywhere in the country, at the touch of a button? With a Maxview Satellite Dome.

While installing a Maxview Dome isn't rocket science, you do need to be a reasonably accomplished DIYer.

The Maxview receiver is preset to the correct satellite for UK channels, but other satellites are easily selected. Once installed, all you have to do it is park, switch it on, and watch TV, with a typical search time of less than 30 seconds.

Picture 1. Adventure Motorhomes' Nick Stevens started by positioning the new dome on the centre of the roof. He then marked the position of each of the mounting points on the roof ...

Picture 2. ... before thoroughly degreasing both the roof, and all of the mounts. He then gunned a top quality adhesive over each mounting point, and repositioned the dome accurately on the roof.

Picture 3. Nick drove stainless steel screws through the mounting holes, having first put a dab of sealant into each hole so the screw thread sealed itself. Be careful: the aluminium is thin.

Picture 4. Inside, Nick had already calculated a wiring route through wardrobe, lockers, and bed boxes, but needed to add self-adhesive white plastic cable trunking alongside one of the window blinds.

Picture 5. Maxview provided a waterproof access point for the cable on the roof, held down with double-sided tape. You may need longer cable, depending on where you locate the dome and TV.

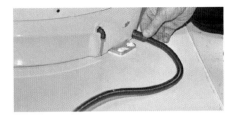

Picture 6. Nick also added corrugated cable trunking, as well as the weatherproof seal provided with the kit, and clipped over the screw-on connector at the base of the dome housing.

Picture 7. The Maxview Free-to-Air receiver supplied couldn't be easier to connect. All of the cables are provided, and are simply plugged in, from the dome, power supplies, and TV.

Picture 8. Small receiver mountings are supplied (a larger one is available), but a Land Rover-type DIN car radio housing and cage make for a neater job. These are standard stereo removal 'prongs'.

Picture 9. With everything connected, Nick tested the system with the dome cover removed. The dish searches, rotating at the correct elevation, then again at different angles, if necessary.

Picture 10. After some whirring from above, the channels appear, arranged in a useful order. The remote 'eye,' which can be fitted to the TV, allows you to tuck the receiver out of sight.

Without doubt, this is the easiest way of watching TV on holiday that I've yet come across. Provided you have a view of the sky, you can pick up hundreds of free digital channels as easily as turning on the TV.

It can receive transmissions from four different satellites, with the equivalent performance of a 60cm dish, and Sky or Freesat receiver can be connected, too.

INSTALLING READING LIGHTS

Here's how halogen spotlights can be added to provide extra illumination when reading in your caravan.

Installing the light unit and running the cable is a job you can do yourself if you're competent enough, but wiring connections should be left to a qualified electrician.

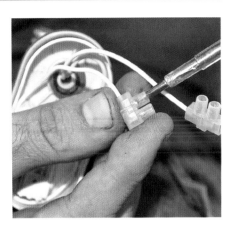

Picture 1. The halogen lights I bought came with bare cables. Dave added small 'chock block' connectors, after trimming off excess cable. The connectors and cabling has to be able to fit inside the housing.

Picture 2. Existing lighting wires ran inside trunking. Dave used a Makita to drill a wiring hole into the locker space. This hole will be invisible when the trunking is refitted.

Picture 3. The other light was connected into a terminal box inside another locker. Here, you couldn't see which was live and neutral, so Dave used a tester before disconnecting the caravan battery.

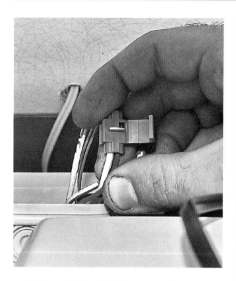

Picture 4. Scotchlok connectors are undesirable where there is damp, but inside a locker, they're the easiest way of connecting a wire without stripping it. Just squeeze shut with pliers.

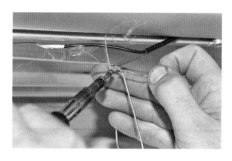

Picture 5. Inside the trunking, there was only enough space for soldered connections. This is a Würth gas powered soldering iron. It can be turned on and off as needed, so there's less risk of burning things.

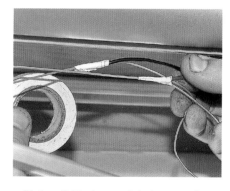

Picture 6. Each completed connection was safely wrapped with insulation tape. Notice how Dave staggered the joints, so that the bulk didn't appear all in one place.

Picture 7. Before attaching the light, Dave drilled pilot holes for the mounting screws with a 2mm bit. We spent ages working out the best light locations – thinking time pays off!

Picture 8. The positions of the pilot holes (arrowed) indicated clearly the position of the light housing, so Dave drilled another hole, this one big enough for the cable to pass through.

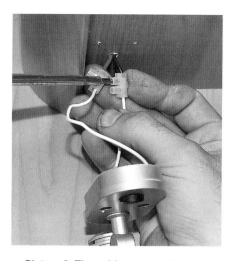

Picture 9. The cable was run through the locker space in such a way that it would be hidden from view, and safe from abrasion. The end was pushed through ...

Picture 10. ... the hole in the locker base, and wire-ends were stripped and inserted into the chock blocks. Cable clips were screwed (NOT nailed), holding the cable safely and neatly in position.

A job of this nature risks causing cosmetic damage if you don't know what you're doing: if you're not competent, don't risk it. And, if you're not a qualified electrician, don't make the wiring connections yourself. You can't fatally electrocute yourself with 12-volt electricity, but you can cause a potentially fatal fire.

Be careful when drilling, because it's easy to damage wall finishings if the side of the drill chuck rubs on them.

Also, take care not to install halogen lamps near curtains or flammable materials: they can get very hot. LED lamps run almost cold, so remove the risk of overheating.

Specialists & suppliers

Adventure Motorhomes, 3 Kings Castle Business Park, Boards Rd, The Drove, Bridgwater, Somerset, TA6 4AG.
Tel: 01278 457557
Mob: 07812390066
www.adventuremotorhomehire.co.uk

AL-KO Kober Ltd, South Warwickshire Business Park, Kineton Road, Southam, Warks, CV47 0AL.
Tel: 01926 818 500
www.al-ko.co.uk

Auto Tec, Walkwood Farm, Morton Lane, Redditch, Worcestershire, B97 5QA.
Tel: 01527 541850.
www.myvehicle.co.uk Also, see www.cobravehiclesecurity.co.uk

Avtex Limited, 22 Merthyr Road, Whitchurch, Cardiff, CF14 1DH.
Tel: 02920 610109
www.avtex.uk.com

Bailey of Bristol, South Liberty Lane, Bristol, BS3 2SS.
Tel: 0117 966 5976
www.bailey-caravans.co.uk

Britool Ltd, Churchbridge Works, Walsall Road, Cannock, Staffordshire, WS11 3JR.
Tel: 01922 702000 Website: www.britool.com

Broad Park Caravan Club Site, Higher East Leigh, Modbury, Ivybridge, S Devon, PL21 0SH.
Tel: 01548 830714 (Open All Year)

Bromyard Downs Caravan Club Site, Brockhampton, Worcester, WR6 5TE.
Tel: 01885 482607

Bulldog Security Products Ltd, Tel: 01952 728171
www.bulldogsecure.com
Email: sales@bulldogsecure.com

CAK Tanks, Aqua House, Princes Drive Industrial Estate, Kenilworth, Warwickshire. CV8 2FD.
Email sales@caktanks.co.uk or Tel: 0870 757 2324 for a catalogue or visit
www.caktanks.co.uk

Calor Gas, Tachbrook Park, Athena

Drive, Warwick, CV34 6RL.
Tel: 0800 626 626
www.caravanning-online.co.uk

Chelston Caravans, Chelston, Wellington, Somerset, TA21 9HS.
Tel: 01823 667 655
www.chelstoncaravans.co.uk

Clarke International Ltd, Hemnall Street, Epping, Essex, CM16 4LG.
Tel: 01992 565 300
www.clarkeinternational.com

Conrad Anderson LLP, 57-59 Sladefield Road, Ward End, Birmingham, B8 3PF.
Tel: 0121 247 0619
www.conrad-anderson.co.uk

CRiS, Dolphin House, PO Box 61, New Street, Salisbury, Wiltshire, SP1 2TB.
Tel: 01722 411430
CRiS charge to register a change of keeper and to check a caravan's status as shown on its records. There's no charge for notifying a change of address

Dometic Ltd, 99 Oakley Road, Luton, Beds, LU4 9GE.
Tel: 01582 494111
www.dometic.co.uk

Dunlop Tyres, TyreFort , 88-98 Wingfoot Way, Birmingham, B24 9HY.
Tel: 0121 306 6000
www.dunloptyres.co.uk

Economical, The Old Pump House, New Street, Upton upon Severn, Worcestershire, WR8 0HP.
Tel: 01684 594981.
www.eco-nomical.co.uk

Elecsol, Energy Development Co-operative Ltd, Unit 2 (The Old Brewery), Harbour Road Industrial Estate, Lowestoft, Suffolk, NR32 3LZ.
Tel: 0870 745 1119
www.unlimitedpower.co.uk

Extreme 4x4 Ltd, (for stainless steel socket brackets)
Tel: 01255 411411.
www.extreme4x4.co.uk

Fiamma. We received notably good service from: **AgentFiamma**, Camperlands Limited, Mill Lane, Northenden, Manchester, M22 4HJ
Tel: Product Service Line: 0161 902 3025, Order Line: 0161 902 3023.
www.agentfiamma.co.uk

Freedom Caravans, Queensville, Lichfield Road, Stafford, ST17 4NY.
Tel: 01785 222 488
www.freedomcaravans.com

Gaslow International Ltd, Manor House Stables, Normanton-on-Soar, Leicestershire, LE12 5HB.
Tel: 0845 4000 600
Email: sales@gaslow.co.uk
Download brochures:
www.gaslow.co.uk

Hauppauge Computer Works UK Ltd, Crown House, Home Gardens,

Dartford, Kent DA1 1DZ.
Tel: 0203 405 1717
www.hauppauge.co.uk

Illbruck Sealant Systems UK Ltd, Trade Division, Coalville, Leicester, LE67 3JJ.
Tel: 01530 835 722
www.illbruck.com

Industrial Plastic Solutions Ltd, Unit 1, Newhall Road Industrial Estate, 2 Sanderson Street, Sheffield, S9 2TW.
Tel: 0114 279 9188
www.ipsluk.co.uk

International Tool Co Ltd, 82 Tenter Road, Northampton NN3 6AX.
Tel: 01604 646433
www.international-tool.co.uk

Keen Electronics Ltd, 202 Aylesbury Road, Bierton, Aylesbury, HP22 5DT.
Tel: 01296 423 203
www.keenelectronics.co.uk

Makita UK Ltd, Michigan Drive, Tongwell, Milton Keynes, Bucks. MK15 8JD.
Tel:01908 211 678
www.makitauk.com

Maplin. Stores around the country.
www.maplin.co.uk

Maxview Ltd, Common Lane, Setchey, King's Lynn, Norfolk, PE33 0AT.
Customer Helpline: 01553 811000
www.maxview.co.uk

Maypole Ltd, 54 Kettleswood Drive, Woodgate Business Park, Birmingham B32 3DB.
Tel: 0121 423 3011
Email: maypole@maypole.ltd.uk
www.maypole.ltd.uk

MCL (Mobile Centre Ltd), Tim Consolante, PO Box 222, Evesham, WR11 4WT
Tel: 0844 578 1000
www.mobilecentre.co.uk

Milenco Ltd, Blackhill Drive, Wolverton Mill, Milton Keynes, MK12 5TS.
Email: enquiries@milenco.com
www.milenco.com

Mobile Technician: Ian Walker, Chase Caravans, Rugeley, Staffs.
Tel: 07951 360260.
Email: chasecaravans@aol.com

Newbury Metal Products, Bone Lane, Newbury, Berks, RG14 5SH.
Tel: 01635 43921
www.carportsnmp.co.uk

Omnistore. The best way of finding an Omnistor dealer near you is to log on to www.omnistor.com, select the 'Contact' option, and either click on the map or enter your county into the search engine. If your county doesn't have an Omnistor dealer, you'll need to try the names of nearby counties until you find one that does! Alternatively, you can email queries to info@omnistor.com.

PaintSeal Direct, Tel: 0871 200 70 70 (costing up to 10p per minute from BT landlines)
Email: info@paintsealdirect.com

Panel Projects, Portview Road, Avonmouth, Bristol, BS11 9LQ.
Tel: 0117 316 7020
www.panelprojects.com

Powrwheel Ltd, 8 Queensway, New Milton, Hampshire, BH25 5NN.
Tel: 01425 623 123
www.powrwheel.com

Propex Heating and Leisure Ltd, Unit 5, Second Avenue Business Park, Millbrook, Southampton, SO15 0LP.
Tel: 023 8052 8555
www.propexheatsource.co.uk

Pyramid Products, Byron Avenue, Lowmoor Road Industrial Estate, Kirkby in Ashfield, Nottinghamshire,

NG17 7LA.
Tel: 01623 754 567
Email: sales@pyramid-products.co.uk

Raydyot, Tel: 0121 561 7000
www.truck-lite.co.uk

Remis. REMIflair IV available from
UK stockists or contact: Ian Fletcher,
Brookfield, Eston Piercy, Chippenham,
SN14 6JU.
Tel: 01249 750045.
See www.remis.de (Click on the Union
Jack for English text and select 'Mobile
Systems'.)

Riversway Leisure, Tel: 01772 729999
www.riverswayleisure.co.uk

Screwfix Direct, Freepost, Yeovil,
BA22 8BF
Freephone: 0500 41 41 41
www.screwfix.com

The Cover Company, 81 St Martin's
Street, Hereford, HR2 7RG.
Tel: 01432 379 357
www.thecovercompany.co.uk

Thetford Ltd, Unit 6, Centrovell
Industrial Estate, Caldwell Road,
Nuneaton, Warwickshire, CV11 4UD.
Tel: 02476 322700
www.thetford.nl

Tockfield Ltd, Pit Lane, Shirland,
Derbyshire DE55 6AT.
Tel: 01773 834968
www.foam.co.uk

Tourershine, Paul Asserati, Stamford,
Lincolnshire.
Mobile: 07849 152411
www.tourershine.co.uk

Tourertech, Rob Sheasby, Mobile
Caravan Service Engineer.
Tel: 01905 29881
Mobile: 07791 017171.
www.tourertech.com

Towsure, Tel: 0114 250 3045
www.towsure.co.uk

Truma UK Ltd, Park Lane, Dove Valley
Park, DE65 5BG. Sales Tel: 01283
586050.
Service Tel: 01283 586020
E-mail: sales@trumauk.com; or
technical@trumauk.com
www.trumauk.com

Tyron Automotive Group Ltd, Stoke
Mill Industrial Estate, Mill Road,
Sharnbrook, Bedford, MK44 1NP.
Tel: 01234 781 525
www.tyron.com

Ultraseal UK, Tel: 0870 240 1280
www.ultrasealuk.biz
www.tyrepressuremonitors.biz

UltraShield Ltd, 11, Lime Hill Road,
Tunbridge Wells, Kent, TN1 1LJ.
Tel: 0845 6014936 (0845 numbers
are generally charged at the rate of a
standard local call.)
www.ultrashield.co.uk

Vision View (in USA), Tel: 001 888
776 6758
www.visionviewmirrors.com

Waeco: Dometic UK Ltd, Blandford
St Mary, Dorset.
Tel: 0844 626 0133
www.waeco.co.uk

Whale Water Systems, Old Belfast
Road, Bangor, Co. Down, BT19 1LT,
Northern Ireland.
Tel: 028 9127 0531
www.whalepumps.com

Würth UK Ltd, 1 Centurion Way,
Erith, Kent, DA18 4AF.
Tel: 08705 987 841
www.wurth.co.uk

ALSO FROM VELOCE PUBLISHING:

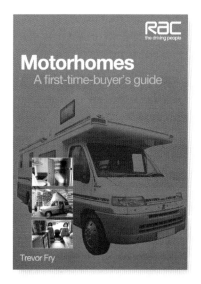

Motorhomes
A first-time-buyer's guide

Trevor Fry

The perfect book for those looking to enter the world of motorcaravanning. This book covers everything from hot water and heating, sanitation, and power supplies, to personalising your motorhome, so you can get the motorhome that suits your needs, and your budget.

ISBN: 978-1-845844-49-3
Paperback • 21x14.8cm • £9.99* UK/$19.95* USA
• 80 pages • 109 colour and b&w pictures

Dogs on wheels
Travelling with your canine companion

Norm Mort

Helpful advice on how to get the most out of car journeys with your canine companion – whether travelling for five minutes or five hours. Packed with original colour photographs, plus information from expert veterinarians.

ISBN: 978-1-845843-79-3
Paperback • 21x14.8cm • £9.99* UK/$19.95* USA
• 80 pages • 90 colour pictures

How your car works
Your guide to the components & systems of modern cars, including hybrid & electric vehicles

Arvid Linde

"Over only 100 A5 pages this book does an excellent job of explaining how our mechanical pets function ... Recommended"
Classic Cars Magazine

"An ideal gift for all new and current car owners with little idea what is under the bonnet.'
MG Enthusiast

ISBN: 978-1-845843-90-8
• Paperback • 21x14.8cm • £12.99* UK/$24.95* USA
• 128 pages • 92 colour and b&w pictures

The Efficient Driver's Handbook
Your guide to fuel efficient driving techniques and car choice

Dave Moss

This book describes in a clear, friendly manner everything today's driver needs to know about choosing and using a car in an economical and eco-efficient way. It explains what matters most to the car buyer when optimum fuel economy and lowest emissions are priorities, and why four wheel drive and automatic transmission present challenges to eco-friendly driving.

ISBN: 978-1-845843-51-9
• Paperback • 21x14.8cm • £9.99* UK/$19.95* USA
• 96 pages • 32 colour pictures

These titles are also available in eBook format:

For more info on Veloce titles, visit our website at www.veloce.co.uk
• email: info@veloce.co.uk • Tel: +44(0)1305 260068
* prices subject to change, p&p extra

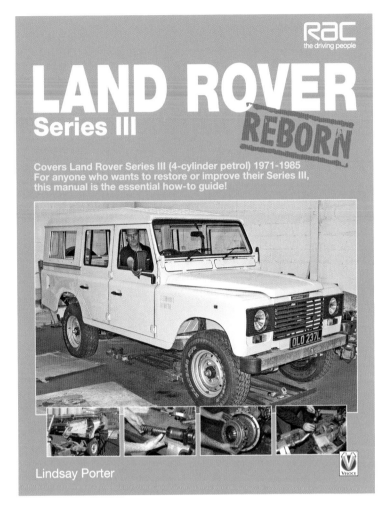

ISBN: 978-1-845843-47-2
Paperback • 27x20.7cm • £30.00* UK/$59.95* USA
• 256 pages • 1749 pictures

Developed from several years of articles in Land Rover Monthly
magazine, this manual is the most detailed package of information
available for anyone thinking of restoring, rebuilding or improving a
Series III Land Rover.

For more info on Veloce titles, visit our website at www.veloce.co.uk
• email: info@veloce.co.uk • Tel: +44(0)1305 260068
* prices subject to change, p&p extra

Index